PENGUIN BUSINESS

Banking On It

'A riveting read. I couldn't put it down! Boden's story powerfully demonstrates how creativity, bravery and determination can quite literally transform an industry. Wow, what a change-maker!' Rachel Botsman, author of *Who Can You Trust?*

'A thrilling account of entrepreneurship, ingenuity and innovation' Tony Fernandes, CEO of AirAsia and author of *Flying High*

'Sent shockwaves through the tight-knit world of UK tech and venture capital' Yahoo! Finance

'A banking blockbuster' *Observer Magazine*

'If there was ever a business book suitable for TV adaptation, this is it' *Financial Times*

'*Banking On It* is the story of Boden's dogged determination to change the way banks do things . . . It is a fascinating insight into how one woman's vision shaped the way fintech looks today' Aisling Finn, *AltFi*

'A fascinating read that will appeal to everyone, not just those interested in fintech or the financial industry. Whether you take inspiration from a fifty-something woman dominating a field full of young men or merely just enjoy the trials and tribulations that come from trying to create a financial institution, *Banking On It* should be top of your reading list' Polly Jean Harrison, *Fintech Times*

'I was left pondering who would bid for the film rights – and this isn't something you often think about a business book. It's a clear-eyed look at the state of banking and how slowly it has moved with the times. Finance is not everyone's favourite subject but Boden makes it accessible' Peter Magee, *Bookbag*

'Boden is a true disruptor, and her big idea for disrupting the banking sector with her digital-only bank is truly inspirational. For women entrepreneurs around the world who want to shake things up with their business ideas and innovations, Anne is a great role model and shows that big ideas combined with tenacity, persistence and hard work can become game-changing realities. This is a must-read book for every woman entrepreneur who wants to disrupt things with their businesses' Melanie Hawken, CEO, Lioness of Africa

ABOUT THE AUTHOR

Anne Boden is the CEO and founder of Starling Bank, the UK's first digital-only bank, which she founded in 2014. She graduated in Computer Science and Chemistry, and started her career at Lloyds Bank, where she helped establish the UK's first real-time payments system. She has held various executive-level jobs in the banking sector, including being Head of EMEA Global Transaction Banking across thirty-four countries for RBS and ABN AMRO, before leaving to start her own bank that could realize the potential of technology in financial services. Anne received an MBE in 2018 for services to financial technology, and sits on the board of UK Finance, which represents more than 250 firms in the banking and finance industry.

Banking On It

How I Disrupted an Industry and Changed the Way We Manage Our Money For Ever

ANNE BODEN

BUSINESS

To my parents, Nancy and Jack Boden, who taught me that happiness must be cultivated and treasured, because those who are always happy are the privileged few.

PENGUIN BUSINESS

UK | USA | Canada | Ireland | Australia
India | New Zealand | South Africa

Penguin Business is part of the Penguin Random House group of companies whose addresses can be found at global.penguinrandomhouse.com

Penguin
Random House
UK

First published 2020
This edition published with a new afterword 2021
001

Copyright © Anne Boden, 2020, 2021

The moral right of the author has been asserted

Typeset by Jouve (UK), Milton Keynes
Printed and bound in Great Britain by Clays Ltd, Elcograf S.p.A.

The authorized representative in the EEA is Penguin Random House Ireland, Morrison Chambers, 32 Nassau Street, Dublin D02 YH68

A CIP catalogue record for this book is available from the British Library

ISBN: 978–0–241–45359–9

Follow us on LinkedIn: https://www.linkedin.com/company/penguin-connect/

www.greenpenguin.co.uk

Contents

Introduction

Sitting in the back of the taxi, my collar turned up, jacket closely wrapped around me and head low, it might have appeared as though I was hunkering down to keep the cold weather at bay. Except I wasn't. Granted, it was early in the morning, but the sun was already climbing steadily in an unusually cloudless blue sky over Dublin. It was July, after all.

No, I was trying to make myself invisible in a pathetic attempt to head off the inevitable question from the cab driver. I need not have bothered. It came anyhow.

'What keeps you off the streets?' the driver said in a friendly but nonetheless insistent way.

In other words: what did I do for a living? I weighed up my answer, aware that he was looking at me expectantly through the rear-view mirror. A number of people had already warned me about this and, since I had asked the taxi to take me to the HQ of Allied Irish Banks in Ballsbridge, the inquiry was inevitable.

'Don't for heaven's sake say what you do,' they'd all said. 'Mention banking and you'll get a thirty-minute lecture about evil bankers all the way from the airport to the office.'

I wouldn't have blamed the driver for being curious, or resentful, just as I wouldn't have blamed any other person in Ireland. The year was 2012 and Ireland had suffered more than any other nation in the EU in the immediate fallout from the global credit crunch. Banks and bankers were firmly in the cross-hairs when it came to who should shoulder the blame.

The fall from grace had been so extreme that everyone had

felt the impact. Just a few years earlier, the 'Celtic tiger' economy was widely viewed as the poster child of the free market and, while no one exactly loved banks, everyone was happy that the much yearned-for boom times had finally arrived. And boom times they were. After years of a stagnant, agriculture-based economy, the nation appeared transformed, virtually overnight. The property sector became turbocharged thanks to the unfettered freedom to borrow and build. Banks were eager to lend and everyone saw an opportunity. To add to the feeling of prosperity, numerous US investors were irresistibly drawn to the Emerald Isle, helped by the shared language and Irish roots of many American investors, as well as a tempting low-tax regime. Anything the global boom threw in its direction, Ireland grabbed with both hands.

Then, of course, it all came crashing down. When the music stopped playing, Ireland was left standing with a frankly terrifying amount of debt. In 2008, AIB, the bank I was on my way to now, held €73 billion of loans, which represented half of Ireland's GDP. After months of wrangling and uncertainty, AIB, along with Bank of Ireland, was forced to accept a €3.5-billion bailout from the government. The scale of AIB's bailout grew over time, when it became clear the initial payout was a drop in the ocean. Eventually it spiralled to reach a dizzying €13 billion. Ireland became, per capita, the most indebted country in the EU and its 14.3 per cent budget deficit was higher than that of Greece. In response, the Irish government slashed public spending by 7.5 per cent of GDP. Public sector pay was cut by 15 per cent, child benefit by 10 per cent and unemployment benefit by 4.1 per cent.

The fall from affluent largesse to desperate poverty was exceptionally hard and fast. People lost their jobs and their homes, with the most vulnerable in society being the hardest hit. And when it came to laying blame, the finger pointed firmly in the direction of the banks. Never mind that an entire nation and professional class had become intoxicated by greed, from politicians to investors to developers to estate agents and, yes, even ordinary folk – it was bankers who had created the environment that allowed this to happen. No wonder my taxi driver eyed me with suspicion. I could have climbed in his cab and asked for a fast trip to Hades and got a friendlier reception.

AIB was undeniably a toxic brand. The bank's appalling reputation exposed it to a number of issues, quite apart from the fact that none of its existing, or potential, customers trusted it one inch. Many of the people who worked there wanted to leave, but were pretty certain they'd never get a job elsewhere with AIB sitting on the top of their CV. Plus, any sort of recruitment was fraught with difficulty. No one in the wider financial sector trusted anyone who was remotely close to what had happened in the run-up to 2008, and promoting from within was never going to happen.

With senior heads rolling left, right and centre, AIB had to refill the posts with candidates drawn from all over the world. When I got the call about the chief operating officer vacancy in AIB, I was at a crossroads in my career, having just left my job as head of Royal Bank of Scotland's Europe, Middle East and Africa (EMEA) Global Transaction Services department. Looking back, I now realize how useful this period was to me. When I was working day-to-day, I barely had time to think. I was perpetually rushing from one crisis to another (particularly during 2008–9), or running to and from airports to fly off for lengthy meetings, or instructing consultants, or briefing my fellow bankers. I rarely had any time to sit down and consider the world around me. Now that I had reached a hiatus, however, I did just that. I stood back, looked at banking and began to wonder if we were all missing the point.

The inescapable truth was that, however shocking and traumatic was the financial meltdown of 2008, most of the banks seemed to have snapped back into business-as-usual without a backward glance. We'd come through the worst banking crisis in living memory and everyone was pretending nothing had happened. Move along, folks, nothing to see here.

While all this was going on, and my fellow bankers' attention was focussed elsewhere, the world had changed around us. Technology was beginning to transform one sector after another. Uber had changed the way we thought about hiring a taxi, Netflix had seen off Blockbuster video rentals and, of course, the tech daddy of them all, Amazon, was transforming everything we thought we knew about shopping. But banking? Technology barely seemed to have changed since . . . well, I hardly knew when. Indeed, many of the major banks sustained such antiquated IT systems it was nothing short of a miracle they managed to function from day to day. Unsurprisingly, there were frequent stories of systems crashing and customers being locked out of accounts for hours. It was costing the banks a fortune too. Among many of the measures to be introduced since the global financial crisis of 2008, authorities had been taking a much tougher line on bank-system outages. In the UK, for example, the Financial Conduct Authority and Prudential Regulation Authority had been imposing fines going into the millions of pounds for each incident.

While I tried to work out what to do next, I started to look into the latest developments in financial technologies, or fintech, as it is now more widely known. Initially, this referred to the technologies used in the back end of a financial institution's business to automate such processes as deposits and account reconciliation, and since technology was my speciality I always kept abreast of what was happening. In recent times fintech had gained a much more significant buzz about it as it described new ways to conduct financial transactions, including mobile payments, money transfers, loans, fundraising and asset management. The more I looked at what was possible right then, the more inspired I became. Things were really changing.

I thought back to a networking event I had attended shortly after leaving my job at RBS. Held in the basement of Balls Bros restaurant in the City, it was open to tech entrepreneurs and bankers, with the idea that the two groups might find a useful way of working with one another. It was an informal evening do with a sit-down meal and a handful of speakers. Since I had received the invite while still at my previous job, my name badge sported the inscription *Anne Boden, RBS*. I saw little reason to disrupt the proceedings by requesting a change. Besides, what would it say? *Anne Boden, Between Jobs*? Or *Anne Boden, Not quite sure what she's doing next*?

I found my seat and saw there was a young man already sitting in the chair next to mine. He turned and flashed a broad smile. Then his eyes travelled to my name badge and the smile wavered. 'Tom Blomfield, GoCardless,' I said, reading his badge. 'Anne Boden.' I put out my hand to shake his.

I sensed my companion was feeling uneasy about something, but couldn't for the life of me work out what it might be.

'So, GoCardless?' I said, settling into my chair beside him. 'I'm not sure I know much about that. What is it that you do?'

'It's a business that helps other businesses collect money,' he said.

'That's interesting, how does it work?' I pressed, still wondering what was making the man nervous. He seemed like a confident and charismatic person, like so many of the new breed of tech entrepreneurs.

'It's a service that makes the back-office operations of small, medium and even large companies more efficient,' he said, looking over my shoulder. 'So they can easily collect recurring payments. Listen, I am very sorry, but could you excuse me one moment?'

I watched as he darted off in the direction of the gents, pulling his mobile from his pocket as he walked. How odd, I thought. I was genuinely interested in hearing more about GoCardless.

He returned after ten minutes, just as the first course was arriving. He still seemed on edge as he apologized, saying he'd had to make an urgent call to his colleagues.

'Never mind, I completely understand,' I smiled. 'Now, where were we? I'd love to know how it all works.'

And so the game of cat and mouse continued. The more questions I asked, the more evasive my dinner companion became. We'd barely got through the dessert course before Tom beat a hasty retreat, saying he had to take another call.

I'm not sure what made me do it, but the following day I called Tom at the GoCardless office.

'Tom? It's Anne Boden, we met last night,' I began. 'I hope you don't mind me calling you, but I still don't understand how your business works.' There was a silence at the other end of the line. I feared he was about to hang up. At last, I heard a sigh.

'OK, let me explain,' he said . . .

He told me that GoCardless were providing an RBS direct-debit facility to businesses too small to buy the services themselves from the bank, but who wanted to give their customers the impression that they could offer such transactions. He'd receive the payment requests and then send them on to the bank. The reason he was so reluctant to talk me through the model was that RBS were unaware of this arrangement. After seeing my name badge, Tom was worried about what would happen if I knew what was happening.

'The reason I disappeared off to the gents was to see if there was some way to get out of the dinner,' he laughed. 'It was a bit awkward.'

I liked Tom and approved of what he was trying to do. He was bright and, now he wasn't trying to hide something, really engaging and full of positive ideas. After setting his mind at rest and talking some more, I agreed to become an advisor at GoCardless and a friendship was made.

This experience really piqued my interest in what could be possible in the banking sector using technology. I travelled widely, knocked on a lot of doors and spoke to whoever in fintech would speak to me. I realized that many of the new companies that were springing up on a daily basis were achieving great things with just a handful of people, whereas big, long-established banks were employing a cast of hundreds to come up with a pale imitation of the same thing. This was really exciting stuff. During the years I had been fixated on dealing with the aftermath of the banking crisis, the world had moved on. Consumers were now operating the financial side of their lives in an entirely different way, but most large banks barely seemed to have noticed.

Although I had lengthy job talks with Microsoft and spent a lot of time in the US discussing a position there, I was convinced that my future career would inevitably be deeply immersed in the fintech area. Then I got the phone call from a headhunter representing AIB.

'Do you fancy going to work for a bank that's been bailed out in the crisis?' said the headhunter.

At face value, it was not the most attractive of job opportunities. AIB were in a mess. The Irish Financial Regulator had recently undertaken a succession of capital assessment reviews across the country's banking system and it had been determined that AIB needed to generate €14.8 billion in additional capital. After a series of capital injections, the government had a 99.8 per cent shareholding. AIB had embarked on a number of asset disposals to raise capital and, as part of the joint EU/ IMF-aided restructuring of the Irish banking system, AIB were also obliged to prepare a viability plan. The next stage in the recovery was a 'transformation programme', which entailed taking a machete to the cost base to reduce it by 20 per cent over two years. This would involve 2,000 redundancies among the 15,000-strong workforce.

The position I was being sounded out for was the new role of group chief operating officer. As COO, I'd be responsible for cutting the workforce and then rebuilding whatever I had left; a challenge not for the faint-hearted and, of course, devastating for those at the other end of this process.

And the compensation for taking on such a gargantuan task? A salary that was capped at €500,000, with no prospect of a bonus. In banking terms, for a role this senior, this was far below the accepted going rate.

It wasn't just the salary that made me think long and hard about taking the job when I was offered it following a succession of interviews and psychometric tests. (The psychometric tests always puzzled me. I wondered what prospective employers expected to get from them.) I hesitated because I had to be sure that it was something I could do, and do well. I also needed to be sure that AIB were willing to change. I confess that my first impression was that there were no obvious signs of such willingness. The huge, sprawling AIB Bankcentre at Ballsbridge was a gleaming open-plan, shining glass-and-metal temple that nodded to past largesse. Were the board really going to put it all behind them and construct a forward-thinking new bank for the twenty-first century?

In the end, I took the job for two reasons. Firstly, I was attracted by the sheer magnitude of the challenge. Here was a once-in-a-lifetime opportunity to take a completely broken bank and turn it round. Secondly, the chief executive, David Duffy, who had been at AIB since December 2010, also impressed me. When we met, he talked inspiringly about the role of technology in modern banking and his vision of how AIB could be more effective for the modern customer. Maybe this was the opportunity to put some of what I had learned into practice as we worked to rebuild AIB and meet their mission to return to profitability by 2014.

I accepted the job, which is how I came to be speeding along in a taxi to Ballsbridge on my first day, evading questions from an inquisitive cabbie.

The onus was on me to hit the ground running. Duffy's strategy for AIB had three main components. The first was to renew the bank's commitment to customers, who ranged from large corporate clients to retailers to the individual on the street. Equally important was a new emphasis on technology and innovation to give customers more choice and flexibility. Finally, we needed to get a grip on income-growth and cost-management measures, to help AIB achieve sustainable profitability. Key to that would be a significant cost-reduction plan, which was where I came in. I was there to restructure, and cuts to the workforce would need to be made quickly.

Even though I needed to reduce costs, I couldn't work blind. If I sat in Ballsbridge with a spreadsheet and just hacked at the numbers, which was the traditional method of cutting costs, I'd be as disassociated from our customers as all the bankers who had come before me. People who banked with us were not just numbers on a spreadsheet. An arbitrary click of a mouse to balance the budget by taking away x per cent of branches, x per cent of customer-services staff and x per cent of back-office assistance didn't nod to anyone's real requirements. That, surely, was where all the problems and lack of trust began?

I resolved that I needed to speak to as many customers and

staff as possible to gauge how any cuts would affect our service and the customer experience with AIB. It was a position shared by David Duffy, who encouraged the executive team to embark on a tour of bank branches. Each month we'd all go to a different town to meet local staff and business clients and generally get nearer to our customers. In addition, I met Irish government officials, finance ministers and international advisors. The European 'troika', which comprises the European Commission, the European Central Bank and the International Monetary Fund, were also stakeholders and came to town on regular visits to assess the state of the Irish banks. The results of my discussions were profoundly depressing. Everyone had a view, but every view was different. Options on the table included higher government spending to artificially stimulate the economy or, the opposite tactic, deflating the economy to reduce growth, or even the nuclear option: defaulting on Ireland's debts. Aside from the gap in expectations, the most worrying part of my discussions was that no one seemed to be working on any significant improvements. Perhaps everyone was waiting for someone else to take the initiative. The inevitable upshot? Nothing changed.

One of the most disappointing manifestations of this micro view of the world came from my own bank. Although desperate to shed its image as an out-of-touch institution that was interested only in profit, rather than the needs of its customers, AIB inadvertently managed to perpetuate this stance, even with their new initiatives.

The most glaring example of this was the new bespoke banking branch in Dundrum's out-of-town shopping centre. On the face of it, the idea was an inspiring one. AIB declared their intention to 'reinvent banking' and it was believed that the most obvious signs of a disconnect with customers were old-fashioned, run-down bank branches. Dundrum was chosen as the location for a complete makeover as the first ever dedicated digital banking store.

The project development was already well underway when I joined in July 2012. The branch had been christened 'The Lab' and I listened with great interest as my new colleagues described this incredible new digital experience. The architect's illustrations of how it would look were pretty impressive too. The refurbishment had more than a passing resemblance to an Apple store, which was not a great surprise since David Duffy was a big Apple fan.

When The Lab opened in April 2013, customers would be able to log on at dedicated terminals and communicate with advisors. There were phones, touch screens and video booths all available for people to fulfil their every banking need.

To the inexperienced eye, Dundrum made a great deal of sense. AIB had 800,000 online customers by this stage and 300,000 were signed up to our mobile banking app. There was clearly an appetite for something a bit more high tech. But, delve below the surface and cracks in the strategy began to emerge. What Dundrum was essentially offering was a service almost identical to the one available on your own PC. If, say, you were after a mortgage, you could go to the Dundrum branch, log on and be put through to an advisor who worked in another part of Dublin. There was absolutely no value added to what you could have done yourself at home.

I kept thinking of something that Ben Horowitz, the American businessman and high-tech entrepreneur, once said. Naturally, new technology is deployed to make something work a lot better. However, to make money out of it, it has to be in the order of magnitude of ten times better than what it's replacing. At least. I had been telling my team about the need to be ten times better, but in reality we were simply polishing up the old stuff with a few shiny new services.

As the days went on, I couldn't escape the nagging doubt that we'd somehow missed the point. Yes, we were opening up technology and the benefits of online banking to those who perhaps had not yet had this opportunity, but did a branch-based system really represent the future of banking? All the research pointed to the fact that customers were using branches less and less. As more people signed up for online and mobile banking, this trend was only ever going to go one way. At this time, around 200 bank branches a year were closing in the UK and surveys showed this was accelerating exponentially. In Europe as a whole, the figure was around 5,500 a year as banks sought to cut costs, with Greece, Spain and Italy reported to be the worst affected regions. You couldn't really blame the banks: branches have a significant overhead cost and with a dwindling number of customers, they don't make as much sense. Among those who have fully embraced mobile banking, many don't step foot in a branch any more than once or twice a year. While Dundrum looked impressively space age and its newness undoubtedly raised the spirits of the organization, I couldn't help wondering if there were more cost-effective ways to encourage digital converts and keep them banking with AIB.

The solution I came up with was surprising to many, since I had long been known to be frustrated with consultancy firms. I hired strategic consultants McKinsey on a three-month project that we dubbed 'Process Reinvention'.

The idea behind it was to look at the customer journey – really look at it – and find a way to give them the best possible experience through digital means. One of the most important things that my previous research with tech companies had taught me was that the focus must always be on the customer. The reason that Apple, Amazon et al. are so successful is they have perfected the delivery of products and services. The entire user experience is seamless. With more and more companies doing the same thing in their own sectors, customer expectations are becoming ever higher. We want to be able to sign into our utilities accounts and see the balance we owe, alongside a read-out of our consumption. When we buy a mobile phone, we expect it to be activated and set up the moment we get it out of the box. When we plug our details into a comparison website to get our annual car insurance quote, we would be very irritated if we needed to start all over again, inputting our personal data, driving history and spouse's situation. It's all stored there, ready to go. It doesn't matter what a business produces, the emphasis needs to be on getting it to the customer in the quickest/simplest/cheapest possible way. In other words, the product or service is there for the convenience of the customer, not the business operator.

What was the equivalent in banking? What did customers rightly expect of a modern bank? More importantly, what was possible at AIB, given our very limited resources?

After discussions with the McKinsey team we all agreed the best way was to think big. We'd put our heads together and come up with a list of the most wonderful processes a bank could have. What would be the 100 per cent perfect solution to a modern customer's every desire? Then we'd work together to redefine it into the most brilliant digital process ever within the consideration of what would be allowed by the regulator and what could be built with our systems in the limited time available.

Something that became evident very quickly was that we needed to go beyond simply automating existing processes. Where we presently were was entirely the wrong place to start. Or, to paraphrase a joke, we were like the tourist who asks an Irish local for directions to Dublin and is told: 'If I were you, I wouldn't start from here.'

Take, as an example, the process of opening a new account. When I first mentioned to the executive team that I was looking at updating and vastly simplifying the process everyone looked shocked.

'That's not going to happen,' one of my senior colleagues said, with an emphatic shake of the head.

'But why not?' I pressed. 'We can't talk about focussing on the customer experience when we make people jump through multiple hoops to open an account.'

'Compliance,' articulated the colleague, with an isn't-it-obvious shrug. But it wasn't obvious to me. Not at all. Then, to make matters even more confusing, another colleague chimed in, blaming 'Central Bank rules'.

When I looked into it, though, what I found was astonishing. Most of these 'rules' didn't actually exist. A lot of what my colleagues believed true was mere folklore, no doubt passed down from generation to generation of bankers. Yes, there were rules. Of course there were. However, the rules were nothing like anyone thought they were, and no one had ever asked for an update.

We needed to think like a start-up and reinvent the whole process completely, cutting the number of steps required, reducing the paperwork and automating as much of the decision making as possible. Obviously, given the limited time and resources available, we couldn't do everything, so twenty processes were identified for the Process Reinvention treatment and I set the McKinsey team an ambitious target of making each process ten times better in terms of efficiency and turnaround times. Shahar Markovitch, then McKinsey's digitalization expert, and the team allocated two weeks to define a best-case-scenario digital version of the application processes for two products: new accounts and mortgages. With the emphasis on thinking like a start-up, they explored the underlying business process, including which elements were essential and which were unnecessary. They also tested each stage of both processes to find out if they were there simply because no one had ever sought to question them. Once they'd found a direct way to get from A to B, the focus switched to finding more agile software approaches.

After the initial analysis, it took six weeks to devise and refine the completely new way of working, alongside the tech side of things. We then moved on to a trial phase to test the new processes with real customers. As far as opening a new account was concerned, this could now be achieved in just ten minutes. This replaced the longstanding (and very sluggish) system that required making an appointment to visit the branch, spending thirty or forty minutes with the staff there filling in an extremely extensive questionnaire and then waiting a further few days before the account was finally live. In the new version, the paperwork was kept to a minimum and the desired result achieved long before the customer began to wonder if it was all really worth it.

The new digital mortgage-application process was even quicker. It used an online calculator that connected to AIB's credit-scoring models to give customers a preliminary offer in less than a minute. Once an offer was received, customers could then access an online portal that allowed them to submit their application and documents, inputting all the required information. The beauty of it was that applicants didn't have to waste an hour of their time laboriously answering a detailed questionnaire, only to be informed that 'computer says no'. This approach not only greatly improved customer satisfaction but also had the advantage of cutting AIB's costs significantly.

Buoyed by the success of the initial trials, Shahar and his team went on to tackle the rest of the twenty processes in the programme, from personal lending to deposits. Each one was given the same treatment, whereby the entire system was unravelled, each step analysed and the unnecessary bits taken out.

What I really loved about the end result was that, to my knowledge, this was the first time a bank had really started thinking about what a customer wanted. After thirty years in banking I had grown used to the fact that data was always used to a bank's advantage, never the customer's. Indeed, very often data was used prejudicially. Now it was finally being used to the client's advantage.

Customers loved it too. In a short space of time after the new account-application process was launched, we saw a 25 per cent lift in accounts opened. That would be pretty spectacular for any bank, but against the background of AIB's terrible reputation in Ireland at the time, it was extraordinary. Couple this with a 20 per cent drop in AIB's account-opening costs and it was easy to see we were on the right track.

By now, I was hungry to learn what more could be done. As well as improving the customer experience and cutting costs, there were opportunities to mine the data we were collecting as we replaced paper documents with electronic ones and manual processes with software. With real-time reports and dashboards on the bank's performance, we'd be able to address any problems before they became critical. We'd be able to understand more about customer behaviour. It seemed to me the prospects were boundless.

Keen to know more, I took a trip to the US with my head of Ops Transformation, Felim O'Donnell, and head of IT Service Management, Paul Sweeney. We visited Cisco, Google HQ, Jive and Adobe, and all sorts of other exciting businesses around Silicon Valley. What we saw there was an inspiration. I was plunged into a world where people were doing things better, faster and cheaper. I was learning about software that had been released in the past few months that had improved many processes in ways previously considered impossible. When we visited Google, I got the opportunity to try out their Google Glasses, but what impressed me most was the line upon line of coaches that bussed in the staff each morning and returned them to San Francisco every evening.

Even as we set off, I realized it had the making of a great comedy skit: two Irishmen and a Welsh woman go to San Jose . . . I should say though, Felim and Paul both had fiercely sharp intellects (albeit with a cruel sense of humour). I was never sure if any of our US hosts could quite figure us out, or even understand the context or humour of the fast-paced commentary from Felim and Paul, but they were very open and welcoming nonetheless.

As we flew back to Ireland I thought long and hard about what I had seen. How far would I be able to apply it all to AIB? I couldn't escape the nagging doubt that I would only ever be able to tinker around the edges. AIB, for all its problems, was a massive organization. Yes, we could make huge improvements by digitizing account opening, mortgage applications and various other processes, but that was never going to be enough. We couldn't truly think like a start-up, or do half of what these US companies were achieving, because we were saddled with legacy issues. Like every large bank, we had a huge infrastructure based on a traditional banking model where customers came into branches to do their banking business. Except they didn't any more. After arriving back in Dublin, I got straight back into the day job, combining the Process Reinvention programme with the gruelling and dispiriting task of restructuring. No one enjoys cutting headcount and I found it very difficult to maintain my enthusiasm against this backdrop. Increasingly, when I got up in the morning and took my shower, I'd ask myself how long I'd have to do this before I could retire. It was becoming harder and harder to justify spending my time on something I wasn't happy about. I always liked to give at least five years to any job, but I wasn't sure if I could stay the course with this one. While I loved the innovative side of it, the restructuring was really taking it out of me.

In the summer of 2013, after months of working twelve-hour days, I took a well-earned break. I travelled to Australia, hoping that a little distance, both geographically and cerebrally, would bring me some clarity about what I wanted to do. Unfortunately, I've never been one for stretching out on a beach with a good novel. In no time at all I found myself arranging to visit bank branches to see what they were up to. As I quickly discovered, the great thing about Aussie banks is, if you turn up at the door and say you work in a bank in Ireland, they welcome you in as though you are a visiting relative. I spent time in the Commonwealth Bank and Westpac, where I was allowed to sit behind the counter and engage with customers, as well as freely talk to staff. Most people seemed a little perplexed as to what I was doing there, but were happy enough to chat.

What I discovered confirmed much of what I had been thinking over the past year or so. The branches were, on the whole, devoid of customers.

'Is it always this quiet?' I asked.

I was behind the counter in a largish branch in the suburbs of Sydney and sitting beside a pleasant, chatty girl called Katie.

'Yes, pretty much,' she said, with a resigned shrug. 'Most of our customers are working, which is a good thing, but it means they don't have the time to come into the branches.'

We were interrupted by a man who arrived at the counter with a bag full of coins. I waited patiently while Katie served him, putting the coins into the automatic counter and then logging them in his account. After waving a cheery goodbye, Katie turned back to me.

'Most of our customers are like that,' she explained. 'Small businesses paying in cash and coins. Yes, we've got the automatic counters for cash and coins, but most of the time they are not quite right for the quantity or type of deposit. I don't know how many years we've been trying to discourage that sort of business, but the irony is, that is all the branches have left.'

'But that will change, won't it?' I said. 'As small businesses move more into taking online payments?'

'It will, and we already see signs of that,' Katie nodded. 'But then who is going to come in and take advantage of our lovely new sofas?'

We both laughed. It did seem faintly ridiculous. The bank in question had clearly spent a great deal of money kitting out the branch with smart colourful carpets and plush new sofas, but fewer and fewer people were coming in and those who did, like the man depositing his small change, didn't have time to lounge around. There was a complete mismatch between what the banks were doing and what customers wanted. It wasn't a problem confined to Australia either. The vision banks were trying to sell to the world was one that customers didn't need.

Others, however, did seem to get it. One of the most interesting characters I met was Michael Harte, the technology guru who was credited with piloting Commonwealth Bank of Australia's modernization programme. He was nearing the end of a $1.5-billion programme to replace the bank's ageing technology system. When we met I felt rather envious as he told me how he had 1,500 people working full time for the past six years on the transformation.

'We've definitely got a bit of a head start over the competition in the tech stakes,' he told me.

Michael has always been seen as a colourful character but he was clearly also passionate about what he'd achieved. He reeled off a list of initiatives, which included a process whereby customers could withdraw money from ATMs using smartphones and a mobile payments terminal that allowed small businesses to take payments while out of the office. In my view, he was coming at things from exactly the right angle: he was giving customers a truly useful service.

'This is exactly the way I'd been thinking,' I told Michael, before describing some of the things we'd done at AIB.

'I'm going to come and see you in Ireland,' he declared when I'd finished.

'Well, we've still got a way to go, but you'd be very welcome, any time.' I smiled, not for one moment expecting he ever would do so.

A couple of days later I was on my way to the Barrier Reef in a bid to finally incorporate a bit of leisure activity into my break, when my phone rang.

'Anne, it's Michael,' said a familiar voice. 'I've organized a team to visit Dublin with me. When am I coming?'

And he did come, too. So many people say they'll do something like this, but they rarely follow through. Harte has since become COO of Santander UK, overseeing their digital transformation, after a period as head of innovation at Barclays. I'm not sure if it was Michael's dogged determination and energy for trying something new that got me thinking, but not long after his visit I started to focus seriously on my own future. I was now certain that there were many, many more things that could be done in banking. In my mind, we were at the birth of a new world. I had to make a choice. I could stay at AIB, doing my best with the hand that I'd been dealt, but in the knowledge that I would never truly be able to create the 'perfect' bank. Alternatively, I could quit and find a way to do it myself, using all I had learned to date. I could start my own bank and attempt to solve all the problems inherent to banking.

As I sat in my office weighing it up, I kept coming back to the same thing: it was a huge, massive, monumental risk. On the plus side, I had enough savings to live on for a while, but even so I would be entering very unfamiliar territory.

'Come on, Anne, what are you scared of?' I chided myself. But I already knew the answer to that question: I was scared of failing. For a brief moment I considered forgetting banking altogether and starting a dress shop. That wouldn't be such a risk. Then I thought again and realized that the probability of failure in that sector was just as high, if not higher. After all, I knew a lot about banks but I was only a consumer of fashion. Besides, my mother had often warned me that fashion was a fickle, cut-throat business.

So that was it. I came to the conclusion that no one can label you a failure when what you are trying to do is audacious. Botching something easy is a failure. Failing in an attempt to achieve something huge is just courageous.

1.   *Find Your Niche*

If you want to make it big as a digital entrepreneur, or indeed any sort of entrepreneur, you need a Big Idea, right? Actually, this isn't entirely true. All you need is *an* idea. Entrepreneurial success is far more dependent on the character and determination of the individual driving the start-up. In fact, most of the world's largest, most profitable digital firms were not built on the back of unique, brilliant ideas that led the market. No, they were built on the dogged persistence of their founders. Facebook was not the first social media platform: it was preceded by Myspace. Google was the *eighth* search engine to appear, after the likes of Lycos, Yahoo and Ask Jeeves. Amazon started life as an online book store, along with dozens of other similar digital retailers. Each business went on to transform its sector thanks to the way their respective founders executed their dream. They *made* it happen. This was the challenge that faced me now.

It is, in fact, very rare that anyone ever has a truly unique idea. The thing that all these businesses have in common is they are *disruptors*. The foundations of their businesses are not unique. They have identified a problem that a large number of people were experiencing with an existing business or service and then found a way to make it more accessible/fast/cheap/efficient. If they pitch it right, in a short space of time, the disruptors become successful enough to replace, or at least displace, the conventional product or service in the sector they've made their own.

I left my job as COO at Allied Irish Banks in December

2013 with a burning desire to create the 'perfect' bank. During my three-decade career in banking I had notched up a lengthy mental list of all the things wrong in my sector. Part of me was mad keen to do something, anything, to get going. There was, however, a little voice in my head that advised me I needed a break first. It had been a tough eighteen months working at AIB in the wake of the worst banking crisis in a generation and I needed time to recover and regroup. I cast around for a suitable venue for a last-minute winter break and chose South Africa. At least I'd be guaranteed plenty of sun and I fancied the idea of a cruise round this country's beautiful coast. Plus, if I was out at sea, there would be no temptation to 'nip into' a few bank branches to do a bit of research.

That was the theory, anyhow. In reality, I was absorbed in banking as much as ever. All hail the smartphone: the invention that means you are never truly out of touch. I managed to rack up a gargantuan bill for using the onboard Wi-Fi (although I subsequently managed to negotiate a discount with the ship's purser). As the cruise ship nosed its way through the beautiful azure waters surrounding Jeffreys Bay towards Mossel Bay and Hermanus, with Cape Town beyond, I was barely aware of the gasps of my fellow holidaymakers as they strained to see the wildlife. I was too busy endlessly scrolling through my newsfeeds, reading everything I could about the latest developments in fintech.

'Surely your office is going to give you a break today,' a loud voice boomed, breaking my train of thought. 'It's New Year's Day!'

I looked up to see a middle-aged man smiling at me. He was wearing shorts and a T-shirt and had the relaxed air of someone who had never, ever worn a suit. Now I remembered, we'd spoken briefly earlier during lunch.

'It's my birthday today too,' I smiled. I was born on 1 January

1960, so was truly a child of the sixties. 'Don't worry, no one is making me do this. I'm doing it all for myself. I'm setting up a business.'

'Oh yeah?' the man nodded. 'Doing what?'

'I'm starting a bank,' I said.

And there it was. I was starting a bank.

'A bank?' my co-traveller asked slowly. 'Don't we have enough of them already? After what has happened over the past few years, I reckon we've got rather too many.'

I understood his point. Banks were still very much in the doghouse. In fact, they'd completely lost the trust of both the general public and businesses alike. Even though the worst of the financial crisis was over, there were still plenty of stories of mis-selling and unhappy customers. The fallout from the credit crunch continued. Consumer confidence in banks was at an all-time low.

'It's going to be a new sort of bank,' I said. 'With a different approach. A digital bank.'

I saw a slight frown cross his brow.

'You do realize banks have apps, right?' he said, as he dug into his shorts pocket to pull out his phone. 'They seem to work OK.'

I laughed as I watched him tap in his pin and pull up his banking app.

'Yes, I am aware of that,' I said. 'I've been involved in making one or two of those myself.'

I realized then and there that I needed to find a way to explain what exactly I was hoping to do. Yes, digital banking had already arrived. Indeed, I had been involved with much of its development while at AIB. I'd seen how powerful a different way of thinking could be. But what I was talking about now was providing a digitized *service* rather than a series of digitized *products*.

By this point, most established businesses had already realized the value of digitizing their output for the new generation
of tech-savvy consumers. This is why newspapers make their
content available online, or in special iPad editions. Likewise,
why musicians sell albums on iTunes and, indeed, why banks
put statements online. However, they are simply taking the ana-
logue version of their products and digitizing them. The result
is an almost exact replica of what is already available. To truly
disrupt a sector, digital entrepreneurs need to go one step, or
indeed several steps, further. In my own case, what I was thinking about now was an entirely new digital banking service.

To do this, you need to start from scratch. I had to consider how to completely unravel the entire concept of banking.
How could I use technology to make the banking experience
much, much better? I was well aware that no existing bank
could even conceive of achieving this at that time. The few
banks that had emerged from the 2008 credit crunch relatively unscathed were too buried in regulations to completely
rethink their business models. This was not to say they suffered from lack of imagination or skill. Far from it. I knew only
too well that the major banks were filled with highly talented
people. Unfortunately, their focus was almost entirely directed
at solving the problems of the past. They also needed to work
with a mountain of new regulations that had been introduced
to see off the chance of any further scandal. With all that going
on, who has the energy, vision, or even time to drive any real
change or innovation?

I needed to figure out what the new version of an established
product would look like from the point of view of customers. It was a given that bank consumers had changed and that
expectations on service were heightened after one sector after
another elsewhere had been transformed by digital. Each time
a sector is disrupted, consumers quickly forget the 'old way'

of doing things. The lure of instant gratification and an easier way of doing things is too great.

As I thought about the new roles a digital bank could adopt, I remembered my recent tour around Silicon Valley and all the exciting things that were being envisaged to service this new way of disruptive thinking. I'd heard the same phrase over and over again when I spoke to start-ups.

First find the problem, then offer the solution.

In other words, the starting point for all these high-tech businesses was finding something that didn't quite work and then putting it right with some sort of bespoke digitized solution. As Paul Graham of Y Combinator fame once said, 'Build something your customers want.'

With this in mind, I thought about how, in an ideal world, people would like to bank today. I'd already gone some way towards answering that question through my work with AIB. Customers had responded well to less bureaucracy and a quicker, more streamlined service, but this was surely just the beginning of what could be achieved.

I was now fully convinced that consumers wanted to see a change in financial services. Research showed that 61 per cent of customers could see no discernible difference between most banks and the younger generation in particular were disappointed by this and desperate for greater choice. In fact, 69 per cent of millennials wanted a greater variety when it came to choosing who to bank with. Most interesting of all, 73 per cent of consumers said they'd be more excited about a new bank offering from Google, Amazon, Apple, PayPal or Square than their own established bank.* The path was laid for new players in the market to supersede the old guard of traditional banks.

* Review of personal current account market, Office of Fair Trading, January 2013.

I thought back to my experiences visiting branches in Ireland, Australia and the US over recent years. Customers' mentality had changed. Hardly anyone saw the need to visit a branch any more. There was plenty of content online to help their decision-making process and many different businesses offering services that were once the sole domain of banks. Consumers had welcomed this development and were now perfectly content to use apps for day-to-day banking, visit comparison sites for purchases like insurance and to shop around the internet for financial products such as mortgages. No one felt the need to be loyal to one financial provider any more, and nor should they.

The corollary of this was that banks no longer had to be one-stop shops. There was no imperative to offer a plethora of financial services, from current accounts to mortgages and insurance. Just as customers could cherry-pick the best products for their needs, banks and indeed any other financial institution could focus on their preferences too. This offered quite an opportunity to anyone able to grasp this concept, since being a specialist means that whatever your product, you have the capacity to offer the best possible all-singing, all-dancing version of it. In my opinion, my new bank had to do only one or two things, but needed to do them really, really well. Today, this process is known as the great unbundling. It's what's happened in the music industry, where albums are unbundled into individual tracks for download, in sport, where viewers can watch individual contests on a pay-per-view basis, and, indeed, in numerous other sectors.

As I did my groundwork, looking at my bank from every conceivable angle, I had what might be referred to as an *Ah-ha!* moment. I was able to see something that others had been blind to, quite possibly because they've been too focussed on the bigger picture in banking. It occurred to me that the biggest opportunity lay in the humble current account. For as long as I could remember, the current account was the most neglected and unloved of all banking services, certainly from a bank's point of view. What, though, if a current account could offer the services people really wanted *and* be profitable to the bank offering it?

Even as I thought about it, I already knew that if I mentioned such an idea to an experienced banker, it would result in a sharp intake of breath.

'You'll never make any money out of a current account,' would be the response. 'It's a loss leader.'

This is a perfect example of the folklore that had always been so readily accepted by my sector. I am sure it must be the same in many other sectors too. I already knew from my experiences at AIB that it is foolish ever to accept any folklore at face value. It pays to ask questions, dig into the detail and find out the truth behind these dogged assertions. In reality, it *is* possible to make money out of current accounts. The reason banks have historically lost money on current accounts is because they heap all the costs of running the entire list of products and services provided to the consumer onto the cost of running a current account. This includes the branch network that is the most expensive side of banking, so it's hardly surprising that current accounts lose money hand over fist. Lose the branches and, hey presto, current accounts suddenly begin to look like an attractive proposition.

A branchless bank using the latest digital technology would have low costs. We would make our money through interchange fees and from net interest margin on the difference between what we pay for deposits and earn from lending as overdrafts.

Working like this would take us away from the accepted banking model, where the revenue drivers are loans and mortgages, to a balance-sheet 'lite' model, where our business would focus on processing transactions.

The goal of my start-up chimed with the central disruptive philosophy of making things simpler and more straightforward for customers. It would be built to help create a more open relationship with money. How many people get themselves into debt because they simply don't know what they've spent, or what they've got left? This sort of scenario can quickly spiral out of control and before they know it, bank customers are 'forgetting' to open credit-card statements, or ignoring messages from their bank. With a digital service current account, where everything is open and transparent, managing finances would become a less threatening, or solitary, experience.

Now I had my core product – the current account – I was able to develop and build on the idea. My vision was to be a financial hub, at the centre of people's lives, where they could instantly see what they have in their account and where they have been spending. The service would be mobile first and always on, delivering a constant live stream of a customer's data into the palms of their hands via their mobiles. Not only that, we'd turn straight facts into intelligent insights to help them manage money. You'd instantly see that you were spending £3 every morning on a Caramelized Pecan Latte at Starbucks and that you had a weakness for popping into Greggs on the way home for a pastry. That's probably why there is always more month than money and you're at least £100 down before payday. Alternatively, if a consumer could get an accurate picture of how restrained they'd been all month, or manually set a threshold spending limit, they'd be able to reward themselves with the odd extravagance.

The service I pictured should not just restrict itself to doing its job and working 'OK' either. It needed to be something that was enjoyable to use. Stressful operations like account opening or setting up payments needed to be super-fast and entirely straightforward. It was important too to give customers all the tools they wanted, so they felt in full control of their finances, rather than always experiencing that somewhat helpless feeling that their bank is keeping them at arm's length.

Thanks to budget-management apps and machine-learning technology, personal debt could become a bad memory. Trends could be instantly spotted in personal accounts and the technology could assist customers in tracking spending on a microscopic level and accessing this information through the digital channels they spend most of their time on.

This would make it easier to identify struggling customers and serve them better. Unusual spikes in late-night credit-card usage combined with low savings rates, for example, would indicate some level of financial stress. Giving affordable credit-limit increases and financial advice to customers tagged by the system could reduce the risk of defaults.

Improved technology would also make financial advisory services more accessible to customers. Robot advisors and artificial intelligence would help take the guesswork out of money management and help a bank's customers stay on their feet financially without too much manual effort.

'But what about if a loyal customer wanted a mortgage?' would be another inevitable question from the naysayers. 'You wouldn't turn down that sort of commercial opportunity, right?'

Well, yes we would. There is nothing that says that a digital enterprise has to be built to mirror traditional businesses in the sector. The joy of being a disruptor is you can pick and choose what you want to be. You're starting from scratch, right? In my case, I was happy to forgo mortgages. However, if our customers wanted a mortgage, we'd be very willing to help; in fact, we'd be a crucial partner. We could work in tandem with approved mortgage companies and would be able to give them a deeper understanding of their potential customer than ever before. With the breadth of data we'd have, there would be no need for mortgage assessors to make informed guesses about customers based on across-the-board market research or stereotypes. The information we'd have would give an instant summary of customer behaviour based on analysis of their payment history. We'd furnish a mortgage lender with intelligent, individual credit assessments based not just on income and expenditure but on a detailed breakdown of where, as well as when, money was earned or spent.

In fact, now I began to develop that thought, I realized that my mobile bank could be a marketplace for all sorts of different financial services, from ISAs, to insurance, mortgages and loans. We would be the central hub offering our customers and their financial partners data at their fingertips. Our understanding of spending patterns would help us give our customers better advice too. If, say, they had a large amount of cash to put on deposit, we'd be able to point them in the direction of the most convenient and profitable place to do so.

Obviously, it would be great to offer a range of financial products to our customers and, all being well, that might be the case in the future. In those early days though, it was prudent to focus on doing one or two things really well. No, not just 'really well'. It needed to be better than anything else that was available in the market. Ten times better.

Or, to quote the billionaire tech entrepreneur Marc Andreessen, who developed Mosaic, the first widely used web browser, in the 1990s and now advises companies from Facebook to Zynga: 'product/market fit means being in a good market with a product that can satisfy that market.'

But was the idea I was formulating on my South African holiday ten times better? Ultimately, there are no acid tests that will tell any would-be digital entrepreneur that their idea is a sure-fire winner, one guaranteed to be hugely successful at that precise moment. Some businesses are brilliant, but just not right for that particular time. If there were such a success barometer, we'd all be running businesses the size of Amazon, and that would never work. Fortunately, experience showed me that there are certain criteria to test an idea against, and check that I was at least on the right track.

One of the most important tests for any fledgling technology business is whether it is scalable. If it isn't, it might be the most brilliant idea ever, but it won't be successful. It's unlikely the enterprise will even make it through the first year. The idea behind scaling a business is simple. If you can add significantly more customers without proportionally increasing your costs, then the business is scalable and will become more and more profitable as it grows. If, on the other hand, you have to add operating costs such as sales personnel, marketing, administration and R&D at the same rate as you grow revenue, then the business does not scale.

Take, as an example, Dropbox, the file sharing/hosting company. Once the technology was built, the only additional costs were for a small amount of cloud hosting. The costs do not increase linearly with each new customer since the process is entirely automated. This is why web-based businesses such as Google Ad Words and Facebook are so scalable: the costs do not increase because they are relatively fixed and additional users don't make a significant impact on them. The same went for my mobile bank idea. Once it was up and running, each new customer who signed up would not represent a proportional increase in costs. Compare this to, say, WeWork, the business that provides shared office space for technology start-ups and other enterprises. While WeWork is marketed as a tech business, it does not follow a scalable strategy and is in fact the antithesis of a digital business. Each time this business targets a new city, it has to spend a considerable amount on marketing. While most of the back-end costs might be fixed, putting more people into more buildings means more costs. Yes, it may well eventually become profitable in each city, but it is a hard slog to make it sizeable. Taking the enterprise worldwide will always incur numerous extra costs in each new location.

There are three acid tests to check whether or not an idea is scalable. They are:

The fixed costs to build. What will it take to start up the business (rough estimates will do at this development stage) and how long before it starts to generate revenues to cover the costs?

Ongoing operating costs. Will there be ongoing monthly, or annual, costs to run the business, and if so, how much? Will these costs increase with each new customer that's signed up? If x customers respond, how many additional staff will the business need to recruit (and pay) in order to service the business?

End-state economics and what it will take to get there. What will the numbers look like when the enterprise reaches its goals? How many customers, or how much revenue, is needed to break even? Will these numbers change if the business grows faster, or slower, than anticipated?

The beauty of most technology businesses is they are relatively easy to scale. They tend to have a core set of assets, such as a website, or app, which are developed early on and can then be monetized at a relatively low cost. Get it right and the top-line growth can become exponential, which is why venture capitalists are generally keen to hear pitches from technology firms.

Another crucial test of an idea, which is related to scalability, is whether or not the potential market is large enough. When casting around for an idea, people often, quite rightly, keep one eye on the competition. What is already in the market? Is it already crowded with start-ups, vying to become the big-name disruptor of the sector? There is a natural tendency to avoid such busy markets at all costs, to try somewhere a little quieter. However, the question that needs to be asked here is: is it too quiet? If the potential marketplace is too specialized, it will be impossible to scale the business properly. It simply won't attract enough customers. While I was the first person to attempt a mobile-only bank, I was convinced that this was something that the market was crying out for. My research at AIB had shown me that customers were very frustrated with what they were getting from their existing service. The sector was ripe for change. If I got it right, I could target the *whole* banking market. That's a pretty significant market: everyone has to have a current account these days.

One more, perhaps too little considered test that any entrepreneur should try is to ask themselves whether they are a potential user of the product or service they are intending to launch. Anyone wanting to begin a business selling, say, the next generation of smart electric scooters should have an interest in, or experience of, those vehicles or something similar. However, anyone with an eye on beginning a new line of personal space rockets (holiday on the moon, anyone?) will be starting from an extremely low knowledge base. Being a user makes creating a business around improving what's on offer much easier. Most importantly, you need to understand where you are, and be prepared to adjust your thinking whichever side of the divide you come from. I had the benefit of being not just a potential user, since I was already a huge fan of fintech, but also steeped in the banking sector, having worked in it my whole career.

I was expecting plenty of criticism as I devised my business model. I anticipated that the majority of people who didn't believe it was possible would dismiss me with a single statement: 'But no one ever changes their bank!'

In the past, that was true. When I started thinking about my new bank in the early 2010s, the big established players looked after 85 per cent of the nation's bank accounts and the position hadn't changed for years. Indeed, the average length of time most people held a current account was sixteen years. When you consider that the average duration of a marriage in the UK is twelve years, the first figure makes bleak reading if you are thinking of starting a bank. (Actually, it is pretty depressing if you are planning a wedding too!) However, the banking situation was beginning to change. The Payments Council had launched a new account-switching service just a few months earlier in September 2013. It guaranteed any payments scheduled in an existing account would automatically be moved over to a new account within seven working days. At a stroke it saw off the age-old fear that bills would get missed. Suddenly, it just became easier to shop around and get a better bank account. There had already been a marked increase in people switching accounts. In the first three months since Switching Services began, 306,000 people had taken advantage of the new procedure. As we all now know, once trends begin to change and people can see what is possible, the status quo crumbles pretty quickly.

I was also very aware that the support for this change in traditional big-bank dominance came from the very top. Since the credit crunch there had arisen a significant will across the political spectrum to shake up banking and remove power from the grip of a mere handful of key players. Steps had already been taken to reduce the market share of the biggest banks, with the revival of previously retired brands such as Williams & Glyn from RBS and TSB from Lloyds. The brands were resurrected in order to sell off branches, effectively reversing all the mega mergers that had characterized the banking industry for the past decades. (The RBS/Williams & Glyn separation was subsequently found to be too difficult, so a fund of £775 million was set up to help smaller banks compete. The bank I would found would later apply for a grant from this very fund. But more of this later.) Politicians openly spoke about the desire to encourage new, smaller banks and were opening up the bank licensing system to assist this endeavour.

While there would undoubtedly be other contenders entering the market, I was pretty convinced that there was no one else who had my unique balance of skills. I understood banking after thirty years plus in the sector and I knew the technology side. I had been at the front line of every single big infrastructure change in modern banking, which surely put me in good stead for the next big leap.

As I weighed up my options, I had to push out of my mind any doubts based on the fact that this was a banking model that had never been attempted before. We were completely ignoring the old way of doing things and totally reinventing a sector without being hampered by outdated, ineffective, irrelevant ideas. Which brings me to what was, undoubtedly, going to be one of the biggest challenges of my digital start-up: the tech side.

Again, I could comfort myself with the knowledge that I had a head start on the big banks. I knew for a fact that every single major bank had to rely on legacy technology that stretched back to the seventies and eighties. Banks had not been able to keep up with evolving technology, not even close. This is not to say they hadn't tried. Over the years, with each new iteration of technology, extra bits had been bolted onto already overstretched systems. The result? A dysfunctional mishmash of disparate systems with outdated code and imprisoned data streams, all held together with an ageing infrastructure.

While there was not a bank CEO on the planet who didn't appreciate that this was a big issue, knowing about it and actually being able to do something about it were not the same thing. You couldn't simply stop everything, strip out the old stuff and insert a whole load of gleaming new machines. That sort of transformation programme would cost at least £1.5 billion, and take between five and seven years, and meanwhile customers would require access to their money 24/7.

'Yes, madam, we are really sorry you can't draw on your salary today, would it be possible to wait until July five years hence? We'll have an amazing system running by then (all being well) and you'll really appreciate the changes.'

There is not a return-on-investment calculation in the world that is high enough to justify a big bank making any of these changes. This meant the only option to major banks hoping to remain competitive was to ignore the core issue and compete in the commodity market instead. By doing so, they amass a staggering amount of products and services, further stretching the legacy IT systems. It's a recipe for disaster, leading at worst to another financial meltdown, at best to a race to the bottom, since there is nothing truly new to offer other than teaser rates and complicated package deals. No wonder banking customers were fed up. They were being presented with delayed access to information, a fragmented view of their finances and very little control over their hard-earned cash.

Although I was starting with a blank sheet, I was certain there was a market for my idea and I knew it was scalable. From what I understood from my research, I believed I could set up an IT system markedly superior to what was currently available for the low tens of millions. It sounds a lot, I know, and that sort of figure brought me out in a cold sweat every time I thought about it. However, measure it against the maintenance and upgrade bill of the average legacy system and it doesn't sound quite so uncomfortable. Of course, tens of millions is tens of millions. Without a big influx of cash, I wouldn't get anywhere. For investment, you need credibility.

I had no doubt whatsoever I was about to take a big leap. In building this brand-new bank from scratch, I would be attempting something that hadn't been done for thirty years. Get it right, though, and this service would be known as banking's equivalent of Google or Facebook, which was pretty amazing by any measure. Best of all, it would be a banking service that would finally empower the customer, a development that was long overdue.

As I neared the end of my South African 'break', I mentally worked through the long list of things I'd need to do. I pushed to the back of my mind any nagging doubts that this wouldn't end well and did my best to forget that I was going to need money. A lot of money. I was 100 per cent convinced I was on to the right idea, but my experience also told me that even with a brilliant, rock-solid innovation, it was more likely that I would fail than succeed. For every fifty start-ups, only one or two ever get off the ground. Of those that do, many don't survive their first five years.

I was more convinced than ever that the only way to test all my assumptions was to get on with it. Funnily enough, I'd bought a copy of Eric Ries's book *The Lean Startup* at the airport on the way to South Africa. It was actually my second copy, but I saw it in the airport bookshop and knew it would come in handy. I reflected that Ries's concepts seemed so close to my beliefs and what I knew to be true but there would be some natural tensions between *Lean Startup* practices and the regulation that I would need to deal with in order to start a bank. I couldn't actually just start trading, I needed a licence first. There would be so much to do before I could actually start working with customers. No industry is more highly regulated than banking and I completely agreed with Ries's exhortation to ignore the magnitude of the task and just tackle it all head on, making progress where you can.

I've heard it said so many times that you should only start a project if you have a really good idea and it is definitely going to succeed. Right then, I couldn't say whether my bank would definitely succeed, but I knew it was a brilliant idea. I wanted to create a bank of the future, a completely different bank that would serve the lifestyles and aspirations of the modern consumer. I would find a way to demystify everything the financial markets did so that it became accessible to everyone, not just the privileged, financially savvy few and would offer products that would vastly improve the way we save and spend. And, in a first for the banking industry, I intended to put the consumer's needs first. All the time.

I thought back again to my American trip. The prevailing view was that it would be a while before financial services got the same disruptive treatment that had transformed industries like tourism, transport and entertainment. While there was widespread agreement that 'something needed to happen' and would do so eventually, it was not on the immediate radar. I disagreed. I suspected I would be doing that a lot in the coming months. The time to transform banking had arrived.

2.   *Get On With It!*

Things I didn't know when I decided to start a challenger bank:

- No one ever 'starts' a bank.
- If you don't have a track record as an entrepreneur, you won't get investment.
- Even if I did have a track record, the sort of money I needed was out of the question.
- Apparently building the tech infrastructure I envisaged was 'impossible'.

Oh, and there was one other, crucial elephant in the room: I was a fifty-four-year-old woman. In a sector dominated by younger men, a female entrepreneur in fintech is a rarity. In the UK, just 1 per cent of venture capital funding goes to all-female-founded teams and that figure remains stubbornly stagnant year after year.* In Switzerland, which has been named the 'most equal country in Europe', companies led by women still only get just over 22 per cent of available funds.† Hardly surprisingly, many women self-select out of the IT sector because of its astonishing lack of gender diversity. While no one ever mentioned this glaring disparity between the sexes out loud, I was very aware that this might easily have been a

* *Financial Times*, 4 February 2019, www.ft.com/content/330b7904-2638-11e9-8ce6-5db4543da632.
† PitchBook Data, www.british-business-bank.co.uk/wp-content/uploads/2019/01/UK_VC_and_Female_Founders_Report_British_Business_Bank.pdf.

contributing factor in making the improbable impossible. If 99 per cent of investments were going to men in their thirties, who would really want to take a risk on a woman in her fifties?

Of course, I didn't really know any of this when I landed back in the UK from South Africa in January 2014. My only fixation was putting all the thoughts that were buzzing around my brain into action.

There were two key components I needed to have in place to get a bank started. One was, naturally, money. The other was a banking licence. That all sounds relatively straightforward (if challenging) taken at face value. However, there was a somewhat fiendish conundrum to throw into the mix. It was not possible to get a banking licence unless you could prove you had money. Meanwhile, it was not possible to raise money from investors to start a bank if you didn't have a banking licence in place. It was a classic catch-22.

On the plus side, the regulatory system had recently been considerably simplified. In March 2013, Chancellor George Osborne had declared the UK banking system 'too concentrated' and introduced a number of reforms to pave the way for new entrants. Potential newcomers were promised 'relaxed' capital and liquidity requirements. The Prudential Regulation Authority (PRA), which took over supervision of safety and soundness in April that year, declared it was committed to 'levelling the playing field' between large banks and their smaller and newer competitors. It was working with the new Financial Conduct Authority (FCA) to revamp the bank application process and make it easier. The target was to reduce the entire process from two years to one. Even so, a great deal of money was still required to get even this far. At this stage my back-of-the-envelope calculations put the figure required at at least £300 million.

So, how could a new bank get started? In an ideal world, I

would be a well-funded entrepreneur. Perhaps I would have already started a business, then sold it for a considerable sum, or floated it. That way I would have a good capital sum to get my newest venture off the ground.

Except this hadn't happened. I was literally starting from scratch. I had no team, no office and no money bar my life savings. I had a house that I had bought in Swansea for my father that was now let out and could be sold if things got desperate, but other than that, my options were limited. With the sort of sums I was looking at, that wasn't going to get me much beyond the first few months.

I had to constantly remind myself that the default state of a tech start-up, indeed any start-up, is dead.* In other words, if you don't get up and do something to make it happen, it never ever will.

Jumping in and just getting on with things was not a culture I was used to. In my old life, working for large corporates, whenever a major new project was announced, the sequence of events went something like this. Let's say, the business was looking to build or buy a new HR system. Initially, a group of people would be assigned to the task and their first move would be to set up a steering committee to discuss it. This committee would come up with a number of options, each of which would be explored in detail by further subcommittees. (By 'explored', I mean discussed and researched, rather than becoming anything like a physical reality.) Eventually, months down the line, a decision would be taken and the HR system purchased.

Contrast that with what happens at a start-up (and indeed what did happen at Starling a little further down the line). Here, someone will mention that, now the business has reached a

---

* With thanks to Paul Graham, founder of Y Combinator, who coined this expression.

certain size, it might be prudent to consider buying some sort of HR system in order to manage things a bit more smoothly. This is the cue for the founder to flip open their laptop, google 'HR system', choose one that looks good and then buy it with their company credit card. Now, it may turn out not to be 100 per cent perfect for the start-up's needs. However, chances are that it would be at least 95 per cent of the way there. And that's good enough. In fact, it will probably be no different in efficiency from the one my big-business colleagues spent many hours agonizing about over several months.

The reason for making this comparison is to introduce the style of working any would-be digital entrepreneur needs to adopt. The somewhat shorter version would be: *Get on with it!*

This was something very much on my mind as I began the first days of what was to become a well-worn, often exhausting, routine. I'd wake up while it was still dark and leave the house before dawn, being careful not to trip over my still-to-be-unpacked South African cruise suitcase and AIB boxes that had now been shipped back from Ireland. I'd drive down the M40 towards London from my home in Marlow, well ahead of the morning rush hour. Once I'd parked outside my flat in St John's Wood, I would head over to Marylebone High Street. I chose it as my 'base' because I had always found its eclectic mix of village atmosphere and metropolitan sophistry quite uplifting.

My preferred breakfast destination became Le Pain Quotidien, where I'd have a soft-boiled egg with granary toast while I read the newspapers. After that, I'd nurse multiple cups of tea while I wrote email after email, each one asking, encouraging and pushing. Between meetings, I would frequent hotel cafés and coffee shops and quickly became an aficionado of the best spots in each London postcode to find free and fast Wi-Fi. If all else fails, I could always write an online guide for aspiring entrepreneurs, I thought. That sort of information can be gold dust when you are desperately trying to get people interested in your business idea.

The majority of those early meetings followed one or another of what were to become two frustratingly familiar patterns. In the first instance, my contacts would give me a hearing and then let me down gently with platitudes such as 'This is not right for us just now,' or, 'It's not an area we are really focussing on.'

In the other camp, however, were those who felt they had an obligation to set me straight and explain point by point just what a ludicrous undertaking this was, particularly for some-one who was not a city grandee. Who the hell did I think I was, imagining I could make my mark on the sector? Where were all my high-profile backers? What chance did someone like me think I stood?

The first few weeks of knocking on doors was a miser-able, soul-destroying, energy-sapping job. Without a doubt, the lowest point came late on one Friday afternoon at the end of January. It was 5 p.m., dark and pouring with rain. As I arrived for my appointment at the law firm in question, people were already streaming out of the front doors and heading towards nearby Liverpool Street station, hoping to make an early start on the weekend. I'm never one to be side-tracked by negative thoughts, but even as I headed towards the reception desk to announce myself, I already had a fair idea of how this was going to go. I could see it now. I would be starting my pitch – 'Hello, I am Anne Boden and I have this idea for a new sort of bank' – and meanwhile everyone in the room would be aching to get away. I wasn't wrong.

Not all my meetings were as miserable as this, though. A few people I did speak to were extraordinarily kind and generous with their time and advice. One who stood out in particular was my fellow Welshman Sir Terry Matthews, who co-founded tech giant Mitel with Michael Cowpland in 1972. (The name Mitel is a contraction of Mike and Terry Lawnmowers.)

'Where are you now?' he said, when we first spoke. 'In your garden? Get yourself an office.'

He explained that, when he started Mitel, people were reluctant to trust a venture that didn't sound stable. He needed an office and someone to answer the phone. He got anyone who was around to pick up his phone and say: Mr Matthews is in a meeting in the conference room right now, can I get him to call you back? Of course, there was no office, let alone a conference room, and no permanent staff answering the phones. Fake it till you make it, was the clear message.

Fortunately, I did have a few funny moments at this stage, even though I must have cut a pretty solitary figure trawling around the City and Mayfair day after day. I realized very early on that I needed to be resilient and find the humour in any situation, otherwise I'd quickly burn out. Thus, when I found myself in the office of a branch of Lloyds Bank opening a business account, I could barely suppress my giggles.

'What is the nature of the business?' asked the earnest young man in a smart black suit from behind his computer screen. He'd already laboriously typed in many of my basic, personal details.

'I'm starting a bank,' I replied, as matter-of-factly as I could.

'A bank?' he repeated slowly, staring at his screen with a hint of a frown on his brow. 'What sort of bank?'

I took a deep breath.

'A bank that does,' I smiled.

The poor man looked utterly perplexed.

The truth is, there were precious few laughs on offer in those early days. Like any start-up founder, I was under the most unbelievable pressure from Day One. The pressure was unlike anything I had ever experienced, even in my senior executive career. The change in status in moving from AIB to set up New Bank (my working title for the venture) was notice-able and jarring. Life was certainly a lot easier when I was going to speak to people as Anne Boden, Chief Operating Offi-cer, AIB, than when I was knocking on doors as Anne Boden from A Bank No One Has Yet Heard Of.

It is tough asking other people for money, or services, for free. Remaining resilient day after day is not easy.

There's a lot of advice around saying that you need to take time out to look after your physical and mental health when you are trying to get a start-up off the ground. The truth is, no one ever really does. For a start, things are moving so fast, and there are so many demands on your time and energy, that looking after yourself always feels like an indulgence. If ever I found myself with a 'quiet' five minutes, I became consumed with guilt that I was not doing enough and immediately started running through my long to-do list. Even so, it's never easy to pick yourself up after a 'no' and head off to another meeting that will almost certainly end in another 'no'. It is horrible and demoralizing every time.

Fortunately for me, I have always been pretty strong minded. In those tough early days, a combination of instinct and trial-and-error helped me find a way through the endless rejection. I developed many personal coping mechanisms. One of the simplest was to immerse myself in books about other entre-preneurs, which has been a long-term interest of mine anyway. I find it hugely absorbing to learn their stories, and it's use-ful to discover how others have withstood the pressures. It's a comfort to know that other entrepreneurs have experienced exactly the same emotions.

When I desperately needed some respite, another of my fall-back positions was to send out what felt like hundreds of emails at a time, asking for help and advice. Often they went out to people I knew, and who were unlikely to be in a position to further my cause. However, their kind and encouraging responses kept me sane at the toughest moments and gave me some valuable breathing space. I felt like I had achieved something too, however insignificant.

I also adopted a series of mental tricks to convince myself to carry on. Whenever the number of rejections threatened to become unmanageable, one of my favoured tactics was to arrange meetings with friends in the banking industry whom I had known for years. Again, these were people who were never going to invest in New Bank or play any sort of role in the business. However, they had the advantage of being long-term associates who would give me a polite hearing and perhaps even a snippet of advice and feedback. What they absolutely wouldn't be doing was doling out abrupt 'no's along with some apparently 'helpful' advice as to why my entire business model was completely ridiculous and would never succeed. Such a meeting would be like food to a starving person, offering a much-needed break from the seemingly endless cycle of rejection. *Wasn't this wasting time?* You may well ask that question. I don't think it was. No one can continue in the face of an endless negative barrage. We all need some respite from it. It's nice to have a pleasant and positive meeting at least once in a while, because it leaves you refreshed enough to tackle what comes next. I also used the conversations to reinforce my belief that I was right and the banking system was wrong.

I think it was also useful to look upon the journey as a series of sprints, rather than a single marathon. Yes, I aspired to grow a significant digital enterprise, but I needed to break that ambition down to bite-sized goals. If I hadn't done so, the scale of the task would have quickly become overwhelming. I strongly suspect that anyone who thinks about their start-up as part of a trajectory towards running a multimillion-pound corporation (with all the personal wealth and prosperity that goes with that) is heading for a fall from the start. Fortunately for me, it was never about the money, or fame, that entrepreneurial success would bring. Neither was an incentive for me then and that remains true today. In fact, if you asked me what was my main motivation then, it was to have a job. People from where I was brought up all have jobs. I passionately believed that the job that I was most qualified to do at that particular time was to begin a bank. If I had been someone who spent time daydreaming about fame and fortune, I'd never have been able to focus on the tough day-to-day stuff I needed to do to get there. But when something did go right, the tremendous mental stimulation and pleasure it brought was often enough to sustain me for days afterwards.

One of my first memorable experiences in this respect was when my persistence did, finally, appear to be beginning to pay off. KPMG, my top pick to help me with strategy and working towards a banking licence, began to show some interest. I'd worked with KPMG before and got on well with Michael Carolan, a director at their London office.

As I'd typed my initial email to Michael, I wasn't exactly sure what reaction I would get. I wasn't naive enough to think that I would write and say, 'Hey, I am starting a bank,' and he'd say, 'Great, let's sort all that out for you.' Perhaps, though, he'd be able to unlock some doors.

Hi, Michael, remember me from Project Prada?*

I wrote.

You may be aware that I've been in Ireland as Chief Operating Officer of Allied Irish Banks. I'm working on a new project and would appreciate a chat.

* The code name I had given to a top-secret but ultimately unsuccessful bid to buy a business from a major bank before I joined AIB. Michael had worked with me on the project.

He replied immediately to say that of course he remembered me and had actually tried getting in touch a few times over the previous months but had been emailing the wrong address.

Well, at least that is a promising start, I thought.

Within a couple of days, I was sitting in the plush boardroom of KPMG at their offices in Canary Wharf. I'd only given Michael the barest hint of what I was up to, but he brought along Giles Adams, one of KPMG's regulation experts. The fact that Giles was there was a real bonus, because the one area where I most needed help was in getting a licence. I needed to know exactly what was required and then detailed assistance in preparing all the plans and submissions for the regulator.

At that stage, I had very little to show my hosts other than a presentation I had prepared that summarized all the thoughts I'd been having over the past months, as well as the research I had put together so far to back my argument. They listened carefully as I talked through what I believed customers wanted, rather than what banks believed they should have.

As I reached the end of my presentation, I held my breath. What was it going to be? *What was it going to be?* 'This is not on our radar right now' *or* 'You don't stand a chance'?

'Well, the first big hurdle to tackle is the initial meeting with the regulator,' Michael began. 'Giles will sort that out for you, but my view is we need to have a workshop to discuss the contents of the presentation to them.'

As Michael listed the next steps, I knew I had to raise the biggest issue of all, which was, of course, payment. There was no possible way that I would be in a position to pay KPMG the going rate for their services any time soon. Just getting to the point of making a full presentation to the regulator would set me back hundreds of thousands. It was money I didn't have and wouldn't be able to get until I secured investment.

'We need to talk about fees,' I said. 'I'd like to discuss the possibility of KPMG working on a contingent fee basis.' In other words, the fee to be paid was deferred to some point in the future and would be payable only if there was a favourable result, i.e. when the bank opened its virtual doors.

Once again, I held my breath.

'That is something we'd be prepared to consider,' Michael nodded. 'Obviously, a lot of people would be involved in a decision like that, but I suggest we start putting together a detailed proposal.'

While it was a huge lift finally to have some positive feedback, I didn't have much time to bask in the glory of having taken a massive step forward. Michael and Giles started asking questions about the business model, which were as intelligent and insightful as anyone might expect from such experienced consultants. I answered them on everything I could and agreed to come back with anything I couldn't confirm at that stage.

By the time I left KPMG's offices, I was exhausted, but really happy too. The people I had just met were experienced, seasoned practitioners. They'd seen the merit in the model I was proposing, which appeared to imply I was on the right track. For once, my age and background had actually stood me in good stead too. And, if I had managed to convince KPMG, that meant it was perfectly possible I'd be able to excite other big names.

Sure enough, my luck did seem to be beginning to turn. As I waited patiently for the powers-that-be at KPMG to make up their minds about working on a contingency basis, I managed to get Clifford Chance to agree to the same terms. After knocking on the doors of literally dozens of law firms, one finally said yes. Clifford Chance was one of the best, too, and their agreement was perfectly timed.

Something else that was high on my list of priorities was the creative side. It might have seemed like early days, but getting the branding and related marketing for New Bank right was crucial. I was preparing to launch an entirely new consumer brand into a highly traditional market where consumers are notoriously reluctant to try anything new. I would need something pretty powerful to convince would-be customers that this was a credible, established brand that they could trust with their money. It was a big ask, and getting the branding right was key. Branding is what gets people to believe in a product and understand its values. A strong identity sends a clear message and should mean as much to customers as the business model itself. This would all, of course, begin with finding a good name for New Bank that would resonate with consumers and quickly become synonymous with a new way of banking. Once I had that in place, we'd need all the related design elements, such as a logo and marketing material, as well as what the actual interface would look like, and how it would all gel together. There was a long list of branding requirements.

Until now, I'd always worked in established businesses with strong branding already in place. Starting an entirely new consumer-banking brand from scratch was a daunting challenge to say the least. However, I reasoned with myself that it was probably no more daunting than anything else I was trying to do. Like all the other components I was tackling, I just needed to find the best possible advisors in their particular sectors and let them use their expertise to put together something that stood head and shoulders above everything else. In the case of the branding, help came quite early on and from a most unexpected source.

One of the people on my long list of contacts was Edward Griffin from Rothschild. I'd first come across Ed back in 2010, when I was trying to establish myself as a non-executive. I was working in the establishment side of banking then and decided that my best career development option was to get a foothold on various Blue Chip boards. The move coincided with noises being made by various people in the City that big businesses needed to be more inclusive. At long last, someone had looked around our nation's boardrooms and thought, 'Hmmm, these are all a bit pale, male and stale.' The thinking went that a bit more diversity and a few more women about the place might actually be an advantage when it came to cutting down on some of the mediocrity, or complacency, that blighted some top companies.

That was the theory, anyhow. It quickly emerged that a great deal of the noise about challenging the status quo was actually hot air. Certainly, I had a plethora of meetings and attended numerous networking activities, but it all came to naught. On the plus side, I did make a few good contacts, which stood me in pretty good stead as I trawled the City looking for assistance with New Bank.

Ed Griffin was one of those contacts and is what would commonly be known as a 'big cheese' in my former world. He was at the top end of the banking business, buying and selling bailed-out banks for Rothschild's clients. His deals were all in the billions of pounds or dollars, so he would never be in the slightest bit interested in a tiny start-up like New Bank. However, Ed was extremely well connected and we'd always got on well, so why not? Indeed, he too had been very helpful during Project Prada. I sent him an email.

> Edward, just to let you know I've left AIB to start a digital bank. There's a longer story to be told but in essence this is what I'm up to. What about a coffee? I'm in London next week on 3 February.

To his credit, he responded straight away. We met up a few weeks later at Rothschild's most luxurious new headquarters in London. It really was a quite sumptuous venue, embedded in the narrow medieval alley of St Swithin's Lane in the City. After we'd briefly caught up, I gave Ed an elevator pitch for New Bank. He listened quietly as I went through it and asked a few questions at the end. I explained that I was really hopeful that KPMG would come on board but was waiting to hear whether they were happy with contingent fees.

'In the meantime, I have got a ton of other things to get organized,' I said, preparing myself to reel off the long list of 'what next'. I must have mentally gone through this list a dozen times each day and each time it seemed to get longer.

'Very importantly, I need to start work on the actual model, so I am starting to twist a few arms among some project management guys I know. Then there is the branding side of things, which, to be honest, is not my area of expertise.'

'I can help you there,' Ed interrupted.

'You can?'

'I'll put you in touch with Martin Sorrell,' he said. 'WPP will put you on the right track.'

WPP? Talk about going to the very top. A personal introduction to the boss of the world's largest marketing communications business? That wasn't something you got every day.

'Well, that would be fantastic,' I said.

Ed said to give him some time and he'd come back to me. I didn't want to get my hopes up too highly, since it was entirely probable Mr Sorrell would turn me down flat, but it was an opening and often that is all it takes.

While I waited to hear from KPMG and Ed, I continued my trawl of contacts. My focus turned to the tech side. It was, after all, a key component of a new, all-singing, all-dancing, mobile banking app. How would the software actually operate? All being well, KPMG would be working on the hugely complex financials, with details such as how much money is being made, the liquidity required and so on, but we still needed someone to actually build it.

Trawling through my now well-worn contacts list once again, I came across someone I knew from Dell. While Dell are well known for their hardware, many people don't realize that they once had a large interest in software and services. I typed out a short email to Sameer Kishore, the vice-president and general manager of Dell Services, and waited to see if he responded. Within a short space of time a delightfully gung-ho email appeared in my inbox.

> We'd be delighted to work with you on this and bring the power of Dell – from hardware, software and services. I would like to involve two of my colleagues – Ashish Shahare (our EMEA Banking Head) and Niraj Singhal (our Global Banking Head) in the discussions.

That looked promising. In a short space of time, I found myself heading to Dell's offices in Bracknell to meet the three men. It quickly emerged that the timing couldn't have been better. The company's founder Michael Dell had recently made a speech about how much he supported start-ups. Having started his own company, he knew the challenges people like me faced and was keen to do his bit to help.

'So, tell us what you want from us,' Sameer said.

This was my cue to go through my presentation, explaining what New Bank would do and why it was so much better than anything else that had gone before. Making full use of the giant whiteboards that were dotted around the Dell office, I explained what I knew about how it would be built, the various timelines involved and the system I believed was required.

The Dell executives seemed enthralled by the idea and asked lots of questions.

'We need a workshop to go through the whole process from a customer point of view,' Sameer concluded.

Of course, there was, as ever, the thorny issue of cost. As everyone in the room was aware, a system like this didn't come cheap. There were not simply software requirements to take into consideration, there needed to be strict anti-fraud protections too.

'How soon do you think you'll be in a position to raise the investment?' Sameer asked.

'Well, obviously, this is something I am working on at the moment,' I explained. 'Something I would like to raise with you, in the light of the comments made by Michael Dell in his speech about supporting start-ups, is some sort of arrangement where Dell invests in the technology in return for a certain percentage of the company.'

Sameer nodded.

'Well, that's obviously not a decision that can be taken here today,' he said, 'but I suggest we proceed as discussed and work on both things concurrently. There is certainly an appetite here to be involved with this.'

I knew from experience that companies like Dell have big budgets when it comes to winning new business. In some cases, they are prepared to spend several millions. If they bought into the idea of New Bank, which they seemed to have done, I could count on the support of some of their best people as we started to build the software. This was another piece of great news. We agreed to meet again soon to kick off the workshop.

The final, crucial piece of the starting-up process was the actual financial model for New Bank. Our early financial needs were, by necessity, quite complex. We were, after all, in the money business, intending to take in our customers' money and lend it out to others. This meant that I needed a financial model from the beginning. In banking this means an accurate idea of how much money will be going in and out each month, so we knew how much we could lend. That might sound quite simple, although in fact it is anything but. On a very basic level, the amount that lands in the bank just after payday is naturally quite different from what is left at the end of the month. Likewise, customers may be relatively flush in the quiet months of February and March, but cleared out in the festive season of November and December. For obvious reasons, banking regulators have very strict rules about how much liquidity a bank must have. If, for example, New Bank took in £1 million of deposits, and lent out £1 million on the back of them, we'd be in a spot of bother if one of our customers went to an ATM and tried to take out £10. There would be nothing left to give them, which is obviously completely unacceptable. Hence there needs to be a carefully thought-out financial model which mimics the way people use their bank accounts, so we'd fully understand all eventualities. We'd also need to take into account our own costs, such as personnel, premises, salaries and software: a business plan and then some.

To begin with, I had a little go myself, tinkering around the edges of what needed to be done, but even though I count myself as very financially savvy, I was honest enough to know this was not the best use of my time. I am not someone who builds financial models. The obvious answer was to get in someone with the requisite skills. At this stage though, contenders weren't exactly queuing at the door and I had barely any money to pay them even if they had been. Nor was it possible to simply buy something off the shelf and adapt it. My bank was an entirely new concept.

I was sitting in my usual café, mulling this over and wondering what to do next. As usual, I had one eye on my emails, in case a new response came in that might lead to another opportunity for my business. I flicked over to the Google home page and looked at the 'search' box. What was I looking for? Banking model financial guru? All-round financial modelling genius prepared to work for virtually nothing?

I typed in a few searches. All the usual recruitment agencies and LinkedIn pages popped up. At the top of the page was a Google Ad for PeoplePerHour.

'Find the world's best freelancers,' it said. 'Post a free project and let people find you.'

I clicked on the site. It's got to be worth a punt, I thought. I filled in the form, listing the requirements of the job as fully as possible, without giving too much away about myself or what I was trying to do. It took about fifteen minutes to complete and as I pressed the 'post job' button, I shook my head. It was a really long shot. Imagine, though, if it did come off. That would be a story to tell.

I started to receive proposals from freelancers within hours. Amazingly, one of the first was from a man called Howard who had previously worked on a banking model for a start-up and was offering his services for just £7 per hour!

It seemed to me I didn't have much to lose in bringing this chap on board. At that point I was still very much a sole trader, but Team Anne could not remain a team of one member indefinitely. There was a lot to be done and there was no way I'd be able to do even a fraction of it on my own. Howard did a fair job too. None of what he did has any bearing on the Starling Bank model you see today, but at the time, it was exactly what we needed. It gave us the bare bones of a starting point and, at £7 an hour, you can't complain.

In March, as the first signs of spring began to appear, I started to get the sense that I was making progress. There was nothing concrete I could put my finger on, and KPMG still hadn't come back to confirm our arrangement, and I still hadn't heard from Ed re WPP either, but it just felt like people were listening a little more closely to what I had to say. Indeed, I was invited to speak at the Future of Retail Banking in Europe conference in Berlin, on the subject of 'working on the launch of a new digital bank for the European market'. I was on the billing beside senior executives from the Payments Council, RBS, Barclays and IBM, so it was gratifying to see that I had not completely dropped off the radar. I decided I would use the opportunity to explain the reasoning behind launching a dedicated mobile-first bank, while not declaring my hand and explaining exactly what I was up to. In the draft of my speech, I laid out my thoughts on the pace of change and the real need for banks to respond to the digital revolution. I would warn that if traditional banks did not react, there were plenty of other potential disruptors waiting in the wings.

To add a bit of colour, I raised the issue of the much-used picture of two successive papal announcements. This was a side-by-side photo comparison of the announcement in St Peter's Square of Pope Benedict in 2005, versus Pope Francis in 2013, which seemed to have been used as an example in every speech I'd witnessed in recent times. In the earlier announcement, we see the crowd staring in front of them, with just one phone in sight. Yet, just eight years later, the almost identical scene is dominated by hundreds of brightly lit smartphones as the crowd strains to get a picture of the new pontiff. These pictures have been cited as proof that we now live our lives through our smartphones, which have gained importance far beyond that of sharing simple memories.

The irony, I would say in my speech, is that no one in our industry really seems to know what is going on, nor is taking this argument to its logical conclusion. Yes, the world has changed. Well done for noticing: but what are you doing about reacting to it? 'When in doubt, show the slide' is not a good enough strategy.

Even as I landed at Berlin-Tegel Airport, I reminded myself that, while I had made good progress with New Bank, there was a very long way to go: not least that I needed to raise millions of pounds. Just getting to the stage of a credible presentation could swallow up £5 million in fees. Without a contingency agreement, I'd be nowhere.

I turned my phone back on as my fellow passengers began to disembark and waited for my emails to load up. As I scrolled through the list of messages, I was oblivious to the people shuffling around me, rearranging their bags. I spotted one from KPMG and clicked on it straight away. This was it. Exactly what I had been waiting for: the draft letter confirming the contingency-fees arrangement. 'Just sign and return,' it said. The wording sounded almost too mundane for such a momentous event. This was the biggest breakthrough I'd had to date. I now had a team from KPMG at my disposal. We could begin working in earnest towards a presentation for the regulator.

With KPMG on board it was inevitable that the workload would increase significantly as we prepared for the meeting with the regulator, but this would also mean we were making solid progress. As I left the aircraft my brain was filled with a long list of 'what next's. I needed to work closely with KPMG to agree the various elements required for the supporting presentation to the regulator and that would entail pulling together a lot of information. After that the anticipated order of events would be, firstly, to hold a meeting with the PRA, who then, all being well, would give New Bank some sort of nod. The next step would be to set about raising a sum of seed funding of around £3 million to pay for some of the initial set-up fees, including KPMG's services, the lawyers and so on. Then, once we were awarded our licence, we could begin the process of fundraising in earnest.

Each step was pretty significant, with its own set of challenges, but the most daunting by far was raising the large capital sum to get the bank off the ground. This could involve finding many tens of millions. It had been hard enough to get this far. How many doors would I have to knock on to raise the investment I needed? For now, though, as I reminded myself as I walked into the arrivals hall, I could at least bask in the glory that there were positive signs that New Bank was on its way.

3. *Know Your Market*

In early April 2014 I'd managed to get a one-to-one with Craig Donaldson, the CEO of Metro Bank. When it started in 2010, Metro Bank became the first new UK retail bank in a century and, not surprisingly, had been keenly watched by other bank start-ups, including mine. Our aims didn't clash, since Metro's business model very much depended upon a branch network, while I was looking at mobile only, but I was curious about their experience of setting up a new bank. What had they learned from the fundraising, start-up process?

Craig was happy enough to give me some of his time. Contrary to what many people believe, banks talk to each other all the time. Yes, we are all competitors in one way or another, but there is a strongly cooperative streak among bankers. I think most senior people in banking have the same attitude as I do: help out people where you can, because you never know when they might be in a position to do you a favour. Or perhaps it is simply good business sense to support a fledgling operation because if, in the fullness of time, it all turns out well, that business will look favourably on those who helped it on the way up.

I met Craig at Metro's Holborn branch and as soon as I walked in it felt like business was going well. There were certainly a lot of people milling around, which was very different from some other bank branches I'd hung out in. This was pretty interesting in itself. I'd long been firmly of the view the branch model was on its way out. Most people never visited their branch from one year to the next and the sites were a real drain on already stretched banking resources.

Rather than steering away from the branch model, though, Metro had grabbed it with both hands and turned it on its head, which was an interesting approach. Gone was the staid and gloomy, identikit interior that you see in NatWest, Lloyds or Barclays from Bournemouth to Blackpool. Instead, Metro had fostered a very airy, open-plan, customer-centric design, with floor-to-ceiling windows. Banking staff didn't have thick screens acting as a physical, and indeed psychological, barrier between them and the customer, but open counters. The welcoming theme extended to lollipops for the children and a dog-friendly policy. They even had machines where people could deposit change: the very thing big banks had been trying to discourage for years.

I was escorted upstairs to the executive suite to meet Craig and couldn't help but notice the doggy theme continued even there, with wall-to-wall pictures of canines. Even though I was not a particular fan of dogs, or the loud red corporate colour favoured by Metro, I had to admit to myself that I approved. This bank was doing something different. It was offering customers choice, which was exactly what I hoped to do.

I was shown into Craig's office and, after he gave me a friendly greeting, we sat down to talk. Once I'd congratulated him on how well it seemed to be going, Craig gave me a brief rundown on the business.

'And you?' he said at last, turning the conversation around. 'How much progress have you made?'

'Quite a lot,' I replied. 'Obviously it is early days, but we're well on the way with our presentation to the PRA. It's been a long journey but I feel quite confident about that.'

'And how far have you got with fundraising?' he pressed.

'I have knocked on a lot of doors,' I began. 'In fact, that was partly why I came to see you today. Don't worry, I'm not here for a loan,' I joked.

Craig laughed.

'I was curious about your experience,' I went on. 'I know this sort of thing is never straightforward. I've seen this from the other side too. How long did it all take for you?'

'We had more than three hundred meetings before we got anywhere,' Craig answered.

Three hundred? And this was a bank founded by American businessman Vernon Hill, who already had considerable financial resources and a record of entrepreneurial ventures. In my mind, the next year or so stretched out before me. I would be doing a lot of presentations in the months to come.

For now, this was not something I could tie myself up in knots about. I had to take one step at a time and the important next step was getting the presentation for the regulator right. With a background of working in large, international banks, I was used to an environment where dealing with the regulator was taken extremely seriously. Getting things right was a very big deal indeed, so it was not uncommon to have dozens of people working on documentation for the banking authorities. Of course, these organizations already had their licensing in place, so were simply fulfilling day-to-day requirements. I was starting from scratch. It struck me I would definitely have my work cut out with my relatively tiny team.

As I listed the various requirements in my head, it seemed to me that the scale of work that needed to be done was breathtaking. To give this new bank credibility, we needed a detailed report into the current and future challenges of fintech, alongside an overview of the economic landscape and the trends in banking. The presentation had to review where we were today, what the big banks had to offer and why it was crucial that a challenger bank like New Bank was given an opportunity to flourish. Of course, we also needed to demonstrate a full awareness of what the big banks would do to ward off competition from an upstart like us. Rest assured, the established players weren't going to let challenger banks come in and mop up a chunk of their business.

Most importantly for me, I wanted to show the regulator that what we would be offering the consumer was entirely different. This presentation needed to show how we would look after the financial health of consumers and help them manage their lives better.

Alongside this, and most importantly for the regulator, New Bank needed to present a credible and comprehensive business model with a breakdown of financial forecasts, liquidity, security, data warehousing, payment details and so on. Plus, we needed to demonstrate how we would adhere to strict banking regulations.

When I spelled all this out to KPMG's Giles Adams, he looked a little taken aback.

'I'm not sure that we need to be that comprehensive on the first meeting with the PRA,' he said tactfully. 'I think it is more of a getting-to-know-you, lay-things-out type of thing.'

Since Giles was our regulatory expert, I had to concede he had a point; however, I didn't want to take the risk of turning up with too little to say. Although I didn't want to seem dismissive of his advice in my response, I was privately terrified that I'd make a hash of this first meeting and not be given a second chance.

'I think we need to show we mean business and that we are a team of professionals,' I said. 'Besides, there are a lot of things here that no one has ever done before. Banks don't usually put customers at the centre of things. I want them to understand that we are different and explain exactly how.'

Giles didn't argue the toss and, to his credit, didn't demur when I said the numbers in the team were not nearly enough to achieve what I believed needed to be done. I was convinced that we needed more help. I was aiming to meet with the regulator by June, or July at the latest. At this rate, we'd be far from ready. I suspect part of Giles's acquiescence to my suggestion of bringing in more people was down to the fact I must have been on the phone and email to him and the KPMG team at least ten times a day. I was constantly asking for updates and adding in requirements. He was probably just grateful for any extra hands on deck.

The big challenge now was that bringing in more help would entail signing up an additional team from another consultancy firm such as PwC or EY to share the load and complement the work KPMG were already doing. Even as I thought about it, I knew this was an ambitious aspiration. KPMG had been incredible, but it had taken some weeks to get them on board and then some further time to get a contingency agreement in place. While the reason for getting in another firm was to speed things up, it could well end up having the opposite effect and delaying things yet further if I had to divert my time to spending weeks making presentations and then chasing up agreements. Nevertheless, I decided that, on balance, it was at least worth a try. Additional experts would make a massive difference if I was successful and if it looked like I was getting nowhere I could always rethink.

On the plus side, just as I was beginning to think about boosting the team, Ed Griffin came through on WPP. He'd passed the request on to one of his colleagues in Rothschild, who had in turn got in touch with Martin Sorrell asking if he was 'interested in helping one of the new challenger banks' that was being launched. The response was positive and, without my ever even speaking directly with Sir Martin (we communicated via email, and frequently so over the years), I was referred to one of the WPP agencies, VML, a specialist in online branding and digital marketing, so this was perfect. A meeting was duly set up and they very quickly came on board on contingency to help with the creative side of things.

I got back on my trusty PC and typed out emails to people I knew in EY and PwC. On the plus side, I was no longer a lone voice coming out of the ether. *Hi, it's Anne Boden here, I am working on starting up a bank.* No, now I could say, quite legitimately, *Hi, it's Anne Boden, I'm leading a start-up bank for Europe. I've got KPMG doing the licence work for me, Clifford Chance on legal, Dell on technology and WPP handling the marketing.*

Obviously, while I was clear in the opening message that I was looking for a partner to work with me on a contingency basis, I didn't mention the £1 million plus I already owed in contingency fees at that stage.

As I pressed the Send key on my emails, I had a brief moment to reflect on how important what I had just written was. I'd barely paused for breath over the past four months. However, I had managed to pull together a formidable team. I had started with zero resources and now I was surrounded by the best in the market. Starting with nothing and creating something was, I realized, the definition of entrepreneurship, which was odd, because I still didn't think of myself as an entrepreneur.

I didn't have long to wait for a response from both companies. In a clear signal of just how far I had come, both of these Big Four firms replied that they would be very interested in holding talks with me. Not only that: they wanted to put together teams to present to me.

'We have a number of experts in this area and extensive experience,' one firm said. 'It would be great to have the opportunity to show what we can do.'

It was hard to conceptualize that these global firms would be prepared to bid for work that they knew they wouldn't be paid for. At least not for a while.

I set up meetings with both EY and PwC.

After two impressive presentations I went with PwC. With an enlarged team in place, it was more important than ever to allocate roles and deadlines. The most pressing task was to itemize fully what we were trying to do and comprehensively analyse each aspect of opening a new bank. What must be done to build this business from scratch?

We required an estimated timeline for each component part of the bank and to work out exactly who needed to do what, and when, in order to launch successfully. The long list of tasks was divided into four areas: customer proposition, which included product development and marketing and branding; technology and operations, which covered everything from how payments were handled to strategic IT to data warehousing; risk and regulatory compliance, spanning the approval process; and finally management and support for the corporate side, from fundraising to governance to intraday liquidity.

It was critical that some of the tasks were fully completed right from the day the new bank opened. However, we did also note that there were things that could be subsequently developed post-launch. Not surprisingly, 95 per cent of the tasks needed to be completed beforehand. The only elements we could push further down the line were such things as company culture and PR. We also had a list of things we'd like to introduce once we got established, like Apple Pay, budgeting, alternative mobile payments and strategic partnerships with other financial organizations. They were nice to have but not entirely critical from the off.

Each area we identified had up to a dozen or more subsections, which all needed to be allocated to someone, with accompanying milestones, an estimate of how long it would take to achieve and a target date. Further notes were added to indicate dependencies that might have an impact on a successful conclusion. If something didn't happen here, for example, what would it mean to something over there? Would everything grind to a halt and, if that was the case, what was the best way to guard against it happening? The plan needed to be incredibly detailed and cross-referenced with a well-documented, stage-by-stage process where nothing could be left to chance.

Take, as an example, our pricing strategy, which was a crucial subsection of product development. Getting the price point just right is, of course, key to any business. Get it too high and no one will buy. Too low and everyone will buy, but there won't be a sustainable business. Meanwhile, as in any pricing strategy, this all had to be understood against a backdrop of what competitors were charging and how much customers would be prepared to pay for what level of service. Thus, in the pricing section we had almost a dozen milestones, from benchmarking against competitors to a risk framework around fraudulent behaviour to research around the levels of service and support customers expected versus the price they were prepared to pay. While any final decisions on pricing would be made closer to the launch date, the foundations all needed to be laid before then.

Naturally, with something as complex as this, several people were allocated tasks on each subsection. On pricing, Paul Rippon (ex-head of banking operations at AIB, who had agreed to help on a part-time basis) was the primary contact, but there was a requirement for input from myself, Gary Dolman (whom I knew from my ABN Amro days and who was also helping on a part-time basis) and others to get each task up to the desired 100 per cent complete finishing line. When you think that a similar exercise needed to be repeated for dozens of complex and intricate tasks, then it's clear to see we were still up against it.

Now we were entering the stage of officially pitching the idea, we faced another pressing problem: what to call this new service. The working title 'New Bank' sounded a little vague, right at a time when we really needed to look on the ball and poised to launch this exciting new service at any moment.

Before joining AIB, I had trademarked the name Social Fintech. I'd figured there would be this big thing about fintech and social media in the coming months, so it might come in handy. Now I thought about it though, it didn't seem quite right for New Bank.

The naming issue threw yet another element into my steep learning curve. Naming a business is an incredibly time consuming and frustratingly intensive exercise. It's not simply a question of choosing a name and building a brand around it. There was also a multitude of considerations around registering and trademarking the name, making sure it was not infringing anyone else's, or sounding too similar and a dozen other rules besides. The only option available to us in the limited time we had was to find a better working title that we could use for now and then find the best name in the months to come. With the clock ticking and so much still left to do, I called VML and asked if we could think about some names at our next meeting.

The session lasted several hours, with all sorts of weird and wonderful suggestions being floated. One of the strongest contenders for a while was 'Open Bank', on the basis that this reflected we were on the side of the consumer.

'That does leave us a little exposed,' I pointed out, after giving it some reflection. 'People might think it means our doors are always wide open, which is a bit of a security issue for a bank.'

'Particularly when there are not any branches,' Chris Wood, one of the VML team, agreed.

It was back to the drawing board.

After going around the houses a bit longer we came up with the rather hopeful sounding 'Bank Possible'. The thinking around the new name went something like this: I was preparing to launch an entirely new consumer brand into a highly traditional market where consumers are notoriously reluctant to try anything new. I would therefore need something pretty powerful to convince would-be customers that this was a credible brand that they could entrust their money to. I also wanted a name that would quickly become synonymous with a new way of banking. Bank Possible seemed the best way to describe our ambitions. It was certainly enough to go to the regulator with and added weight to our argument that we were pushing forward into a new way of banking, opening up new opportunities.

The initial appointment with the regulator was fixed for early June and although this was way ahead of the official application, which would require extremely detailed documentation, I was determined to leave them with a good and lasting impression of Bank Possible.

By the time we reached the date set for the meeting, I'd managed to put together what I felt was a pretty detailed and credible twelve-page document outlining what I hoped to achieve. As I headed over to the PRA offices in Moorgate along with Gary and Paul, I felt quite confident about the presentation. Despite Giles's assertion that this would be more of a coffee and 'getting-to-know-you' type chat, rather than a crunch-time pitch, I believed what we'd done would look pretty respectable up against comparable pitches from much more established organizations.

My well-rehearsed presentation went well and when I'd finished I was curious about the regulator's reaction. Had we made the impression we'd been working so hard to make? I couldn't have been more surprised by the response. The PRA representative immediately started to explain the process and timelines in a very matter-of-fact way. Even though I had already carefully researched the process (and been briefed by Giles), I let him run through the requirements. I was impatient to get to the next stage, though, and hear some feedback. Yet, instead of making any specific comments on Bank Possible, the PRA man moved seamlessly on to outlining what would happen next. What he said at this point stopped me in my tracks:

'If you are to come to the next meeting . . .' he began, as he went through his list.

If? The penny began to drop. This regulator had seen literally dozens of would-be new banks, but barely any had made it past the stage of this first meeting. Presumably once the contenders saw all the onerous requirements of actually starting and running a bank they'd had a change of heart.

For a short while I was a little irked. Then I thought about it properly and realized this was simply the environment we were now in. I've always thought that the world separates into several different camps. There are the people who see everything as just too difficult, so never try. Then there are utter realists, who see the world the way it is and will only ever try if the outcome is a dead cert. Then there are the eternal optimists, who will blunder from one thing to another, convinced the next opportunity will be 'the one'. When it doesn't work out, they'll go on their way with no real regrets. It seemed to me that, to succeed in something like I was trying to do now, one needed a mix of optimism and dogged determination, which is a rare combination. It's the duo that drives entrepreneurs to succeed, though. I very much hoped that I had these two qualities because I could see that I would need them a lot in the months to come.

Overall, the initial meeting with the regulator had gone well.

All we could do now was put our heads down and get on with the task of proving how serious we were about the bank. This meant building on what we'd already done and making a start on the document that outlined the long list of processes and timelines that had been explained to us in that first meeting.

Our big sell for Bank Possible, 'the first digital native bank delivered through mobile and tablet', was that we were at a tipping point in the current-account market. Our disruptive model would open up the potential of the multitude of data that is now available about each and every one of us and make it work in our favour. Plus, because we weren't hampered by having to use an infrastructure that was many decades old, we could use the latest that technology had to offer to harness the innovative power of the app market.

The theme running through the pitch that we began to develop in earnest was that we weren't in the market to sell as much product as humanly possible to our customers. We would be enabling our customers and giving them the freedom to choose among the pick of third-party providers.

We obviously needed to put some numbers into the mix and put a stake in the ground declaring what share we intended to take of the estimated 65 million UK current accounts (of which 51 million are active). We said that we were aiming for a 4.3 per cent share of this market within five years, which translated to 2.2 million accounts. For comparison, Metro Bank and TSB, the other significant UK challengers, had respectively 0.6 per cent and 4.5 per cent of the market. This, in our opinion, was doable, particularly since the introduction of The Payments Council's current account-switching service (CASS), which had seen 5 per cent of accounts moved in the twelve months before our document was written.*

The other important statistic to support our entry into this market was the exponential rise in smartphone ownership. By the summer of 2014, 70 per cent of the population owned smartphones. Meanwhile, tablet ownership was fast on the rise too, with a quarter of the population now owning one. Smartphone users were already comfortable with downloading apps and a growing number of mainstream banks already offered their own versions. Ours would just be a lot better!

Listing the services we'd be offering made an impressive read. Our vision was for securely linked multiuser facilities, so parents could keep an eye on children's spending, or make payments to an elderly relative's care home. Customers would be able to pool their financial data in one place, regardless of the provider, which would give them a much better snapshot of their monthly spend and hopefully help avoid nasty surprises. The simple-to-use app would allow them to tag individual spends, via photos or receipts, so they actually meant something as they scrolled through to check their balances. We envisaged (carefully controlled) interconnectivity with other apps to make everything more manageable.

Naturally, the part the regulator was most interested in was the financial side and governance. Running a bank is a huge

---

* There was a 22 per cent increase in account switching in the first twelve months after the service was introduced in October 2013; the following year switches fell back and in January 2015 were 16 per cent higher than when CASS was first introduced: www.fca.org.uk/publication/research/making-current-account-switching-easier.pdf.

responsibility. People give a bank money as a deposit, while the same bank lends that money to other people. If a bank makes a mess of it, the government needs to step in and make everybody happy by giving them their money back through the Financial Services Compensation Scheme. Thus, a large part of our initial documents included a breakdown of projected profit and loss, through a series of spreadsheets showing our financial position, capital model and liquidity, as well as details of our experienced senior banking team and the governance and controls we'd have in place.

With a second meeting with the regulator booked in for November, I asked the guys over at VML to make a short video presentation showing exactly how the product would operate from a consumer point of view. They worked with Jason Bates, one of the newer members of the team who had come from a background in big transformational programmes at organizations such as Accenture, Google and Facebook. We'd met up in May and he'd been genuinely excited about the idea of Bank Possible, agreeing to join almost straight away, which was great because he was an excellent project manager. I loved the video that VML and Jason managed to produce really brought things to life. Also, it worked perfectly for those people who have a very visual approach and just need to see something real, rather than hear detailed descriptions. I was, however, in the minority on that one.

'Don't show the video!' was the almost unanimous verdict, when I shared it with the rest of the team.

'It's a little corny,' was the general pronouncement from the team.

'It is a bit, er, overkill,' Giles concurred tactfully when we showed him the video. 'I really don't think they will be expecting that level of detail.'

I let it go. Even so, I did think we were missing a trick here.

Working day and night, we completed the main presentation document ahead of the date set for the second meeting with the regulator in November. Just.

I met with Giles, Gary, Paul and Jason in a Starbucks across the road from the PRA offices. I couldn't help noticing that everyone looked pretty exhausted. Conversation was thin on the ground as we all waited for the appointment time. I found it quite hard going making small talk. A big part of me just wanted to get this bit over with so we could move on to the next stage.

The clock ticked achingly slowly to just ten minutes ahead of our appointment. Then we gathered up our things and headed out into the busy street. After navigating our way across the road that was jammed with a mid-morning mix of delivery vehicles, buses and taxis, we made our way into the PRA building. Next up, we had to navigate through the extensive security checks, which included scans of all our cases of documents. Finally we were shown up to a meeting room for the long-awaited, second audience with the regulator.

I almost laughed when I saw the room we'd been allocated. It was tiny and dominated by a large, eight-seater table running almost the entire length of the room. There was hardly any space between the chairs and the walls, and what followed was an almost comical scene as the Bank Possible team and those from the regulator tried to shuffle past one another with their large cases of documents and find a suitable seat. Bags were then emptied and unceremoniously squeezed into spaces below the chairs and table. In a way, it worked out quite well because, by the time we'd settled down, the earlier tension my team felt had all but dissipated.

I didn't even look at my notes as I confidently went through the timeline behind Bank Possible and the numbers that went with it. I was pleased to see that the regulator team seemed to be receiving it all quite well and were even agreeing with me on a few points. Unable to resist, I reached down and pulled out my laptop from the bag below my chair.

'Before I finish, there is just one more thing I'd like to show you,' I said as I quickly keyed in my password.

I heard a barely audible gasp from my colleagues.

'We've had a short video made that will give you a better idea of how it all works,' I said, pressing the 'play' button and swinging the laptop around to face the group.

I glanced at Giles, who raised his eyes ever-so-slightly heavenward and then followed up with a barely perceptible frown. I smiled back. Corny or not, I wanted Bank Possible to show exactly what it could do.

Once again, the meeting had gone well and the regulator reiterated the next steps of the process that needed to be achieved before we got to the following stage. It meant we now had a long to-do list to get to grips with and, very importantly, we needed to get started in earnest raising some investment. While I had no doubts about my ability to knock on doors and to make things happen – indeed I had already proved that – I couldn't help feeling it would be quite useful to have someone on board with a bit of start-up experience. Someone who had already been through a similar process and fully understood the pitfalls and opportunities. That sort of knowledge could really speed things up. But who?

Then I had the most unexpected virtual knock at my door.

I was on my way to a meeting with the PwC team in More London Riverside. It was one of those deeply depressing taxi journeys during which the London traffic was frequently at a standstill. The driver hared off on a completely circuitous route, which was really starting to irritate me because it seemed that we were now going in precisely the opposite direction to where I needed to be. As a distraction, I immersed myself in my phone, flicking through the incoming emails to see if there was anything of interest. I noticed that there was one from Tom Blomfield. I hadn't heard much from him since I'd helped out on his GoCardless venture what felt like years before. I knew he'd gone off to the States to work on the dating site Grouper, but we hadn't spoken in months. I clicked on the email, wondering what he was up to now.

Hi Anne. I'm back in London. Can I come and see you?

I quickly typed a response.

I'm just on the way to a meeting at PwC in More London (if I ever get there) but should be free by 11.30, if you are nearby.

He replied to say he'd meet me there and I wondered what could be so urgent.

I did eventually make it to PwC and Tom was already there when I arrived. He stood out a mile among the PwC crowd, who were all in smart navy and grey suits. He was dressed casually in jeans and a shirt and sporting a battered old backpack. It was good to see him, though.

'Well, since you are here, you may as well join the meeting,' I said with a smile after we'd greeted each other.

I respected Tom and thought it would be useful to have his perspective. I knew from experience he was never afraid to speak his mind, so it would be interesting to get his take on where Bank Possible was now. Sure enough, he was characteristically blunt in the meeting, which no doubt ruffled a few PwC feathers. I let him speak, though, because he had valuable experience of a start-up.

After the meeting was over, the two of us went for a drink at a nearby restaurant. I'd barely ordered before Tom was inundating me with questions. What was I doing about this? Had I thought about that? The penny dropped; he was on the market, looking for a new fintech venture to get his teeth into, and he had heard about what I was doing.

Less than twelve hours after we re-engaged, Tom Blomfield became the newest member of the Bank Possible team. It was great to have an experienced fintech professional like him on board. I'd worked with him before and trusted him. With his input we would surely increase the chances of achieving our goal.

4. Bid for Investment

Early in September 2014, *The Times* broke the story 'Newcomer Promises Mobile Challenge to Banks'.

The mainly positive piece went on to describe how the mobile bank would work, what sort of service it would offer and just why data and connectivity were so important.

The Bank Possible team were elated. Now it was there in black and white in a serious newspaper like *The Times*, it felt so much more real. One person, however, was not quite so thrilled.

A few days after the article appeared I received a sharp rebuke via email from Martin Sorrell. He'd been none too happy to be taken to task by Ross McEwan, the CEO of WPP's significant (and paying) client RBS. McEwan had raised an eyebrow over the fact the newspaper piece mentioned that Sorrell's business was apparently backing Bank Possible.

'I made it quite clear that this was not the case, although we were providing marketing services to you through VML,' he wrote. 'In any event, Ross would be very interested in talking to you about your launch and your plans and your business approach.'

Naturally, I apologized profusely for the miscommunication.

Interestingly, one of the other things that the *Times* article raised was the fact that we were not the only new mobile bank working on being granted a licence. He noted that Anthony Thomson, a co-founder of Metro Bank, was also looking at a branchless model using the latest technology. His service, Atom Bank, had started in April 2014 and was also busily preparing its banking licence application.

Anthony was not our only competitor. I'd also come into contact with an Australian entrepreneur by the name of Ricky Knox, who had founded Tandem Money a year earlier. His vision was for an app-based, full-service retail bank with all sorts of bells and whistles, such as alerts when bills increased, or payments came in, advice on switching utilities and break-downs of available spend. Ricky meant business and, most importantly, he had strong backing. One of his co-founders was Matt Cooper, who was chairman of Octopus Investments and had founded Capital One, one of the ten largest banks in the US.

When Ricky and I met in the summer of 2014, we compared notes on what we wanted to achieve. I'd explained that our next big challenge was finding investment and it soon became clear that he considered himself a bit of an expert in this respect. It couldn't be denied that he had somewhat fallen on his feet with Matt Cooper.

'I knew Matt for fifteen years or so before this,' he explained. 'We met after Matt had just retired from Capital One at the ripe old age of just thirty-five! We talked about starting something then, and spoke on and off after that. It wasn't until I went to live in Bali to think about what I was going to do with the rest of my life that I really made up my mind. I called Matt and told him. He said, "Awesome, I'm in."'

I couldn't help thinking how great such a straightforward investment journey would be for us. I liked Ricky, though, and we've met again a few times since. He invariably turns up wearing motorcycle leathers and is always a bit late, but he's a charming guy.

With rivals circling, it was now more apparent than ever that we really needed to make some ground towards our own launch. The pressure was on. Our bank licence application was proceeding steadily and we had high hopes that we'd have something in place by early 2015. Following the meeting in July, the regulator had written laying out the requirements to reach the next stage. As well as articulating how the mobile app would work, we also needed to produce:

- A detailed business plan and timeline showing viability, profitability, product offering and forward plans. This included market analysis.
- Information about where the capital was expected to come from and the impact it might have on the firm and its governance arrangements. In other words, would there be additional shareholders who would need to be approved by the regulator?
- A breakdown of operations, IT and outsourcing, showing how the systems would work, who the providers were and what governance there would be of the systems.
- Complete details on governance structure and controller structure.
- Background information on all the key individuals within Bank Possible.

I couldn't help reflecting that there was a fine balance between the stringent requirements of the regulator and what our potential investors would like to see. For the PRA we needed to be people who had done it all before, who knew how the committees and governance processes worked, and who were fully aware of our responsibilities to look after our customers' money. On the other hand, for the private equity (PE) world we needed to appear as hard-headed business people who were going to sweat the assets and run a traditional high-return banking business. Meanwhile, any potential venture-capital investors would be on the lookout for a bunch of smart people who wanted to change the world. We just needed to fulfil each and every role somehow! Or rather, some people on the team would have to be all three people on the same day, while others picked a side and stuck with it.

There was a lot of work to be done, even in the light of what had already been achieved with our presentation and in building the model. However, the most pressing issue by far now was fundraising.

I knew from experience that the biggest challenge when it comes to borrowing money is that you need to have money in the first place. To borrow £50 million you usually have to match it with £50 million of your own. This was, of course, £50 million I didn't have. Worse still, I was rapidly running out of what money I did have. My home in Swansea was already on the market since my savings were rapidly evaporating. At this stage, the burn rate (the amount I was spending each month) was around £60,000. Oh, and not to forget I owed around £2 million in contingency fees.

It was good to have Tom on board now we were going into the fundraising phase. One of the best assets you can have in a venture like this is a great chief technology officer (CTO), with knowledge and credibility. Even though Tom wasn't strictly a CTO, he was a start-up expert. We'd ticked the boxes on regulatory matters but now we needed to tick some boxes in the start-up world too. Having founded a number of businesses, Tom was very experienced in working with the venture-capital community, and that previous experience would get a big tick from the VCs.

It was refreshing to have him around for another reason too. He was insanely enthusiastic about Bank Possible. He told me very early on that the prospect of building a bank was so powerful and exciting it actually kept him awake at night. I knew that feeling well.

My faith in Tom appeared to bear fruit, because one of the

very first investors he introduced me to was Passion Capital, who said they were very interested indeed. After we showed our investor presentation to Eileen Burbidge, one of the fund partners, she said they would almost certainly want to do something and promised to come back to us shortly with an offer. She indicated that they'd be considering putting in £3 million on a £9 million valuation. Eileen also suggested that Daniel Korski, an extremely well-connected Downing Street advisor to David Cameron and someone who had a great interest in tech start-ups, should be invited to our meetings. I turned this proposed introduction down because I (perhaps naively) thought there needed to be a firm boundary between a bank applying to the regulator for a licence and politics. It didn't seem right that Cameron's advisor would be part of a commercial deal.

Even so, it seemed like a cracking start, although both Tom and I felt Eileen's valuation was a little on the low side. We were not out of the woods yet, though. VCs like Passion Capital generally only deal with start-ups, so will only ever be able to invest a few million or so. The normal way of things is for start-ups to get such a cash injection and then, when they've proved their mettle, go back and try to borrow a greater sum. Unfortunately, fledgling banks can't really do this since they need something like £50 million before they can sign up a single customer. To get an investment like this, we'd need to go to multiple sources, which was challenging for a number of reasons. Firstly, there was no guarantee we'd succeed, since I had no track record as an entrepreneur and no one on the team except Tom had ever started their own business. Secondly, as I quickly discovered as Tom and I began the rounds of VCs in London, investing in banks is not high on the list for angel investors because it is not tax efficient. This is primarily due to the fact that investment in a business like ours would not be eligible for the Enterprise Investment Scheme (EIS), a tax relief designed to encourage investment in small, unquoted companies. To compound matters, we were looking for a great deal of money and the probability of our investors recouping their stake quickly was zero, since Bank Possible was still many months away from launch thanks to the regulatory process.

The alternative would be to go for larger-scale investment, which was the preserve of PE firms. I'd dealt with many of them during Project Prada and they had been very helpful then. However, as I quickly discovered, raising money to buy an established business is very different from raising money for a start-up. These companies invariably bought billion-dollar businesses, installed new management to turn them round and then either sold them or floated them on the stock market. They weren't interested in getting involved in a relatively tiny operation, in an entirely new and untried sector. It was just too risky. Besides, even if they were minded to take a punt, they would only be interested in a start-up that was planned and executed by an established entrepreneur. By established entrepreneur, we are talking someone of the calibre of Richard Branson or James Dyson.

Aside from Passion Capital, we were getting no interest in London. Although we knocked on countless doors, the response was always a polite, 'Thanks but no thanks.'

'We need to go to America,' I said to Tom. 'We'll have a much better chance there.'

I'd been considering this for a while now. My visit the previous year had shown that there was a real appetite Stateside for disruptive businesses like ours. A digital bank called Simple had launched in 2012, claiming to be a 'forward thinking, tech-enabled alternative' to traditional bricks-and-mortar banks. The mobile app looked pretty slick and had won more than 40,000 customers. While there had been talk of teething troubles with occasional outages and glitches, there was clearly a lot of faith it was going in the right direction. It was acquired by Banco Bilbao Vizcaya Argentaria (BBVA) in February 2014 for $117 million.

Another mobile bank constantly in the news was Moven, which had been founded by Brett King, who also happened to be the author of a number of fintech books, such as *Bank 2.0*. Moven had already secured more than $4 million in seed investment.

At the time everything was very new and everyone seemed to be taking a different approach, but it just felt like the Americans were more receptive to new ideas on the future of banking.

I have also always thought that women often do better in countries away from their home base, which is perhaps why there are so many foreign female executives on FTSE boards. Maybe company bosses feel more comfortable with a woman who doesn't sound like their wife or mother, and therefore believe they are able to do that big job!

There was another good reason for going to the US: we could finally lock things down with Dell. By this stage I'd had a number of meetings with Sameer Kishore and his team. We'd held workshops and discussed the business endlessly, but hadn't really got as far as I would have liked. Each meeting would be punctuated by Sameer asking how things were going on fundraising, and me admitting the process was still ongoing. I was still holding on to the hope that Michael Dell might pitch in with an investment, but that would entail my taking up the open invitation to visit him.

The last weeks of September were pretty hectic. Tom and I were planning our trip to the States, where we were going to travel from West Coast to East, taking in Dell in Austin, Texas on the way. We were trying to set up as many meetings as we could in advance. Meanwhile, the business was about to move into its first ever dedicated premises.

We moved into Bank Possible's own office on 23 September. It was a real red-letter day for me. As the *Times* article had mentioned, the team was now up to ten people working full time, both paid and unpaid, and until now we'd all been working either at home or in various bars, hotels and cafés. For the most part, though, we'd been camping out in the very plush customer lounges at KPMG and PwC. Both firms had been very generous in letting us stay around for days at a time. However, this state of affairs couldn't go on for ever. Even though we still didn't have any money coming in, we needed a permanent home.

The Bank Possible HQ arrived courtesy of another of our partners, this time WPP, who rented the new offices to us. Not to sound the least bit ungrateful, because I'm not, but this warehouse-style office in Peter's Lane was something that estate agents might describe as 'having potential'. We rented the upper of the two available levels of number 22, and it was pretty humble to say the least: wooden floors, broken heating (which was a worry as we went into autumn) and Wi-Fi via a domestic router. I managed to fill it with second-hand furniture that I picked up from here and there, but unfortunately the mismatched chairs and tables did little to absorb the sound of conversations that used to bounce and echo around the office. It was a far cry from the Google HQ I'd visited the previous year, that was for sure. The most comical aspect of the whole thing was the really complicated entry and exit procedure, as well as how we locked up at the end of the day. The only entry was via an external fire escape (not easy in high heels, but I managed it) and the front door needed to be bolted from the inside. The only way to exit the building then was to climb over the fence. This was impossible for me, so I had to be sure I was not the last person to leave at the end of the day.

With a permanent home, we were able to start recruiting developers. Within a short space of time a number joined the team, including Matt Heath, Jonas Huckestein, James Nicholson, Mike Kelly, Stephen Best and Simon Vans-Colina. I began to grow used to the look of utter confusion when each new recruit first arrived at the office seeing this fifty-year-old woman in charge of a banking start-up. None of them had any experience in banking and they were awestruck both by what we were trying to do and the freedom with which they were allowed to do it. They were each given a brand-new MacBook Pro (with due ceremony!) and told to get on with it. Build a banking app. We needed to launch asap. Oh, and that woman sitting there in the middle? That's the CEO. If you want anything, or have any questions, just ask. Not that there was any hollering across the room. All the new guys wore headphones to listen to music as they coded, and communicated using the private online chat service HipChat, even when addressing someone sitting right next to them. It was a million light years away from my previous life in the traditional banking sector.

5. Bank On America

On 1 October 2014, I flew from London Heathrow to Austin, Texas. I used some of the last of my air miles from my previous life to pay for my flight. Tom had travelled on ahead of me, having funded his own flight. We'd booked separate accommodation too, with me opting for hotels and Tom choosing a range of Airbnbs for our time in America. We had agreed to meet that evening for supper to discuss strategy for our meeting at Dell's offices at 8 a.m. the following day.

It was strange being back on a plane again, after the weeks of frantic activity back home. It was much more like my old life as a banking executive, when I was rarely out of airports. I'd been sure to use my Executive Lounge privileges at Heathrow, acutely aware that this was the last time I'd be doing anything like that for a long time unless we were successful in raising money and getting Bank Possible off the ground.

The flight went smoothly and I met up with Tom that evening for supper. He'd chosen a restaurant he really wanted to go to, although when we arrived by Uber it seemed that the Austin locals didn't share his enthusiasm since it was virtually deserted and remained so all evening. Tom barely seemed to notice. On the way to the restaurant he'd spent twenty minutes extolling the virtues of Uber, even though the driver we had that evening was among the worst I'd ever experienced. Before she even arrived to pick us up she got hopelessly lost. We tracked her on the app as we stood outside the hotel waiting and saw her going round and round in circles. She did eventually manage to find us, but we'd had to direct her through the city using our phones. Once we were in the restaurant, I was keen to deliver a brain dump of all the work I'd been doing on the flight, but Tom was still eager to explain his views on Uber. I felt a little irritated that he seemed so distracted but supposed he was worn out from the trip.

The unproductive evening went from bad to worse when we turned out to be completely unable to raise an Uber for the return journey. No cars were available for love or money. (Apparently we were 'out of area', we later discovered.) Technology didn't seem to be on our side and it took ages to get back to our hotel in Austin, which was the only accommodation we had in common for this trip. Privately I hoped this somewhat unsatisfactory evening was not a portent of things to come.

Early the following day a black people-carrier picked us up and took us to Dell's headquarters in East Parmer Lane. It comprised a series of quite nondescript, low, two- or three-storey blocks and certainly seemed very different from the flashy glass-fronted towers favoured by investment banks, or the more quirkily architectured buildings that housed many of the tech giants I'd seen in San Francisco the previous year. The emphasis at Dell seemed to be on function, not style, which, I mused, mirrored the difference between Dell and Apple computers.

When we arrived, we were asked to sit on soft benches in reception before being shown up a winding staircase to the first floor. There we found two friendly PAs whose desks flanked the doors to a pair of large offices. One, as I learned when I peered inside when its occupant came out to greet us, was Michael Dell's personal office. Once inside, I couldn't help but notice the large poster on the wall for the iconic film *Wall Street*. Had Michael Dell's face really been superimposed on the spot where Michael Douglas's was supposed to be, or was

I imagining it? The other office was the Dell boss's meeting room, where Sameer was already waiting for us.

'Sameer tells me you are going to change the world of banking,' Michael said, getting down to business almost straight away.

'That's the intention,' I said, settling into the seat he indicated at the other side of the meeting table.

After first apologizing to Sameer, who had heard the Bank Possible strategy at least half a dozen times by now, I took Michael through the investment presentation. He listened carefully, but his expression gave nothing away.

'Obviously, we are keen to formalize this relationship and, as you know, we've already talked with Sameer about some sort of partnership with Dell.'

Michael nodded in agreement, which I took as a good sign.

'Your vision for Bank Possible is certainly interesting,' he agreed. 'This is the sort of model we like to see. I can definitely see some sort of partnership going forward.'

I stole a glance at Tom, who was maintaining a fixed expression, listening intently.

'I think this will probably take the form of some sort of agreement where we offer you tangible services up to an agreed limit on the condition that you agree to reciprocate by committing to using our services on an ongoing basis. Dell would be Bank Possible's IT partner.

'In other words, a tranche of any investment would release a return to Dell in the form of services consumed.'

I nodded to indicate this sounded like the sort of thing we were thinking about. In fact, it was exactly the kind of help we did need and had been working towards for months.

We talked about how this arrangement might work in practice for a little longer, before Tom excused himself and left the office. He'd been feeling unwell since he'd left London.

'And how are you getting on with finding principal investors?' Michael went on after Tom had left.

'We've had a bit of interest in London, with Passion Capital,' I said. 'However, we thought we might have more luck in the States. We believe investors this side of the Atlantic will be much more open to this sort of idea.

'Obviously, we've only just arrived, and you're our first meeting,' I went on. 'We've got a number of presentations set up in San Francisco, which is where we are heading when we leave here.'

'And New York?' he pressed.

'Yes, New York too,' I nodded. 'That's after San Francisco, although we weren't as successful at setting up so many meetings there. We intend to make calls en route.'

'I may be able to help there,' Michael said. 'I know a few people you should see. When exactly will you be arriving there?'

I could hardly believe it. Not only had Michael Dell agreed to invest his company's considerable resources in Bank Possible, he was now opening his no doubt highly impressive contacts book to introduce us to investors in New York.

Strangely, Tom had not returned to the meeting by the time it was over. This was not entirely unusual. He could occasionally be quite withdrawn and thoughtful and, if he was ill, that was not something that could be helped. As always, I focussed on the positives.

I'd been entrusted with introductions to half a dozen or so people in New York. They were all pretty high-level financiers. One of the names on the list did cause me to do a double take, mind: it was John Thain, the former chairman and CEO of Merrill Lynch, who had joined just at the start of the 2008 financial crisis and overseen its sale to Bank of America. Although the deal saved Merrill Lynch, Thain had become a controversial character after accelerating bonus payments of $4 billion to Merrill employees just before the deal closed. The move later earned a public rebuke from President Obama. What had really captured the eye of the media, though, was the $1.22 million of corporate funds he'd spent in early 2008 to renovate two conference rooms, a reception area and his office. The sum included an eye-watering $141,000 on rugs, $68,000 on an antique credenza, $35,115 for a gold-plated commode on legs and $1,100 for a waste basket. (I wondered what he would have made of our office in Peter's Lane.) Thain had subsequently apologized for his 'lapse in judgement' and repaid the costs. While analysts predicted the Merrill boss would be able to get the company back on track, there was tension between Thain and Bank of America CEO Ken Lewis, and Thain resigned in January 2009. He was now at CIT Group, which he'd joined in February 2010, and Michael Dell certainly thought he was a person well worth speaking to.

In the meantime, we had a number of meetings in San Francisco to get through. Tom and I had set up presentations to both VCs and private equity houses, even though we knew the former might be reluctant to invest because our proposition was too big, while the latter would be concerned that the opportunity was too small.

As I caught up with Tom and we headed back to the airport, I felt quite positive. The Dell meeting had gone better than expected and as I left Michael said they would come back to us later in the month with a formal proposal about their investment. That was great news because if we could tie all that up in October, we could really start to accelerate our progress.

Despite our promising start in Austin, things didn't seem quite so positive in San Francisco. Although we were in the one region of the world where good, new disruptive ideas were valued most highly, investors just didn't seem to be able to get their heads around Tom and me. I guess we must have seemed like an odd team: a thirty-something bearded hipster type and a fifty-something former member of the banking establishment. I was a bit disappointed that no one appeared able to get past that. I certainly wasn't challenged by any especially intelligent or insightful comments about our plan for Bank Possible.

I started to feel quite deflated as we went from one meeting to the next. Tom was the same, and constantly complained of feeling unwell, even bailing out of a meeting and returning early to his lodgings on one occasion. When we were together he seemed increasingly anxious and distracted. I couldn't blame him. We obviously weren't getting anywhere. There seemed to be some general misunderstanding about what banking actually was. One financier seemed utterly incredulous that we'd be lending out our customers' deposits.

'What, so you'll take all these people's money and then give it to other people?' he said. Yes, because that is what a bank does!

'Isn't that a bit risky, lending it out to people?'

Again, that is what a bank does . . .

I tried to keep my spirits up by playing spot-the-executive at the various private equity houses we visited. Invariably, the San Francisco PE firms were based in large, gleaming, high-tech glass-and-chrome deco offices, yet we barely ever saw a soul. After waiting in a cavernous yet comfortable reception area, we would be invited by the young lady behind the front desk (for it was always a young lady) to enter the boardroom. During this entire period and then on the way out, we never saw anyone other than the PE executives who would join us after we had been securely deposited in the boardroom. Where was everyone?

The venture capitalists' natural abode was the polar opposite: all exposed brick, with brightly coloured furniture and a fair smattering of table-tennis tables. Here, dozens of young people in designer clothing milled around perfecting the somewhat awkward compromise of looking wildly busy yet supremely relaxed.

We left San Francisco with nothing more than a few vague promises. Mind you, VCs and PE houses never actually say the word 'no', even when they are certainly not going to say 'yes'. A negative response would close off any future possibilities should anything change. However, Tom and I were both left in no doubt that, as things stood, we'd come away with nothing.

The situation in New York was no more productive. We had to begin our visit by going out to buy Tom a smart jacket. John Thain fell firmly into the bracket of 'old school' banker and I would have put money on the fact he'd have taken a very dim view of anyone turning up in a check shirt and jeans. Tom wasn't keen on the new outfit, but he was curious to meet John.

'You do know he's not going to invest though, right?' he said.

'Ed Griffin was never going to invest,' I reminded him. 'But he brought us WPP.'

To say the meeting with John was somewhat toe-curling would be an understatement. John was hugely welcoming and friendly and brought along a few members of his team. For some reason I couldn't quite fathom, Tom decided this was the moment to relate his views on what caused the global financial meltdown in 2008/9. The faces of the bankers opposite us at the table were a picture of disbelief. My business partner, on the other hand, was quite determined to have his say. I felt a bit embarrassed but there was little I could do. I had no idea why he felt compelled to say what he said, but I could hardly contradict him in public. As Tom spoke I knew it had gone too far for me ever to fully recover the meeting. The only comfort I could take was that I had a fantastic story to tell and would probably be able to dine out on it for years. The time my business partner took one of the world's top bankers to task.

After spending nearly an agonizing hour with John Thain, we moved on to Thrive Capital. Thrive Capital was founded by Josh Kushner, and one of its big backers was his brother Jared, who is well known today as Donald Trump's son-in-law. The firm focussed on media and internet investments, and at that time managed over $600 million in investments in businesses such as GitHub and Instacart. Once again, although the meeting seemed to go better, we came away empty handed.

As Tom and I hailed a taxi to take us to the airport I felt a little dejected. We'd seen dozens of people and achieved precisely nothing. It was hard to know where we were going to go next with this. I racked my brains as I settled into the bright yellow cab, trying to think what we could do or say differently. Clearly, I was missing something by not being able to interest investors in what was (to me, in any case) a fantastic idea. I pictured myself having to go back to Peter's Lane the following day and deliver the bad news. The team were putting everything into this project and I felt like I was letting them down. I reminded myself that at least we had something positive from Dell, so it was not all wasted time.

'I'm sorry if I have been behaving a bit oddly,' Tom said suddenly. 'My girlfriend's here.' I turned to face him, unsure if I had heard correctly.

'She wanted to see me,' he said.

He explained that she had, in effect, been mirroring our trip, staying with him in the Airbnbs, following us from state to state. No wonder he'd been more than a little distracted. Apparently their relationship had been in crisis and the two of them had been working out if they had a future together. As I digested the news of the underlying background to our trip, it did all seem a little strange. What an odd new world I had immersed myself in. I listened sympathetically as he told me more about what had been going on, but I wasn't really sure whether he wanted my advice or just a friendly ear. Either way, we didn't speak of it again after we got out of the taxi.

We reached London and went into the office to explain what had happened and how we had come back with nothing. Everyone was hugely supportive, but it was easy to read the disappointment on their faces.

'Metro had to see 300 investors before they got their funding,' I reminded the team, even though I was very conscious I had somewhat overused this line already. 'We're not even up to triple figures yet. There are plenty more people to see.'

I pushed to the back of my head a voice that was saying, *Oh yeah, so who and what will get them interested?*

After doing our best to gee up the team, I turned my focus to beefing up our investor deck and continuing preparations for the regulator. The past week had been disappointing, but we had to put America behind us now and resume our search for opportunities closer to home.

6. Build Momentum

A week or so after we'd returned, I received an email from Sameer detailing the Dell offer. They were prepared to invest services to the value of $5 million. This would include engagement and support from Michael, Sameer and his team; their hardware and back-office facilities such as their customer briefing centres; 'services assets' such as industry and technology consultants, solution architects, developers and testers; and assistance from Dell's digital and 'user experience' experts. Basically, all the software support we needed to get started.

Sameer was at pains to point out that their investment was not a 'discount' or 'delayed payment', but a 'real and material' commitment to Bank Possible. In return, Dell expected the digital bank to reciprocate by agreeing to employ Dell's services on a commercial basis going forward, making Dell Bank Possible's IT partner.

It was a real relief to get the offer and to see that Sameer was 'flexible' on the period it could take for Dell to make a return, saying anything up to five years was fine. It felt like at last we were really starting to get somewhere. As always, there was precious little time to reflect in the glory of another small step forward. There was just so much to be done.

I had just finished discussing some more details of the regulatory submission with my lawyer when I received a call from someone I had never spoken to before. He said he was calling from a London law firm.

'I have been talking to Route 66 Ventures,' he explained. 'It's a Washington DC-based private investment firm which focusses on the fintech sector.' As he spoke I was googling the name Route 66. Disruptive technology? Yeah, we love it, was the banner on their website's landing page. That sounded promising.

'They've heard about what you are trying to do and wondered if you would like to have a conversation?' the lawyer went on.

A lot of things ran through my head at this point, most prominently, *Hell yes, I'd like to have a conversation*, and also that maybe our American trip had not been such a waste of time after all.

'Definitely,' I replied. 'I am always open to talk about Bank Possible.'

In a very short space of time a conference call was set up with Pascal Bouvier, who was responsible for fintech investments for Route 66.

When we spoke, the difference in tone was noticeable, compared with many previous potential investors we'd sounded out. Pascal was enthusiastic from the beginning. He'd followed our progress closely and seemed to get what the business was about. Although it was difficult to do the full investment pitch on the phone, I explained where we were in the process and what we were hoping to do.

The conversation opened up a series of talks with Route 66, each one seeming more positive than the last. We were aware that they had invested a small sum in one of our rivals, Tandem, but no one seemed to think this was a big problem. Bank Possible was also still in on/off talks with Passion Capital, the investor Tom had brought in months earlier. Then, out of nowhere, I received a call from Christian Hernandez from White Star Capital, another investor we'd approached some time before. We were now talking with three potential partners.

'Best-case scenario: they start competing,' I told Tom after I had spoken at length with Christian. 'That'll drive up the valuation.'

It was such a relief to feel like we were finally making progress on the money side. Our monthly spend was now up to £80,000 and most of that was coming from my now almost completely depleted savings, as well as Tom's. I knew for a fact that some of the guys, particularly Jason and Paul, were getting very nervous indeed about our perilous financial situation. Everyone wanted to see Bank Possible succeed, but there was a real possibility we'd run out of money before that happened.

While juggling the interest from Route 66, Passion Capital and White Star, as well as compiling details for the regulator, Tom and I continued to see other investors. Now we were 'in play' we seemed to get a vastly different reception. Doors that were previously closed began to open. Mind you, we might have had at least one narrow escape.

One potential investor we were introduced to was Ifty Ahmed, who at the time we saw him worked at Oak Investment Partners. I met him at the Dorchester in Park Lane and rather liked him. He was very charming and affable and quite different from many in the VC world, who are often rather blunt and abrasive. Ifty was as keen to know as much about me personally as the business and seemed very attentive and inquisitive throughout our meeting. Even so, the discussions eventually came to naught. However, it later emerged that Ifty was under investigation by the US Securities and Exchange Commission (SEC) over allegations that he had manipulated Oak investments for his own financial gain. He was accused of doctoring deal documents and faking invoices on at least nine companies. According to the SEC, in one instance Ifty convinced his employers to write a $20 million cheque for a stake in one company, when in reality the deal was for a $2 million investment. Ifty, who vehemently denies all charges, subsequently fled to India and has been waging war on the SEC to unfreeze his assets. He insists he expects to be fully vindicated at some point.

Then, towards the end of November, our ongoing discussions with Passion Capital foundered. I ended the talks after discovering that one of its three founders, Stefan Glaenzer, had been placed on the Sex Offenders Register in 2012 following an assault on a woman on the London Underground, a charge he admitted, claiming to have been high on cannabis at the time and for which he received a suspended prison sentence, a fine and a ban on using the Tube for eighteen months. I was not being judgemental: it just didn't seem appropriate to get involved with this business, particularly when key personnel in the bank would be under such close scrutiny from the regulator. Eileen Burbidge offered to structure any deal so Stefan wasn't involved, but it seemed too much of a risk to me with regards to our future reputation.

By this stage the pressure was really on in terms of finances because I had only recently formalized the relationships with the team. Up until December 2014, I had been the only shareholder of Bank Possible. Now Paul Rippon, Gary Dolman, Jason Bates and Tom Blomfield became consultants to the company in return for equity. It formalized matters and meant that Paul, Gary and Jason were able to spend more time on the business. It was all done in a bit of a hurry, with lots of copies of documents being passed round the office for people to review and sign. Each of the developers was also awarded a small amount of equity to incentivize everyone to be part of the team. Leah Templeman, who was an ex-girlfriend of Tom's from their university days and who had joined us a few weeks earlier, helped me sort through all the contracts and paperwork. Together we made sure that by the end of the day it was all done. Leah, who had previously worked at a company specializing in coconut water, also persuaded many of her old colleagues there to help us on customer research, which was a real bonus. It did also mean that for a long while the only beverage available at Peter's Lane was coconut water.

While I didn't articulate it to the others, I found the burden of being responsible for so many people's livelihoods huge. Even though I had managed thousands of people in my career and made many redundant in the name of so-called cost management, if anything went wrong here, there would be no one but me to blame. It was all very well me spending a couple of years of my life trying to pull this together, but these people had young families, mortgages and all sorts of other commitments. They trusted me to deliver and there was no going back. It was often a little overwhelming. Meanwhile, I was still the only director of the company and the responsibility for paying the debts remained mine. We now had a team of ten and a large salary bill each month. I was really running on vapours in terms of finances. I couldn't see anything past Christmas because by then I would have completely run out of cash.

Although we'd had regular one-to-one contact with Christian Hernandez at White Star, strangely, no one at Bank Possible had met anyone from Route 66 yet. Until now, all the negotiations had been done over the phone. All this was about to change. Pascal Bouvier sent me an email to say he would be in Frankfurt with his Route 66 partner Michael Meyer on 20 November and asking if they could visit myself and the team the following day.

'Assuming all goes well during due diligence and we have mutual business chemistry, we would have appetite to invest between £10 million to £15 million over several rounds,' he wrote. 'Once we meet, and assuming mutual interest is still strong, we can then move very swiftly and fund a significant part of the £3 million first round.'

This all looked really promising, particularly the part about moving swiftly. After that, even though the work that needed doing for the regulator and business model was intense, we did everything we could to make a show-stopping presentation to the Route 66 pair.

We met up at an office near One New Change, the retail and office development in the shadow of St Paul's Cathedral, and had lunch together afterwards. I felt it had gone quite well, but after that it was simply a question of waiting.

Then, within a short space of time, things began to get very serious. Both Route 66 and White Star Capital began a period of intense negotiations. We saw the valuation of Bank Possible creep up from £10 million, to £11 million and then £12 million.

While all this was going on, Paul, Gary and myself, together with KPMG and PwC, were working and reworking the next stage of the Regulatory Business Plan. We'd had to produce detailed information for the Internal Liquidity Adequacy Assessment process (ILAA). This examines whether there will be enough capital to withstand customers not paying us back and whether we'd be able to pay people out if they all wanted their deposits back at once. These documents were submitted in stages, the first part in November, another in December and one more due to go out in the New Year. It had been a major piece of work and hugely labour intensive. It was a good feeling to be getting to the end of that too.

We'd had a bit of a blip on the actual naming of the new bank. After applying to trademark Bank Possible, we were informed there might very well be objections. Sensing a lengthy legal tussle for which we didn't have the money, time or appetite, we decided to switch tack. Jason was put in charge of managing the project. I enjoyed working with him. He was always very diligent and courteous.

Finding a good name was a challenge. We started with another day-long brainstorm with VML, during which we came up with a list of new contenders. VML encouraged us to think about a name that connected with what we did, in other words that described our core proposition in some way. Obviously, it had to be very different from all our rivals' and not infringe any copyright or trademarks. We were also told to come up with some 'bad' names as part of the thought process. Thus, we quickly managed to discount anything that sounded like an old family name, or a traditional bank, or words like Doobop or Mooney that just didn't mean anything.

We were advised that a good name does more than just trying to 'sell' the business. It should 'speak' to the consumer and be sure to say something worth saying. Oh, and have nerve, ambition, personality, a mission and a little bit of a risk to it too. All in all, quite a lot to expect from a single word in anyone's reckoning.

One of the early runners was Bank Carrot, which followed the fashion at that time of naming brands after fruit or condiments. It hadn't worked out too badly for Apple; then there was Orange, Nutmeg and many others. At the time we had a bit of a rabbit theme going too (rabbit–carrot – geddit?) so it seemed logical. Plus, everyone thought that if normal banking is about 'stick', carrot would indicate a more enlightened attitude. Even as it was mooted, though, I did wonder if I would ever be able to get up on a conference platform under this moniker and be taken truly seriously.

'Good afternoon, my name is Anne Boden, CEO of Carrot Bank.'

Other names that got an airing included Rhythm, as a

shorthand for people's daily, weekly and monthly spending habits; Reflex, because it reflected a fast response to anything life throws at you; and Alfred, the banking personal assistant in a nod to Batman's faithful butler.

Another name that came up during the session was Starling, although no one could remember who first suggested it. I liked the sound of it immediately, and it certainly sounded less frivolous than all the other options. The birds themselves are sociable, adaptable, friendly and strong, all qualities we wanted our new bank to have. Plus, it is a hugely successful bird, which arrives in great numbers in each new territory and displaces the old guard.

Jason took charge of running all the names through the lawyers and came back to me late into the night on 13 November. Three of our shortlisted choices were unavailable, including Carrot, but Starling was given a green light. The various Starling domain names were available too, so it seemed like the obvious choice. Starling it was.

The real icing on the cake was the fact there would shortly be an article about Starling in the *Financial Times*. Journalist Sally Davies visited the office in December to interview me for an article to be published early in the New Year. After hearing about Tom she'd spoken enthusiastically about it being a great news story: a traditional woman banker starting a bank with a tech start-up guy. There was a little uneasiness about this in the office, not least since it somewhat elbowed Jason, Paul and Gary out of the way. I completely understood this viewpoint, but by the same token it was clear Tom had bags of potential and it was a good, newsworthy angle at the same time. Sally loved the atmosphere and location of our office too, with its stand-up desks, coffee, beer and talk of Silicon Valley, all based in one of the most interesting and vibrant parts of the capital. Her enthusiasm was infectious, and made us all stop for a moment to appreciate that this was, indeed, something pretty incredible. We'd come such a long way.

For my own part, I was enjoying being surrounded by this group of highly intelligent and affluent millennials, all of whom seemed to see life differently from the traditional banking community that had been my world for so long. Even though I was always rushed off my feet, I did enjoy a spot of people watching now and again. In particular, I was fascinated by their attitude to money. I was curious about how it was different from my own attitude, and indeed that of our potential customers. My worries about the day-to-day finances of Starling seemed lost on them. They talked casually about amassing enormous wealth, as though it was almost inevitable, whereas I knew most of our would-be customers would be 'ordinary' people carefully eking out their budgets each month. This is not to say my team were not giving it their all. They were. At the same time, they were also very idealistic about their achievements. The pressure to succeed while at the same time fixing the world was ever present in our office.

Even though it was apparent that good things were happening, the closer we came to Christmas, the more agonizing each day became. We still seemed a long way off from securing our investment. While the rest of the nation threw themselves into the festive season and pretty much downed tools, we were working long hours every day and going back and forth providing information to White Star and Route 66. All the while, I was only too conscious that we would not be able to continue work in January should neither of them come through. After coming as far as we had, we could still shortly grind to an ignominious, juddering halt having completely run out of money.

Fortunately, the team continued to be very mutually supportive, although Tom and I had a few tiny disagreements about the best way forward. Tom was, for example, quick to add his voice to the others about hating the demo video we'd had done. He maintained his stance that there should be an absolute ban on showing it to anyone. I didn't feel the same way. Sure, it might have been corny, but I think it gave us a human edge too. It broke up presentations that would otherwise comprise only spreadsheets and graphs. Another thing Tom opposed was getting on the first tier of Faster Payments. This was the scheme, introduced in 2008, which enabled instant payments between one bank and another, replacing the system whereby such payments could take three days or possibly more to clear. There was a strict process for becoming a member of the Faster Payments Scheme, but I felt that for a mobile service like ours it was critical that we could offer such real-time transactions. Tom saw this as a waste of our resources and reckoned that we'd be fine piggybacking on an established bank. I disagreed entirely, but with so much else going on let it drop for the moment. Tom had given some great input to the business and brought in some good people, so I wanted to demonstrate that his views counted for something.

Determined to show him my support, I agreed to host a pre-Christmas dinner at my house. It had been Tom's idea. He'd read in a book that many Silicon Valley start-ups have a ritual of going around to the CEO's house for lunch on Sundays and said we should do the same.

'But you are cooking,' I insisted, agreeing to the Sunday before Christmas, thinking it could double up as a bit of a festive celebration for the team.

I've got all the fancy kitchen stuff at home, but I rarely cook. A few days later, Tom emailed me a list of everything he needed. I don't just mean the ingredients list of chicken, potatoes, veg and so on; he also prescribed the exact utensils he would require in order to pull off this culinary masterpiece.

I suppressed a giggle when, an hour later, he sent me another email containing pictures of said utensils, just in case I had misunderstood.

Sunday came around and a Tesco delivery van duly dropped off the ingredients a few hours before everyone was due. A while later, the invited guests started to arrive, all of them a little late. While Tom got to work in the kitchen, I handed out glasses of champagne to the assembled throng and pretty soon everyone seemed quite cheerful and relaxed.

We were finally called to the table late in the afternoon, by which time a few people were quite merry, having waited so long for their food. Unfortunately, as it turned out, there was not nearly enough 'lunch' to soak it all up. I'd ordered faithfully from the prescribed list, but somewhere along the line there had been a bit of a miscalculation. There was just one chicken between the ten of us and a very meagre portion of vegetables to go on the side. Frugal doesn't come close to summing it up. Suddenly, it all became very intense and everyone began discussing cryptocurrencies.

Needless to say, it was not the most successful lunch party ever. I made a private vow that the practice would never be repeated.

The following day, Monday 22 December, White Star dropped out of the process, having come as far as they cared to go. Route 66 had won the bidding war and let it be known that they would be sending something over later in the day. It was a shame we wouldn't be working with White Star, since I particularly liked and respected Christian Hernandez, who had played it fair throughout the process, but I was confident we'd got a good agreement with Route 66.

I felt almost sick with nerves as I waited for Route 66's official offer to land and was glued to my email inbox so I could see the moment anything arrived. Tom seemed to have found a way to conquer his nerves. He was sitting three desks away from me playing some sort of online war games with his mate Dave, a professional poker player who mainly worked from his home. Every so often the normal murmur of office life was punctuated by Tom shouting 'Attack! Attack!'

Late in the evening, an email landed from Route 66. I held my breath and clicked on it. We'd got our £3 million invest-ment. Starling was in business.

As I headed back to Marlow to begin my Christmas break I felt more relaxed than I had done in months. It wasn't just that I was about to take a few days off and had a trip to Ireland planned (albeit to see if I could recruit some more people), it was the fact we finally had funding in place. I'd signed the term sheet with Route 66 and told the regulator that we now had the investment. It was a huge relief.

7.   A Near-Death Experience

It's a well-known fact that many business start-ups fail. More than half don't make it through the first year and many more fall by the wayside in their second, third and fourth years. What is much less widely known is that even the most success-ful start-ups go through at least one near-death experience. They get to an absolute rock-bottom moment where they have one of two options. They can watch everything they've worked for collapse and walk away, either to start again or to give up on the entrepreneurial world altogether. Or, they can find a way to make it work. While not very enjoyable at the time, the upside of a near-death experience is that it is the cata-lyst to find a way to make the business model work. Very often it is the signal to start again from scratch with an entirely new direction. And it is this new direction that guarantees the suc-cess of the company. I didn't know anything about start-up near-death experiences as we headed into the colder months of early 2015.

I returned to the office on Friday 2 January, raring to get started. We still needed to complete due diligence with Route 66, but I was hopeful that Pascal Bouvier's earlier promise of a swift deal still held true.

Over Christmas, Pascal handed day-to-day contact to his colleague Michael Meyer. Emails went back and forth steadily during the festive break with questions asked and answers pro-vided. It was looking promising for everything to be finalized by early February, which was good news, not least because Starling was still spending money at an alarming rate.

Then, out of nowhere, an issue emerged. A serious issue. Michael Meyer raised concerns over how much we owed KPMG and PwC. The firms were, of course, working on a contingent basis and Starling had put a considerable amount of fees on the tab. Michael's argument was that Route 66 was not willing to put in £3 million and see a third of it paid out in historic fees. They wanted their investment to go towards building the business, not covering past losses.

The question being posed was very clear: could we renegotiate the valuation of the business based on these debt obligations? Instead of the pre-money evaluation of £12 million, they wanted to change it to £9 million.

For me the idea was a non-starter. We'd agreed terms and it was completely out of the question to change them at this stage. It's the way the process works with investors: you do the preliminary work, agree a non-binding term sheet, which sets out the deal in some detail, and then do the due diligence where the lawyers pore all over it. More than 90 per cent of term sheets go on to become fully executed transactions.

But not this one.

In a matter of hours, the Route 66 deal fell through. They subsequently invested more cash in Ricky Knox's digital bank, Tandem. I had played hardball and they had walked away. It was a devastating development. We were back to square one, scrabbling around to raise even a small amount of money so we could stay in business. Tom said he would be prepared to put in what funds he had, and his father and uncle also offered to invest. Earlier on, a group of angel investors had offered around £1 million, which we'd declined as being too little. We considered going back to ask if they would be prepared to re-engage, but of course there was now a high probability they wouldn't want to know. Tom also raised the possibility of returning to Passion Capital, but I still wasn't keen to risk our reputation. Whichever way you looked at it, Starling was in serious trouble.

After an intense couple of days, we somehow managed to get an outline agreement with an alternative investor, Inflection Ventures, a company introduced to us via team member Jonas Huckestein. The deal, negotiated at breakneck speed with Inflection Ventures' Nash Islam, depended on Starling management covering all the deferred fees and me personally injecting an additional £183,000. It wasn't ideal, but it was the only deal on offer.

Monday 2 February kicked off a week I will never forget. I had spent the weekend in Marlow, but driven to London early that morning. I stopped off at my small flat in St John's Wood on the way to the office. The moment I saw my front door, I knew something was wrong. When I turned the key and pushed to open it, it hardly moved. The security chain was on from the inside, which was all wrong since no one was supposed to be at home. My heart was beating hard in my chest as I poked my hands through the gap and tried to work the chain free, which I managed after a minute or so of awkward manoeuvring. I took a deep breath, pushed the door open and walked in with no idea what to expect. I'd had this flat for thirty years and never had any trouble before now.

It was a mess. A real mess. Drawers had been ransacked, cupboards emptied and my stuff was strewn all over the floor. Even my bed had been turned over and the bare mattress was forlornly half sticking in the air. The flat had clearly been thoroughly searched. I looked around, taking a mental stock count. As far as I could tell, nothing had been taken. In fact, there was £60 in notes left lying on the floor. I'd never kept many possessions in the flat; nothing of real value, anyhow. It was somewhere I could sleep during the week and grab a quick meal. It certainly wasn't full of home comforts, gadgets and entertainment equipment, since I rarely had time to relax. I guessed a burglar in St John's Wood would normally anticipate a more impressive haul in such a well-to-do area, whereas all I had of any value here was a large pile of banking strategy books. Even so, it was a horrible feeling to have had someone go through all my stuff.

The police were called and I arranged for someone to come over to let them in when they turned up. Galling though it was, there was no way I could spend the day hanging around to wait for them, since I had another busy day ahead trying to raise funds, as well as a photo session booked in for Tom and me to get pictures to go with the *FT* piece by Sally Davies.

The atmosphere in the office was subdued when I arrived. It had been this way since everyone had found out that Route 66 had gone off the radar. It was no secret that we were fighting for our existence.

I told my colleagues about the burglary, but didn't make a big deal about it, so no one else did either. The day kicked off with a management meeting between myself, Tom, Jason, Gary and Paul. After the morning I'd already had, I didn't have too much problem being quite blunt with them.

'We need to talk about diverting the team to more time-critical tasks,' I began. In other words, we needed to prioritize things that would demonstrate critical value, that would prove to investors that we had made progress.

'We need to show something concrete because we may not be around in a fortnight if we can't close this deal with Inflection,' I went on. I could see straight away that Tom was irritated by the suggestion, or perhaps felt it didn't need stressing. Meanwhile the others began to say that things were not that bad and we had probably already turned the corner. I found this all a bit frustrating. No one but me seemed to appreciate the seriousness of the position we were in.

The meeting ended inconclusively because we did not have enough time. I had been late into the office thanks to the burglary and now Tom and I needed to get to the photographer's studio.

Tom was almost monosyllabic as we left the office and walked the short distance to the studio. I saw the time together as a good opportunity to talk through some plans going forward, but he seemed very unwilling to respond.

The photography session was not much better. The photographer had been briefed to get some slightly wacky pictures of the 'odd couple' together. The establishment banker and the tech dude, side by side. I didn't mind. I thought it was all a bit of fun and if it helped to get Starling noticed, so be it. Tom, though, was having none of it. He made it very clear that he was not buying into this process at all, and when the photographer did coax him into standing next to me, he stood shoulders slumped, hands in pockets like he'd rather be anywhere else but there.

'Come on, Tom,' I chided. 'It's not that bad.'

Tom looked away. His facial expression was thunderous. Between takes I kept a constant eye on my phone to see if any progress had been made. On anything. I saw there was an email from the PRA and opened it up. Scanning the first few lines, I smiled. Good news at last.

'This is positive,' I said to Tom, who had found a seat as far away from me as possible. 'We've got a challenge session set with the regulator.'

A challenge session is where the regulator reviews all the documents sent in and literally goes through them line by line, asking challenging questions on every aspect of what has been written. Once we'd got through this session we'd be allowed to put in our application. Tom nodded, but said nothing.

'It's a very big deal,' I coaxed. 'It means that the regulator is happy to meet with us because the documents we have produced meet the standard required. In other words: the last twelve months of hard work and the bill for KPMG and PwC for their help in this have been worth it.'

Tom nodded again, but it didn't take a genius to realize he wasn't as over the moon as I was. He still very clearly felt uneasy and agitated about what had happened with Route 66. As far as I was concerned, though, we now had an opportunity to put this behind us. We were so close to getting regulatory approval that we'd become a much more enticing proposition. It should be easier to get funding.

When the photo session was over, we left the studio together for the walk back to the office.

'Let's grab a coffee,' I suggested as we passed a Costa.

I needed to know what was up. Why, just when we seemed to be getting so close to a positive resolution, was Tom so distant? Tom agreed to my suggestion, but he was obviously not keen. He barely looked at me as I bought two coffees and stayed silent as we settled into one of the empty tables by the window. He then stared dolefully into the coffee I put in front of him, head and shoulders slumped low.

'I thought it would be quite useful to have a chat outside the office,' I began. 'You are obviously not happy about something.'

Tom's head jolted up and he looked at me properly for the first time that day.

'I'm just sick of your knee-jerk behaviour,' he said tersely. 'In the office . . . this morning . . . it's just not necessary.'

I opened my mouth to respond, wondering even as I did so what I would say.

'Oh, forget it,' he said, standing up, his chair clattering behind him. 'I'm going.'

With that, he turned on his heel and left his untouched coffee without a backward glance. What was wrong? Yes, Tom had been fed up since Route 66 had walked, but why was he so especially unhappy today? I couldn't understand what had happened to make our situation worse. Arguably, after the news from the regulator, we were actually in a better situation.

When I arrived back in the office, Tom approached me and abruptly resigned. I was stunned.

Naturally, I asked why he was leaving, but he was low on detail on the reasons why, other than the fact he could not work with me with my 'reckless' behaviour. He also emphasized his disappointment at the fact I had curtailed spending on a couple of projects I felt were unnecessary at this stage. The straw that appeared to break the camel's back was my proposal that morning to shift priorities in the light of our cashflow issues. He simply couldn't agree with my argument that we needed to swap things around to focus purely on aspects that would make us seem more investment-worthy. He had ideas that were important to him and wasn't prepared to drop them. Yet, even though there was a reasoned argument to explain our difference of opinions on all of these matters, he didn't want to know. It felt like whatever I wanted, he wanted the opposite.

Tom certainly didn't want to discuss any options now though. He just wanted out and he wanted out now.

Even as I watched Tom's retreating form as he strode out of the office, I could barely believe what had just happened. Why was he walking away now?

The enormity of this turn of events was almost too big to contemplate. Without Tom, or rather without a CTO, the challenge session, and therefore all hope of funding, would be a non-starter. There was no chance of finding a suitable replacement CTO in the time we had. Starling would cease to exist. Everything we'd all worked so hard to achieve would come to nothing.

That wasn't all. I had already invested everything I could easily raise. I still had my home and my pension, but the rest had been eaten up by Starling.

Looking around, I could see that everyone in the office was as shocked as I was. 'We have to change his mind,' I said, my brain spinning.

I turned to the team, looking for people in Starling to whom Tom was closest and whom I might ask to talk him round. In the end I chose Jason and Gary. They immediately got to their feet and followed him out of the building, promising they would do their best to persuade him to change his mind.

My stomach was in knots as I watched them leave. I couldn't shed the nagging feeling I was missing something. As a team we'd been through so much at Starling: ups, downs, extreme triumphs and crushing blows. We'd weathered them all. We'd been stressed, almost to breaking point at times, but we'd got through it. What had changed now? Arguably we were, if not in a brilliant position, at least poised for a breakthrough.

I thought back to a conversation I'd had with Jason a week before. We'd been in the conference room alone, working on yet another iteration of our presentation to investors. We'd been talking about something that was happening at one of the rival challenger banks when, out of nowhere, Jason had asked if I knew about Tom's plan.

'What plan?' I said, still looking at our presentation, our deck, in front of me.

Our industry was always rife with insecurities and intrigue. Tech seems to attract all sorts of weird and wonderful theories, which is partly why it is such an interesting field to work in. Some of the time they were right, but mostly they were 180 degrees wrong. As a consequence, I never really took much notice of hearsay.

'There has been talk . . .' Jason began, and his voice tailed off.

'Of what?' I said, suddenly alert. I could see something was troubling him.

'Just vague stuff really.'

I stayed silent. He was obviously finding it hard to get the words out.

Jason looked embarrassed.

'That Tom was working on a plan to get rid of you and then me too.'

I frowned. At the time this seemed utterly inconceivable. 'How is that even possible?' I said. 'I'm the sole director and have invested everything I own into this bank.'

And I had dismissed the idea. It was just too unlikely. How on earth was it possible that Tom could even contemplate taking over the business I had started? The very idea seemed absurd. Now, though, I realized I may have been wrong.

Jason and Gary returned to the office a few hours later and I could see before they even said a word that they had been unsuccessful in their mission. They had, however, managed to persuade Tom to meet me that evening, so we could talk things through properly. That was something at least.

If I didn't hold out much hope before I left the office to meet Tom at Grill on the Market in Smithfield, I had even less when I saw him face to face. He would barely give me eye contact and still seemed utterly furious. The restaurant was surprisingly empty for 7 p.m. on a Monday evening, so the waiter was quite happy to give us a table tucked away at the back where we could drink and talk undisturbed.

'Can you just tell me what has changed?' I coaxed. 'Things are going in the right direction, you know that.'

'I do know that,' Tom said. 'But I just can't do this with you. I can't work with you. Your way of . . . well, it's not the way I like to do things.'

'But why hasn't this come up before? We've worked together a long time on this and then on GoCardless before that.'

Tom just shrugged and shook his head.

It was an uncomfortable drink. Tom very clearly just wanted to get it over with, while I tried everything I could to get him to open up and tell me what was really going on. I was still convinced there was more to this than met the eye.

The waiter had barely arrived at the table to offer us a top-up of our glasses before Tom asked for the bill.

'I need to go,' he said.

So, that was it. Not even a small chink of hope. What now?

I had very few cards left to play. In fact, one of the few options left seemed to be to place my fate in the hands of Jonas Huckestein, who was a good friend of Tom's. Tom had brought Jonas into Starling a couple of months earlier, since he was a talented developer. Jonas was away in Germany, visiting family, but when I had called him before leaving the office he'd said he was flying back to London the following day and would lend his voice to those trying to convince Tom to change his mind.

I slept fitfully that night, partly because my flat still didn't feel safe, but mostly because I kept going over and over in my mind what I would do next if Tom really couldn't be persuaded to stay. I woke in the early hours, my head still spinning.

The only firm conclusion I had managed to reach was that I needed impartial advice. It was almost impossible for me to come up with a solution alone. I was too close to it. The same went for all those around me at Starling, and even from within our partners such as KPMG and PwC. The people who had supported me there all had their reputations invested in the bank too. However, it was difficult to go further afield, because I didn't really want to alert the world to what was happening. There was still a possibility we'd be able to pull it back from the brink. I needed someone I trusted.

By a stroke of luck, I had a meeting arranged the next day at Deloitte with Ian Steele, to whom I had been introduced through another partner there. The meeting had been arranged a week before, but couldn't have been more timely. The subject matter might just be a little different from the one Ian and his team were expecting. I was not looking for assistance to launch my bank: I was trying to save it. I headed over to the Deloitte office, doing my best to ignore the knot of apprehension that was now ever present in the pit of my stomach.

When I arrived I was shown to a meeting room, where Ian and his colleagues were waiting. After the briefest of introductions, I launched into a full explanation of where I found myself today. I explained the long process to find investment and how we were nearly there, only to have it all fall apart at the eleventh hour when Route 66 departed. Then there was the lengthy engagement with the regulator, which had finally seemed to bear fruit. Meanwhile, we'd been busily putting a business model together and working on the software. Now, just as we were primed to succeed, my CTO and key consultant to the company had just announced his intention to quit.

The Deloitte team listened quietly as I went through it all. They'd shown very little reaction while I spoke. When I finished, though, the room erupted with questions.

'What is your run rate?' (In other words, 'How much are you spending each month?')

'Who else do you have in the pipeline on investment?'

'If Tom goes, is there a likely successor as CTO?'

I answered each question, acutely aware how bad everything I said sounded. Saying it out loud seemed to unite and bring alive the negative thoughts that had been running through my head during the previous night. I had a clear line of sight into the future and it all looked pretty bleak. It was now Ian Steele's turn to speak.

'Your business is hanging by a thread,' he began bluntly.

Even though I knew this, my heart sank as he said these words. It seemed so final.

'You have eight people on payroll, a large amount of debt and without Tom you have no funding. You are the only director: you must act to start cutting your costs now. Unless you raise money quickly Starling is dead.'

They were right. I'd already known this, but it was devastating to get an impartial view. I was so invested in the business, emotionally and financially, that it was difficult to be 100 per cent rational about it. Even as Ian spoke, I knew that if I were an outsider looking in, this was precisely what I would have said. I was experienced enough to know exactly what needed to be done when a business was in a horrible mess: attack the cost base, look for fresh funding and start again.

Feeling a little more confident, albeit still stunned by the turn of events, I returned to the office. I called everyone around me and put them on one week's notice.

'Without Tom, we don't have much of a business,' I said. 'If anyone is able to help me persuade him to stay, please do. It would be in all our best interests. Failing this, we will need to raise money quickly. By quickly, I mean within the next week. If we don't have funds in place by next week, we will have to pay everyone off because the business can't keep going. In the meantime, we'll need a new CTO, and the obvious choice is Jonas. I will talk to him when he comes in after having a go at making Tom reconsider.'

As I spoke, I knew very well that what took place over the next few days was going to make or break the business, and that how I played it would be critical. It was crucial that I remained publicly supportive of Tom, even though I was very aware he was inviting my IT engineers to off-site meetings. If there was any public sign of a rift between us then we would not be able to raise money. Anything that smacked of me bad-mouthing Tom would work directly against the interests of the company.

Inevitably, everyone was stunned by what was happening. The atmosphere in the office was awful.

I did my best to temper the bad news by reiterating that there was at least some hope. We did still have the challenge meeting set up with the PRA/FCA and we had already made some progress in terms of building the technology and apps.

'We are on a path to success,' I said to a room full of disbelieving faces. 'I still believe it is just around the corner. However, I cannot do this without Tom. He is one of the finest business people I have ever met and I am not prepared to embark upon this journey without him.'

I ended the meeting by saying that everything that was happening was highly confidential and, for now, we needed to be extra careful not to allow the news to get out. I explained that I had decided to go to my house in Marlow for a couple of days, to give Tom space to come back to the office, where, hopefully, his colleagues would manage to engage with him.

Late that evening, after I had arrived home, I received an email from Jason, who, while sounding devastated about what had happened, seemed to offer some good news.

He wrote:

Tom is fully engaged, as is Jonas, they will definitely give it their all tomorrow, calling everyone they have ever met for funding. The team are rallying/bonding around them.

However, as I read on, it was clear that all was not what it seemed at first glance. The email from Jason went on:

If they get funding and you don't come to a deal, I think that they will still leave to do something else, probably with the team in tow.

They? Tom and Jonas? Come to a deal? And now the whole team too?

In an instant I realized I had made a tactical error. I am, by nature, an optimist and I had hoped that, given space, a way forward would be found. In reality, I had missed all the obvious signs. The rumours about Tom working to be rid of me were true. By leaving the office to come back to Marlow, I had allowed him space to engineer what was nothing less than a coup.

While I was in Marlow, Tom, Gary and Jason met with Eileen Burbidge and Stefan Glaenzer at Passion Capital and agreed a deal. Key to this deal was the fact I would be asked to leave. (I was later told by Jonas that Stefan had personally recommended that the team reduce the value of my shareholding from 32 per cent to 5 per cent and that they begin by offering me 2 per cent to go.) There also seemed to be an understanding that Starling would be able to walk away from its obligations to PwC and KPMG. Over the following few days, things started to unravel at a dizzying rate. Jason announced that he would be siding with Tom. I couldn't blame him personally. Tom was apparently offering to double Jason's equity in the bank under his leadership and Jason had financial commitments to consider. He couldn't work indefinitely for nothing for a company that might go under at any moment. Jonas Huckestein said pretty much the same thing, but with the added kicker that, since Nash Islam at Inflection Ventures was a personal friend, he would be recommending that Nash pull out of any agreement with Starling.

According to a series of messages that began to flood my email inbox, Tom had made it clear to everyone around him that he was not able to work with me going forward. While

Eileen had initially said she wanted us both on the team, she now said that if it came to a choice between us, she would prefer to have Tom on board, not me. She had known Tom before she met me, having backed him at GoCardless, so her loyalties stayed with him.

It was all such a shock. I'd turned my back for a couple of days and somehow Tom had taken my place, Passion Capital was in and I was out.

Over the weekend of 7/8 February, I was sent details of an offer to hand the company over to Tom. I felt a slight detachment from reality as I read it. How had it possibly come to this? Somehow they'd managed to concoct an argument that it would be for the good of the company if I went. Perhaps it was this that swung it. I couldn't say for sure. I suppose there was still a part of me that was desperate for Starling to succeed. If the only option for it to do so was without me, then so be it. If I went, Nash Islam would be brought back to the table and they'd be able to move things on. I'd still have my equity and assumed they would treat me fairly if I made this huge sacrifice. I would have fulfilled my duties as a director.

I called Baroness Denise Kingsmill. She'd been my first choice to be chair of Starling and earlier she'd been given 2 per cent of the company in shares in anticipation of this. I'd already asked her to speak to Tom but she said she had been unsuccessful. She'd also spoken with Jonas, Jason and Paul, but had come away empty handed. Now I needed her advice on what to do next.

We met at Peter's Lane and Denise said that the only option was for me to leave. Things had gone too far now. 'I'll help you write your resignation letter,' Denise said quietly. And that is how we did it. Denise dictated the words and I typed them.

It was surreal. The letter, which was addressed to Denise as chair, but copied to all involved, read as follows:

Dear Denise,

Thank you for coming in this morning and helping all of us think through the options. I would like first of all to say how energized I have been by what we have built.

I have now considered the way forward and would like to suggest the following:

- I resign as a director and CEO today with immediate effect.
- I continue as a consultant but with no executive responsibility.
- As founder, we will agree that I will be granted 10 per cent fully vested equity as part of the restructuring soon to take place.
- I am referred to at all times as the founder of Starling or of any successor.
- I am released from all financial obligations past, future and present, in return for which I will work to negotiate and reduce any liabilities contingent on funding.
- I will also use my best endeavours to support Starling in all regulatory matters.

This is a brief outline of the terms, no doubt this will be put into a formal agreement in due course.

Regards
Anne

When it was all done, I simply clicked Send and that was it. My involvement with Starling was over. Just like that. I felt sick to my stomach.

Within less than two hours an email came back from Tom to Denise.

Denise,

Thanks for helping us through this. I'm hopeful we can come to an agreement that works for everyone. I'd like to first state how happy I am that we're back to the table, talking about options.

I need to talk with the management team about their views, which I will do immediately. I've arranged a brief call this afternoon with some lawyers to help us shape a deal that works for everyone – Anne, creditors, investors, employees etc.

I need to emphasize that I cannot accept Anne's resignation as a director or CEO until I've talked with the team and taken legal advice. I hope this is acceptable to you both.

We will work together towards a deal, but it will obviously take a few days. I've given a commitment to Anne that no further liabilities will be incurred, on top of what's already owed. This should hopefully give her some comfort to help us all shape a binding deal over the next few days.

I hope that is acceptable to everyone.

Cheers,
Tom

It didn't take long to find out the real stumbling block to Tom et al. accepting my offer. In the event of such an agreement, they required me to take responsibility for all the debts of the company.

I almost laughed when I heard this. I had created the bank, brought the team together and been responsible for making something awesome. I had invested all the money meant for my future in the process and I had sold my home in Swansea to pay for it. There was a million plus of debt outstanding to KPMG and PwC too.

After discussing it with Denise, I replied that, while I was willing to resign, there was no way I was going to indemnify the team for all the costs to date. It was a ludicrous suggestion.

This was a time when the other side of the 'negotiation' really started to up the ante. Instead of email correspondence, I received a flurry of HipChats pressurizing me to take the 'offer'.

There is only one right thing to do.

was a typical example. Or this one from Jonas:

It's a long shot, but it's worth trying.

To which he added:

And 5 per cent of the world's best retail bank isn't nothing.

The main selling point appeared to be that the bank would have a future. No one seemed to get it that this might not be exactly to my advantage, since I would not be part of it. Put it like that and it didn't seem that attractive a proposition.

The HipChats continued unabated throughout Monday. On Monday evening it became evident that Tom had shifted tack and was now working on a plan to liquidate the company altogether and/or resort to some sort of prepack arrangement.

He emailed me late on Monday evening:

We just spoke with lawyers – they think that while the arrangement with creditors etc. is messy, we might be able to make something work.

This is now the priority for everyone – I'd like to chat
tomorrow about strategies for each creditor – who
approaches them, what we can offer etc.

I kept thinking about what this was doing to my reputation.
If Starling went under it would leave it in shreds and take
away any chance of my running a new bank, or even a traditional bank, at any time in the future.

By Tuesday, I'd had enough and headed out of the house. I
just needed to get away, have some peace and quiet and time to
think. I headed down to Marlow High Street and the familiar
environment of Starbucks, my regular haunt whenever I spent
time at home, which had been rare until now.

It was still quite early in the morning and the café was pretty
quiet. I was waiting for my coffee when I spotted a friendly face
sitting at a corner table behind his newspaper. It was my friend
Ken Blackman, whom I had known for some years. He's a tech
entrepreneur and we'd often chatted about the trials and tribulations of Starling over the past months. He waved me over.

'Hello, Anne!' He smiled, then a slight frown clouded his
brow. 'Forgive me, but you look terrible. Are you unwell?'

He probably had a point. I had hardly slept for a week and
wasn't exactly looking after myself.

'It's been, er, quite a few weeks,' I said, settling into a chair
opposite with my drink.

'What's been happening?' he asked. 'I think last time we
spoke you were feeling quite positive. Weren't you in due
diligence?'

Due diligence with Route 66 seemed like such a long time
ago. So much had happened since that all fell through. Taking
a deep breath, I began to explain to Ken what had happened. I
trusted him completely, so left nothing out.

He listened in silence as I spoke. When I had finished, he

nodded. 'So, let me see if I have got this straight,' he began, deadpanning. 'You've had a great idea, you've convinced people to back the idea and pulled together a brilliant set of plans and documents which mean that you are very likely to get a banking licence. Meanwhile, you've invested a huge sum of your own money, not to mention a year of your life, getting to where you are today. Now you are being forced out?'

'That's about the size of it,' I agreed, smiling despite the despair I felt.

'Well, I don't think you have any choice then,' he went on.

I was about to say there was no way I could sign an agreement that would mean me taking on all that debt, when I realized Ken was still speaking.

'You have to walk back into the company you founded and take back control.'

I stared at Ken, weighing up what he had just said. I'd felt so browbeaten by the chain of events, this possibility had not really occurred to me.

'OK, let's put it another way,' Ken continued. 'What would you do if you lost Starling?'

'I'd start a bank like no other,' I replied, almost without thinking. The only thing that mattered to me was Starling.

'You don't need to start another bank. You already have one.'

Ken was entirely right. I needed to take back control.

We spoke for a little while longer, but now I had made up my mind, I wasn't really focussed. I thanked Ken profusely for his advice and promised I'd update him on what happened as soon as I could.

'Just give me a shout if you need any help,' he said as I left. 'You know where to find me.'

I practically ran the short distance home, gathered up my laptop and got into my car. Within half an hour of leaving Starbucks I was on the M40 heading into London. An hour later, I had parked outside my flat in St John's Wood and made my way to 22 Peter's Lane. The office fell completely silent as soon as everyone saw me. Some of the team had the good grace to look a little embarrassed, one or two even managed to say 'hello', but most of them looked down at their keyboards.

Some members of the team were sitting on a sofa in the corner. As I glanced over, I had to suppress an ironic smile. That sofa and the coffee table in front of it had been brought over from my flat in Dublin. For a brief moment I imagined them all sitting in my sitting room.

'Tom, can I have a word?' I said as I drew closer. 'In the meeting room?'

He looked surprised, but got to his feet and walked over, following me in. We sat down on opposite sides of the table. 'I've given this all a great deal of thought,' I began, looking at him steadily. 'I've decided I am going to terminate your contract. I am the CEO of Starling and I am not going anywhere.'

Tom looked stunned but didn't say anything.

'I'm going to leave the office, so you can get your things together, but this is the way things are,' I said.

I got to my feet, walked towards the door and then beyond to the stairs. Only then did Tom seem, at last, to find his voice.

He appeared at the top of the stairwell and I turned to face him. He was bending over to look at me, since I was already halfway down.

'The money you owe is huge,' he shouted. 'We have worked it out; Starling owes too much money. You are in an impossible situation.'

This was not the time or the place to argue the toss. I had made up my mind and I had said what I was going to do. Now we all needed to live with that decision and do what we needed to do as individuals.

When I returned to the office the following day the place

was all but deserted. Nearly everyone had left. Shortly afterwards I received three almost identically worded emails in quick succession from Jason, Gary and Paul. The gist of them was that they were all resigning, but would like to make one last effort to beg me to reconsider the original deal and hand the company over to them.

Months later I found an email exchange in the system that started with a message from Tom to Gary and Paul. He said Stefan Glaenzer had recommended that they all leave me to it:

> Just spoke with Stefan at Passion for thirty mins. His advice is to sit tight for a day or two. Don't engage with Anne, but also don't provoke her. I think once she realizes that she has no support, she'll come back to the table. Obviously there are difficult questions about how we deal with her once she does want to talk again.

Jason, who had always been so supportive, seemed the most saddened by the turn of events in his resignation email:

> The tragedy is that everyone knows that this could work given half a chance. As you said just a couple of days ago, we had a great team, the finance was lining up, and a challenge session with the regulators, 'It was all so near . . . it is all within arm's reach.'

The conciliatory tone was somewhat spoiled by what came next:

> But as I said yesterday, I can be very clear, going forward I will not be involved with Starling – if you are involved . . . I do hold out a small tiny chink of hope that you will re-evaluate the options, change your mind, or that I'll wake up and find out that this was all a bad dream.

But with that said, please don't use my name with the regulator, investors or suppliers, or by omission imply that I'm still involved.

Paul Rippon in his resignation letter nodded to the great loyalty he had always shown to me:

Many times at AIB and while building the bank I have said 'I trust you'. By this I meant not just bank decisions but also my career, my finances, my reputation . . .

However, the same dry warning was added:

To be clear, I am out and please do not use my name in connection with the bank without my prior agreement.

Gary's email was the briefest of the three, noting that it had been a very stressful time for everyone and recognizing the 'huge effort' that I'd put in to get Starling to this point. He did at least offer to help me wind things down in an orderly way.

Wind things down? Nothing could have been further from my mind. I was here to make sure Starling did succeed.

Mind you, my situation did not look good. By then, the one-week notice period I'd given all the software developers was up. Nearly everyone had left, bar two contractors: Hugo Cornejo and Mike Kelly. I heard that everyone on the team had gathered in a bar near Passion Capital's base in White Bear Yard. They were knocking back gin and talking about how they'd start a bank together.

While I felt a sense of relief that I no longer had responsibility for a team that so clearly wanted rid of me, I was also intensely conscious of my awful position.

Tom, the man who helped instigate this situation, now had a full team, backing from Passion Capital and a full set of documents and plans from Starling.

Me? I had no team, no money and millions of pounds of debt.

While Mike set about securing the software we had, I reflected on how we had ever managed to end up in this situation. Perhaps I had gone too far in my efforts to be inclusive and build up everyone's ego and status in Starling. I had trusted and liked Tom, and never imagined he might do something like this. What annoyed me most about what had just happened was that I now realized I had shown too much weakness when Tom threatened to resign. I should have just let him go. By chasing after him, I had left myself open to the coup that he orchestrated shortly afterwards.

If I had been less trusting, I would have seen that Tom was always eager to be CEO. Of course he was. He was an ambitious, clever young entrepreneur. Unfortunately, we were never going to see eye-to-eye on the moral obligation to pay organizations such as KPMG. Perhaps his biggest miscalculation was his erroneous belief that I had a personal responsibility to pay off any debts to the company. I didn't, and I knew that now. My obligations were only ever to do the right thing by everyone. It was a position I was comfortable with.

Even now I could hardly believe how close I had come to losing Starling. Indeed, it was by no means certain that things had not gone too far and I might never be able to recover from what had just happened. Although we'd been so close to being able to launch the bank I had first envisioned on my trip to South Africa, we were now so far away it was devastating to think about. Whichever way I looked at it, I was effectively starting all over again.

8. *Last Woman Standing*

Starting again was a challenge. I had no one on the team, zero prospect of investment in the foreseeable future and the regulatory process had returned to square one. As I arrived in the office on Thursday 12 February 2015, for my first day after losing the whole team, my head was filled with lists: who did I want in my new team, what did I need them to do and what did we have to achieve? Most pertinently: how long would it take to get Starling back up to the position it had been in just a few days earlier?

Before I could even contemplate confronting these future challenges, I needed to tackle the business's more immediate concerns. Urgent legal advice was required to unravel the situation with Tom and the team he'd taken with him. There was no way I was going to let them use anything they'd developed at Starling as the basis for their new venture. It wasn't just morally wrong, but it would also put Starling at a severe commercial disadvantage at a moment when it was already in a dangerously weakened position. Equally urgent was the need for me to fulfil my contractual obligations to everyone who had just left. During all the intense negotiations of the previous week I'd barely had time to give a second thought to such things as issuing P45s or bringing expenses up to date. That had to be a priority too.

Failure of any sort is hard to live with. It can leave you feeling vulnerable and questioning your own abilities, which is never a nice place to be. What do you do when, despite doing everything you can to secure the success of your start-up, it just doesn't make it? Mine wasn't the first start-up to go through this. There are no guarantees of success and, indeed, 70 per cent of start-ups fail, often within twenty months after first securing financing.* Perhaps they run out of money, or fail to secure investment, or customers don't quite get what they were trying to achieve. Or, as in my case, the team breaks apart. Fortunately, in the tech world, there are always second chances. In fact, there are third and fourth chances too, if needs be.

There is a great tradition in this sector of start-up founders coming back and trying again with a different model. There is even a saying that the more start-ups you do, the easier it gets, and this isn't a bad way of looking at it. In fact, some investors view start-up founders who have tried and failed as better prospects than complete beginners. The thinking goes that they have more experience of the highs and lows of digital entrepreneurship and so are more aware of the potential pitfalls.

To give you an idea of just how OK it is to fail, you only need to look at the Silicon Valley tradition of writing up the story of failures. Shortly after any start-up takes its last breath, the founder invariably writes about it on the Medium.com website. I imagine there was originally a need to do so on a central website, since the digital entrepreneur's own website would have been taken down as part of the process of closing up shop, but after a time the tradition just stuck. These post-mortems have become known as 'goodbye letters' and if you want to take a look at them you will see they are deeply personal and honest accounts of what went wrong. The idea is to put your heart and soul into the write-up to draw a line under the experience, then you can park it and move on.

* www.cbinsights.com/research/startup-failure-post-mortem/28 February 2019.

The goodbye letters are so much more than simply a cathartic experience for the founder of the failed start-up though. They can provide incredibly useful pointers and advice about the good things as well as the bad. Very often we learn more from failures than if something has gone brilliantly well.

As I sat down at my desk and looked around the deserted office, it was hard to dismiss the overwhelming feeling of disappointment and sadness at what had happened, but I knew that I had to. Forcing myself to focus, I turned to my laptop and started writing a list of the people I should contact. I didn't need to write a goodbye letter. I still had my business. I just had to rebuild it to be better than before.

I was about to make the first phone call of the day when I was disturbed by a knock at the open door. I looked up to see it was my good friend Alan Chandler. I'd known Alan for years since we'd worked together at ABN Amro and then RBS. Ironically, I'd even spoken to him about joining me at Starling a few months earlier. Unfortunately, when he'd met Tom in November, Tom had not warmed to him at all, so that was that. Nevertheless, I'd kept talking to Alan since then and had shared Starling's business plan with him.

'I didn't want to disturb,' Alan smiled. 'You looked like you were pretty absorbed. I just wanted to hear how it was all going. I brought coffee.'

I smiled as Alan set down a large Starbucks beaker on my desk.

'Thank you,' I said gratefully. 'As you can see, I am on my own. I'm pretty much the last man, well, woman, standing. You are looking at the entire personnel count of Starling.'

Alan nodded slowly and settled into a chair by my desk.

'What happened?' he asked.

What happened? Where was I to begin?

I sat back in my chair and did my best to explain the events of the past few weeks. It was strange going through it all again. It felt like the more I told the story, the less believable it seemed.

When I finished recounting everything, Alan looked thoughtful.

'So, what now?'

'Well, now I start again and make Starling the great bank I know it is going to be.'

'But, in the short term, you've got a lot of things to sort out, yes?'

I nodded and glanced at the lengthy to-do list on my screen. Alan got up and glanced over my shoulder at the list.

'OK, why don't I tackle the P45s and all that stuff, while you get on with talking to the lawyers?' he said, slipping off his jacket as he spoke. 'Point me towards a PC and I will get started.'

'You choose, they're all free,' I said, laughing in spite of myself. 'Are you sure you've got the time?'

'Absolutely. It would be my pleasure. Just point me in the right direction to find the relevant details.'

I felt quite emotional that someone could be so kind after all that had gone on – and also supremely grateful. It was great that it was Alan who had appeared on the scene too. The reason I'd tried to bring him in last November was because I believed then that he was exactly what Starling needed. He was an exact sort of person, a details man I suppose you'd call it. He was tenacious too and always held people to account, as well as being constantly curious and enthusiastic. Starling had lacked much of this over the past month or so. Most of all, Alan was highly principled: a quality I appreciated more than ever right now. It was a real bonus that he was able to step in and help right at that moment.

While Alan got on with sorting out the staff paperwork, I got in touch with my lawyers. This, of course, meant going through the whole story yet again, but oddly it seemed to become easier each time. In all the telling and retelling, it began to feel like I was relating something that had happened to someone else entirely.

The lawyers advised that I needed to write a detailed account of what had happened to date, along with breakdowns of the company's structure, its shareholdings and the various players involved. Even before I got stuck into this process, I was advised to offer Tom mediation. If this all ended in legal action, the courts would want to see that Starling had made efforts to solve this amicably.

It wasn't easy writing an email to Tom offering mediation. Right then, I felt anything but conciliatory. However, there was also a part of me that did want to sort things out between us in a good way. We'd worked closely together in the most intense circumstances and that stood for something. Ultimately, we had both wanted the same thing: to launch a fantastic mobile bank. Sadly, a huge divide had opened up in how we both felt this could be achieved.

This has been a roller coaster,

I began, with masterful understatement.

While you asked me to resign and I terminated your contract with the company, we have been through a lot together and I believe in my heart that we can still pull this around. My primary motivation is to ensure the survival of the business: I think that we share this enthusiasm.

I went on to offer to breach the impasse by supporting Tom as CEO in the short term, provided that if he was unable to secure the support of the regulator by June 2015, he would agree to step down and agree to the appointment of a new CEO. This was, I believed, a pretty generous offer. It was predicated on the basis that I had 5 per cent of the outstanding shares immediately following the lifting of the regulatory restrictions and that if a new CEO were appointed he or she would need to be incentivized through Tom's shareholding.

> I hope that this offer forms the basis of something we can discuss,

I concluded.

> If you think it beneficial I am willing to talk to you directly or for us each to appoint 'spokesmen' to mediate for us. If we go with the spokesman route it probably makes sense for us each to choose somebody who has no historic involvement with the business.

I sent the email on Friday 13 February, hoping this was not an omen of more bad things to come. By then, Alan had made good headway with all the staff admin and had diverted to begin helping me with other items on my to-do list. I kept telling him to go, but he insisted he'd stay until I was back on my feet. (Alan ended up working unpaid for almost a year; a sacrifice for which I will always be monumentally grateful. He dropped by with a coffee and never seemed to leave.)

There was no reply to my offer to Tom until the following Monday afternoon. When it landed, it was a firm no.

> We're all committed to bringing a new challenger bank to market, and it seems that the best way forward is for us to start a completely separate and distinct bank from Starling,

Tom wrote.

> It's a big market out there, and we feel that there would be more than enough room for another player.

To this end, Tom laid out two potential options going forward:

1) At the very least we'd like to suggest putting an agreement in place that formalizes everyone's position, so that we can all go our separate ways, reputations protected. A clean break, so that we can all focus on building great banks.
2) If you choose not to take Starling to launch, we would be interested in talking about buying company assets and taking the licence application forward.

We'd be willing to buy certain assets for £200,000 in cash. At first glance, the assets would be:

– IP [intellectual property rights] in the code & designs
– IP in the regulatory documents, plus an orderly handover of the application process
– Limited pieces of IT equipment

So, this didn't seem very promising. Perhaps the most telling part of the communication came in the closing paragraph:

We need to agree our approach & start communication with the regulator by this Wednesday, so please get back to me before then if you would like to talk.

Wednesday? Tom and his team were moving quickly. Yes, they'd be starting again in the regulatory process, but thanks to all the work that had already been done, they knew exactly the steps that needed to be taken. Even though I was not entirely convinced that Tom and his team would be able to start a bank, it didn't detract from the fact they were going to give it a bloody good go.

Of course, I needed to speak with the regulator too. Only, instead of informing them that I was kicking off the process of launching a bank, I had to bring my application to a full stop. I needed to update them on the status of Starling's executive team, which had shrunk considerably and now consisted of just me. I typed an email outlining the bare bones of my situation and received a reply inviting me to participate in a conference call with the PRA and FCA the following day. Another hurdle crossed.

The next big thing was to recruit a new team. The experience of the last twelve months had shown me that I needed a range of different skillsets on board. I got on the phone and made a few calls to headhunters. Luckily, a good contact of mine was able to see me virtually straight away. I put on my coat, picked up my bag and headed out of the office.

I was waiting in the reception of the headhunters' Mayfair office when my phone rang. I fished my phone out of my bag and looked at the caller ID. It was Sally Davies from the *FT*.

'We're running the piece tomorrow,' she told me almost as soon as she'd announced herself. 'Obviously the angle has changed a little since we first spoke.'

My heart dropped. This was my worst nightmare. I knew the story of the past few weeks would eventually get out into the public domain but this seemed like the worst possible scenario. We'd given the *FT* full access to Starling in happier times, so who knew what this journalist would write now.

'I assume you've spoken with Tom?' I said, keeping my voice steady.

'I have, but obviously we'd like a comment from you on what next for Starling,' Sally said. 'I understand there has been a parting of ways. Tom has left along with at least three members of your senior management team, Gary Dolman, Paul Rippon and Jason Bates.'

I stayed silent as Sally clearly had more points to make.

'I'm told that the fundraising deal with Route 66 fell apart in January,' she went on. 'This was the falling-out over Star-ling's decision to earmark at least £1 million of the initial £3–4 million for consultants and advisors, as part of the approval process.

'There were also question marks over your decision to build IT systems in-house from scratch, rather than buy software off the shelf, which is the route taken by the likes of Atom and Metro.'

Sally had been very well briefed. There was not much she didn't seem to know.

'What do you want to say to all of this?' she pressed. 'To start with, the most obvious question is: is Starling going to continue?'

I paused, weighing up the right response. There was little point issuing a curt 'no comment'. That would just make a bad situation worse. The best damage-control option would be to sound as positive as possible.

'We are looking at the overall management structure,' I began. 'We are trying to figure the best way forward, but Star-ling will continue.

'We have made huge progress on our technology build and huge progress in preparing our regulatory submission. We are now in a situation where we need a different organization with a different skill base.

'That's all I can really say for the moment,' I concluded.

This seemed to largely satisfy Sally, but she still fired a few more questions in my direction, in an effort to get to the bot-tom of the story. I suspected she already knew most of it, so I didn't rise to the bait.

'OK, thanks for this, Anne, and all your time earlier,' she con-cluded at last. 'I'm sure we'll speak again soon.'

And that was it. I'd have to wait until the following day to find out how badly this would reflect on Starling. My instinct told me that whatever the piece said, it would not be good. Plus, it would inevitably alert other media outlets, which meant that very soon the story would be everywhere.

There was nothing I could do to stop it. I just had to keep my head down and get on with things. I went into the meeting with the headhunter and tried to push the *FT* piece to the back of my mind. It wasn't easy.

I woke early the next day and logged on to FT.com. There it was in black and pink with a banner headline:

BANK POSSIBLE'S FUTURE IN QUESTION AS STARLING TEAM FLIES APART*

As I read the article I felt sick to my stomach. It was worse than I could ever have imagined.

> It was called 'Bank Possible'. The aim was to challenge Britain's biggest lenders with a digital-only current account made for the smartphone generation.
>
> But the founding team of the start-up bank, created last year by a former chief operating officer of Allied Irish Banks and a financial technology entrepreneur, has broken up before it even obtained a licence . . .

I noted that Tom had 'confirmed he was no longer employed by Starling' but had said he was unable to comment under the terms of his departure. Interestingly though, Sally had managed to find two people 'close to the situation' who were able to give her a great deal of background information. One of those two people managed to deliver the most personal lines of the entire piece.

* FT.com, Bank Possible's future in question as Starling team flies apart, 18 February 2015, by Sally Davies.

It wasn't so much strategic differences of opinion. The breakdown came down to tension between Anne and Tom.

The piece ended with the announcement that the 'departed Starling executives' were planning a rival service.

I read and reread the piece trying to work out what it would mean next. It wasn't good. That was obvious. But would it stymie my chances in the future? I supposed I would get answers on at least some points later in the day, since I still had the conference call with the regulator. And how would the wider world of potential investors respond?

Even though it was tough, really tough, there was little else that I could do other than to keep going and meet each challenge as it came.

I realized that I would get the opportunity to gauge some of the reaction sooner than I'd like to. Not long before, I had been speaking to financial commentator Chris Skinner, who runs the influential Finanser.com blog. In January, Chris had invited Jason Bates and me to one of the regular Financial Services Club dinners. It was being held on the evening of 25 February at the Italian restaurant L'Anima at 1 Snowden Street and I had already said I'd go. In the meantime, Chris had interviewed me for a piece for Finanser.com.

Should I still go? It would be publicly humiliating, since everyone in the fintech world would know what had happened. At the same time I had little choice. If I was going to relaunch, I had to go along with my head held high. It would be one of many tests of courage in the weeks to come. To make it just that bit more challenging, on the day of the dinner itself I noted that the 'Finanser Interview: Anne Boden, CEO of Starling Bank'*

* https://thefinanser.com/2015/02/the-finanser-interviews-anne-boden-ceo-of-starling-bank.html/ by Chris Skinner.

which had earlier been published on Chris's website, now sported the addendum: 'Since this interview took place, there have been a few changes at Starling Bank, as outlined below.'

And there, tacked onto the end of Chris's hugely positive piece about Starling was Sally Davies's *FT* article. Fantastic! I would be walking into a room filled with digital luminaries from more than a dozen organizations from Nutmeg to Lloyds Banking to Fujitsu and I had this *FT* piece following me around like a bad smell. There was nothing for it but to get dressed up, put a confident smile on my face and tell anyone who asked (and everyone did) what a great future Starling had. Looking back, I was glad I did it. Having to make such a challenging first appearance made everything else that came after it seem just that little bit easier.

Not that anything about my situation was truly 'easy'. Now I was on my own, save for Alan, I would have to fulfil many roles for the moment. One of those roles would be external relations, which was something that was more pertinent than ever in the light of the *FT* article. Previously, Jason had made a good job of keeping our Twitter account active from day to day and had secured a good few followers. They were mostly early adopters, keen to see the next iteration of disruptive technology, but these were the very people who were most likely to make up our early customer base.

Tweeting was not something that I had had much practice with. In a big bank, the PR department would tweet on behalf of the executives. Messages are all carefully crafted for the right balance. Things were different now though. There was no one else to do it. The website, Twitter, the technology: it was all down to me.

Twitter was also the medium by which I received constant reminders of my new rivals in the challenger bank world. At the end of February, Eileen Burbidge tweeted a photo of Tom,

Gary, Paul and Jason, the four ex-members of Starling, who were all at the Passion Capital office in White Bear Yard. This was no big shock: I knew they'd been working there since they'd left Starling. It was just odd to see them go public and tell the world they'd been backed by Passion.

Not long after the *FT* piece, I met with the various consultants and advisors who had been helping me over the previous year. Both KPMG and PwC said they would need to cut back their commitment to Starling, which was understandable in the circumstances. VML too pulled away after explaining that, from a practical standpoint, they could not continue to support us. We hadn't moved on far with Dell, following their offer of assistance, because Tom was never keen, but I knew this was probably not going to go any further now either. I understood everyone's positions completely. I would have probably done the same if it were the other way around. I was grateful for their help until now and, on the plus side, at least Starling's bills or outstanding debts were no longer increasing. That said, it added another bunch of to-do items to my already lengthy list. I would need a new group of partners going forward.

Overnight I became the CTO, CRO, CFO and pretty much any other role you care to name. Strangely though, I loved it. It was hard work, yes, but it also wasn't that difficult to pick up from where everyone had left off.

The important thing was to take my time and recruit judiciously. I was very careful not to jump in and take the first person I could find. I needed to select my team thoughtfully. Plus, as I constantly reminded myself, so much of the groundwork had already been done.

Then, just as I was daring to believe I was getting somewhere, the oddest thing happened. It was the afternoon of 31 March. Alan wasn't in the office that day and I had popped out for just twenty minutes to meet a potential recruit for the CRO position. I always made sure to meet interviewees outside the office, since it could be rather off-putting for a candidate, arriving at a completely empty office. Not exactly a great way to sell Starling as a thriving bank. This time, after a brief chat at Leon, the fast and apparently healthy food café, we both realized we were not a good fit so I went straight back to the office. I sensed something was wrong the moment I got back, because the door was wide open. I felt sick.

Starling had been burgled.

Except it was the strangest burglary. The only item missing was my laptop. The people who had stolen it had left two other laptops behind – even though they were clearly visible. He, she, or they had also forced open a locked filing cabinet, but, as far as I could tell, had taken nothing.

The most worrying aspect of it all was that whoever had done this had entered via the front door using a key. There were no signs of forced entry whatsoever.

I immediately called the police. They arrived remarkably quickly, but when I explained the circumstances they were as mystified as I was. The policewoman warned me it was unlikely they'd find out who was behind it. There had just been so many people coming and going at 22 Peter's Lane over the past months.

I felt utterly stumped. What was going on? One thing was for sure: I didn't feel safe staying there. I didn't want burglars feeling like they could come and go as they pleased. Someone had access to our front door key, so our tech equipment would never be safe.

I rang our landlords at WPP and they were very understanding. A promise was immediately made to help us find new accommodation in a hurry and, in the meantime, they offered to change the locks.

Great: now I had to add 'moving office' to my to-do list.

In reality, it was probably a good thing to be relocating. The top-floor office was certainly too large for our needs right then and to me it symbolized what had gone before. How better to signal that Starling was making a fresh start than to begin again in new premises?

In preparation, I penned a brief email to Tom and his team, reminding them to pop over to pick up their remaining personal possessions, since we'd shortly be moving on. Under the subject header 'Various items', I briefly went through the circumstances of the strange burglary that had taken place at 3 p.m. that afternoon, and explained that the police were investigating.

Over the past six weeks, relations had become matter of fact with the old team. Initially, my legal advice had been geared solely towards stopping them progressing with their rival bank, on the basis they'd be using much of the material and knowledge gained through Starling. It soon became clear that this would turn into a messy and protracted process. Not only would it cost a fortune (even getting this far with it had cost another £100,000) but it would be a huge distraction just at a time when I needed to be fully focussed on reviving Starling and getting it back on track. In the end, I dropped it after Tom and his team signed undertakings that they had destroyed any materials taken from Starling and would not use any confidential information from their period there.

In the joint email to Tom, Jason, Paul and Gary, I said if they let me know when they wanted to drop by, I would arrange for someone to let them in. I sent it on the evening of the burglary, but didn't hear back from anyone.

The following day, I headed to a coffee shop at 8 a.m. I pushed the odd burglary to the back of my mind and started to get on with my long list of tasks. I was a woman who wore many hats at this stage, and one of my first jobs of the day was always to check on the various emails that came into the office addressed to all and sundry. It was only a matter of weeks since everyone had left and their Starling email accounts were still open. Former members of the team were still receiving messages that were important to Starling, so I had little choice but to keep an eye on them.

I noticed straight away that Tom had received an email from Paul Rippon. That was pretty odd, since the pair were working together at the new venture based in Passion Capital's office in White Bear Yard. Why had Paul emailed Tom at his old Starling address? I clicked open the email, which had the subject header 'Re: Various items'. The message was clearly in response to my email the previous day.

I could barely believe what I was reading.

I'm at WBY and a team of police officers, one armed, has arrived seeking signed witness statements about where we all were at 3 p.m. yesterday.

I actually went out for a coffee and so they have informed me that I will be taken in for questioning. As I was unable to vouch for your whereabouts they have asked me to instruct you to go straight to Holborn police station.

When you arrive they will be taking urine and DNA samples so please don't where [sic] any heavy clothing.

I stared at the screen in front of me, my mouth completely dry with shock and surprise. Did the police really suspect foul play from my former colleagues? They'd clearly jumped to entirely the wrong conclusion and I had no idea how they'd got to that place. There was no way the burglary could have been anything to do with my old team. I was horrified by the vision of armed police raiding White Bear Yard and arresting Paul and the rest of my former colleagues.

I forwarded the email to my lawyer, asking for his view. We needed to stop this spiralling out of control and ending up in the *Sun*. How had it come to this?

I found it very difficult to work efficiently that morning. I kept going over and over the email in my head. Half of me wanted to call Tom and his team to see what was happening, but the other half thought that I might just make things worse.

Then, two and a half hours after the first email from Paul to Tom, another appeared under the same subject header. Steeling myself, I clicked to open it up, wondering if this could get any worse.

> Oh yes and of course it is critical that you attend Holborn
> police station this morning, the 1st of April :-o
>
> April fools
>
> Kind regards,
> Paul

'April fools?' Paul's original email was an April Fool's Day joke? I certainly didn't feel like laughing. I felt foolish, angry and upset, all at the same time, which was a heady mix of emotions.

This jolly jape had taken me to hell and back. After all that had happened, it was really chilling even to think there was any suspicion about my former colleagues. How could people who were once my friends think this burglary was in any way a laughing matter?

What should I do now though? What was the best way to respond? I forwarded the second email to my lawyer, since he had already seen the first, and asked what he thought I should do.

> Make sure you don't respond in any way to this, or let them
> know that you were aware of it,

he counselled.

> Wait and see whether you get a proper reply to your email.

He was right, of course. It didn't make it any easier though. It was hugely hurtful that these people thought to laugh at my expense when I had been through a difficult enough situation with the burglary.

The old team never did respond to my message about the burglary, but they did turn up to collect their belongings as they were asked. I may have been a bit paranoid, but I noticed Jonas and Tom were wearing matching black-and-white, convict-style stripy shirts. Again, if it was a joke, I didn't find it at all funny.

In the days that followed, the mystery around the burglary seemed to deepen, if anything. Alan received an email from Simon Vans-Colina, one of my former team, who had heard about the break-in. He got in touch to say he'd received a call to his mobile on the day from someone who said they'd locked their keys in 22 Peter's Lane and asking if he could let them in. Simon had told them he didn't work there any more and asked how they'd got his number, but the caller had rung off. Fortunately he'd taken a screenshot of the anonymous caller's number and I passed it on to the police. The whole story seemed to be getting stranger by the minute and we weren't any closer to solving the mystery. I called the number: the person who answered said he was based on the south coast and knew nothing about a burglary in Clerkenwell.

Once again, I just had to get my head down and get on with things. In early May, Starling moved to new premises at the corner of Clerkenwell Road and St John's Street. By now Tony Ellingham had taken over the post of CRO. Tony had been recommended to me by another senior banker. He was what the press would no doubt call an 'establishment' banker, having pursued a long career in banking and finance, most recently at Lloyds Banking Group, but in my view he had exactly the mixture of experience and gravitas that Starling needed. Tony was quite a private person and I could already see it would take a bit of time to get to know him on a personal level, but he certainly seemed to have all the qualities, and knowledge, Starling needed. As well as being very calm, solid and stable which was crucial, he was also prepared to work for no salary to begin with.

It wasn't easy to recruit a new group. I felt that I had been blighted by the fact my entire team had walked out en masse. Now it wasn't just a question of selling the brilliant idea behind Starling, I also had to persuade prospective recruits that there wasn't something odd about me. I'd have conversations with people and I could almost hear their minds working it all through: *She's a bit quirky, but I think she is OK*.

Fortunately, after Tony agreed to come aboard, it began to feel a little like we were returning to normal. While he very quickly swapped to become CFO, rather than CRO, there was a really determined and focussed atmosphere in the office now. We'd moved once more – this time to 222 Grays Inn Road, beside the ITN building – and hired a number of contractors. It was clear things were beginning to move in the right direction. Everything was geared towards re-engaging with the regulator and seeking out new investors.

One afternoon, when I returned to work after yet another meeting with a potential investor, I noticed a new face in the office. I had never seen this man before and had no idea who he was. He did seem to be gainfully employed though, staring intently into his laptop, so I assumed he was something to do with WPP, since they were our landlords. I was so busy it was a couple of days before I went over and introduced myself. I then found myself involved in the most bizarre conversation.

The man was called John Mountain and his background involved many years working for clients such as Lloyds Bank and Bank of America at IT consultancy BJSS. He explained that he'd become frustrated with the inefficiencies at trad-itional banks and had been looking around for something to challenge his skillset and excite his interest in an industry that, in his view, had grown very stale indeed.

'I spoke to a lot of people, from the banking industry and outside,' he said. 'I told them I wanted to work for a digital bank and asked them what they thought. They pointed me in the direction of Atom and Tandem. They said Starling was in the market too, but would never launch so I would be mad to try and join. So, I decided to come here. It turns out I am quite contrasuggestible.'

I had to smile. I'd been searching for the 'right' person to sort out our IT strategy and John had chosen us.

'And what do you think?' I asked. 'You've obviously had a few days to look around.'

'Well, I've looked at the code base that's been done to date and I don't like the language, the architecture, tools, well, pretty much everything actually,' he said. 'You need to start again.'

This somewhat blunt approach, as I quickly learned, summed up John's character to a T. To say that John was a man with strong views was an understatement and he was not shy about expressing them. You didn't need to spend long with him to rec-ognize he had a brilliant brain and would stubbornly search for a solution until he found one. A Cambridge maths graduate and son of a NATO executive, he just seemed to get what we were trying to do with no one really explaining it to him.

He arrived, joined the team, decided what needed to be done and just got on with it (his favourite expression turned out to be 'It is often easier to do it than talk about it'). I gave him completely free rein as he began writing code for Starling from scratch. Over the next few weeks Starling seemed to grow before our very eyes.

Once I got to know him better I used to joke that he had a half-finished boat, a half-finished house and a half-finished bank. Happily though, Starling was well on track to be the project that crossed the line first!

Then, one day I discovered yet another new face in the office. It was a not dissimilar situation to John's arrival. There was a man sitting at a desk, working away at a laptop as if he'd been there for years. I discovered that he was called Steve Newson and he was an old colleague of John's. The pair of them used to work at a firm called CHP (today renamed Alfa), which wrote leasing software for banks. Like John, Steve was a talented coder (he'd started aged eight) and they had been all over the world together coding for banks.

John explained to me that he had reached out to Steve to help with the coding.

'I told him there were nine people in a room trying to build a bank,' John said. 'I said: they've got nothing and I'm going to need a hand.'

Apparently that was enough to tempt Steve along.

With the pair of them working in tandem, the pace quickened even more. It was exciting to watch. There certainly seemed to be a buzz about the place now.

The next big hire was Julian Sawyer, who joined as Starling's chief operating officer. He had previously run his own financial services consultancy, Bluerock, which he had sold in 2012, and was looking for his next challenge. Julian, who was in his forties, tall, mature and, above all, noticeably calm about pretty much everything, seemed to provide the perfect balance to the other characters in the office. Besides, three different sets of people had told me that Julian would be an ideal COO, so I couldn't really ignore their advice.

I also had to build a new bank board. My first recruit here was Mark Winlow, whom I had known for more than twenty years. He'd been a partner at KPMG, AT Kearney and EY and managing director of Zurich Financial Services. I put head-hunters onto the task of finding a chair and they came back with a somewhat ambitious suggestion: Oliver Stocken, CBE. Oliver has more than fifty years' experience in the finance industry and corporate world, on the boards of everything from Standard Chartered Bank to GUS to Rank and chairing organizations from the Natural History Museum to Care International. It was an optimistic ask even by my standards. What followed was quite funny. The headhunter ran into Oliver outside a Tube station and took the opportunity to ask if he'd be interested in chairing a fintech start-up. Amazingly, Oliver agreed to talks and soon he was on the board. He seemed to get it right away, too. In his mind we were never just a small team of people trying to start a bank, with no money and no customers. To him, we were always going to be the next Standard Chartered, or even better. It was only a matter of time until we were the best bank in the world.

While I was fortunate that good people found me, as much as me finding them, I didn't just say yes to everyone. Every hire truly does count. I always did my due diligence thoroughly with anyone who might join the team. It may have appeared that beggars couldn't be choosers in the days following the loss of my entire team, but that doesn't mean I was ever going to just throw caution to the wind and align myself with the first person who said 'yes'. I always looked very carefully at what someone had done before and what other businesses he or she had worked with. The type of stuff people have had a hand in previously gives a valuable clue as to whether they are truly committed to your area of business, or simply here as a stopgap while they look for their next opportunity in their preferred field. It's also crucial to look closely at how their previous firms did and their true involvement in those businesses. It's not uncommon for people to talk up their role in a start-up that built fast and exited for a significant sum, but were they as influential as they claim to be? If someone lies about their past, how can you rely on them to be completely frank in the future? This type of character could easily have a tendency to cover up or try to ignore project mistakes. Honesty and openness are qualities I can't afford to overlook. If my gut feeling says I can't trust someone, I always heed it.

As I rebuilt Starling, something I was very certain about was that we'd never have an IT department. This was a practice very different from anywhere I had ever been before. To many people this may sound odd, especially since we were a digital start-up. It was a very deliberate strategy though. When I first joined the banking workplace, at the start of my career, coders sat in among the people who needed the software they created. Over the years though, I'd become very aware that these two groups had moved further and further apart, with many technical functions eventually being outsourced and offshored. Today, this has gone full circle and technology companies are, quite rightly, bringing things back together again.

I remember talking to John Mountain shortly after he joined Starling about what he liked about us.

'I joined because you'd written on the website that Starling didn't have an IT department,' he said.

If technology is in *everything* you do then you don't need to have a department for it: it is everything you do. That is the way it should be too, certainly if you want even a chance of success in your start-up.

While I was lucky in that many of my new team found me, this period was also a brilliant test of my powers of persuasion. It's a skill crucial to any entrepreneur, so it was good to get some practice. It wasn't just the vision that I needed to persuade them about either: it was me. They had to trust and believe that I was the right person to deliver that vision. They had to be convinced that I was the one who would deliver them to the end of each month and produce a pay cheque. It's a big ask of anyone to join any start-up. We all have financial commitments and it is a rare person indeed who can go for much more than two or three months without any form of income.

Fortunately, a large number of highly talented people did agree to join Starling. Very quickly, Alan, Julian, Tony, John and I formed a close-knit group, which we dubbed Team A. The moniker was a sly nod at what had gone before: those who had walked out in February were the B Team. This team now: this one was the first team. The A Team.

Incredibly, just four months later, we were ready to meet with the regulator once again. The clock had been reset to zero and this time we went without advisors in tow, but we were making progress. It was a remarkable turnaround from a time when I had gone from being on the brink of launching a brilliant new bank to nearly losing everything. It had been a dreadful experience, but we'd come back stronger than ever.

9. Go for the Big Money

Most digital start-ups begin with a financial blank sheet. It can be quite a sobering experience when you start to add up just how much you need to develop your product. I can still remember the surge of fear that arose whenever I thought through my calculations for Starling.

My goal was to set up an IT system markedly superior to those that powered mainstream banks, which had struggled for years with legacy systems. To do that, though, I would need in the region of tens of millions. Raising that much money for a product that no one had ever heard of, and would most likely struggle to understand, was a frightening prospect. And after picking myself up, dusting myself down and starting again, I was still faced with the same issue: I didn't yet have investment. This meant starting the rounds all over again, although this time I had the added hurdle that investors would inevitably want to know exactly what went wrong with Starling's first round. I would have to offer some sort of satisfactory explanation before I could properly begin any pitch.

This was not the only challenge with funding, as I knew only too well by now. Investors generally like to see evidence of a track record as an entrepreneur before they take anyone seriously. More importantly (to them) they prefer it when the entrepreneur has already won backing elsewhere. This gives VCs peace of mind, since it proves that the entrepreneur is a good bet. This is somewhat of a catch-22 for the poor entrepreneur though, if they haven't yet received any investment.

Even as we prepared to go into the fray again, I already knew the main objections that Starling would face. I had heard so many of them before. VCs prefer to invest in a tried and tested idea that ticks all the boxes but to date no one had started a mobile-only bank. We were entering uncharted territory and that made them nervous. Then there was the issue that investors generally gravitate towards people who look just like people in whom they have already invested. In the main, this means they are more receptive to teams of three thirty-something men with an idea to solve a problem they've had personal experience of.

In the UK, less than 1 per cent of venture capital funds go to start-ups run entirely by women, while all-male founder teams get the lion's share at 89 per cent.* While VCs have publicly made much of their diversity initiatives, there is still very little evidence of them taking effect. Either way, Starling, and particularly I, definitely didn't tick enough boxes. As a fifty-something woman who wanted to start the first ever app-based bank I was a somewhat unusual proposition.

Whatever your background or experience, it is always extremely difficult to get any attention from VCs. Why is it that VCs appear to be so single-minded and inflexible when it comes to making investments? It is always helpful to know just why the odds are stacked against you. It gives you a chance to push them, at least a little bit, in your favour.

So, what is it that VCs are looking for? Simply put, it is a numbers game. VCs raise money from their own group of high-net-worth individuals. Often these individuals will be ex-entrepreneurs themselves, or perhaps former investment

---

* 'Women Awarded Tiny Fraction of UK Venture Capital Funds', *Financial Times*, 4 February 2019, www.ft.com/content/330b7904-2638-11e9-8ce6-5db4543da632.

bankers. They will look to make up a certain amount in a fund, perhaps say £100 million. Each of the high-net-worth individuals will get an asset allocation according to the proportion of money they put into the fund. VCs will also charge their investment partners 2 per cent of the fund as an administration fee and have a written agreement that they'll take 20 per cent of the profits.

When it comes to making an investment, VCs count on the fact that just one, perhaps two, start-ups will ever reach any scale. Out of every 150 start-ups they see (and they pass over opportunities to see many hundreds more), they'll only consider ten as even worthy of a second glance.* If they do agree to put money into those ten, they know that three will go under, possibly fairly rapidly. A further four will most likely be sold for less than the original investment. Of the remaining three, at least two will be sold at a small profit, but no more than twice the initial stake. That leaves one, solitary investment out of the 150 they originally agreed to see, and the ten they subsequently invested in, that will pay any sort of substantial return.

The holy grail of VC investment is that a single investment will reward the fund with what is known as a 'venture rate of return', yielding a 10x return. In other words, if £50 million were invested, the VC would get back £500 million. That's what that one remaining winning investment has to achieve in order to prop up an awful lot of failed investments and time expended. And this is why VCs tend to be so choosy.

In a sense, it is all a bit of a lottery. If VCs knew the magic sauce that would pick a winner every time, they'd only ever invest in winners. But they don't, so all anyone who is seeking funding can do is enter the lottery and do as many things

* https://medium.com/datadriveninvestor/understanding-startup-valu ation-a393f6fadc6f.

as they can to reduce the odds in their favour. That is exactly what I did.

By June 2015, the pressure to find backers was mounting from all sides. The regulator made it clear that our application was not deemed fully complete until we could name Starling's investors, since they were integral to the application assessment process. So I not only urgently needed investment to seal the revival of Starling under the new team, I also needed to stay one step ahead of my rivals. As Eric Ries, entrepreneur and author of *The Lean Startup*, once said: 'The only way to win is to learn faster than everyone else.'

Starling was not the only business in the running to launch a mobile bank and my competitors were moving forward at pace. There were at least half a dozen players who were well on the way. Atom had been granted a banking licence in June 2015 and was talking about launching in November with a full range of products, including current accounts and mortgages for retail and business customers.

While Ricky Knox's Tandem had yet to secure a licence, it did have the security of Route 66's investment and was beginning to build up a waiting list of potential customers. It was also promising a full-service retail bank with additional built-in budgeting features such as bill alerts and advice on switching to the best utility suppliers. And then there was Mondo: Tom's start-up.

It was hard to avoid the progress reports on Mondo. Pretty much every media report on the new bank was accompanied by a reference to the team's former position at Starling. Both parties had remained stubbornly silent in public about what had happened but this didn't stop the media constantly digging around. Steve O'Hear, a technology journalist at TechCrunch, was all over it and, naturally, keen to explore any potential rivalry between Tom and me. He messaged me to say he was 'digging into Tom Blomfield's new thing' and wanted to reference Starling in his piece. He was quick to reassure me that while he'd 'love to know what actually went on' he didn't plan on dwelling on it. He was merely curious about what I was up to now. Steve included a list of questions about Starling and why we thought we'd be better than existing banks and banking apps. Oh, and while I was about it, who were Starling's investors? Good question.

I answered as expansively as possible, explaining that Starling was going to be a full-stack bank, not an app bolted onto some other institution's banking licence. We intended to offer a single bank account that people could easily manage on the go.

> It is a disruptive enterprise in that it simplifies the
> banking process that is defined by transparency and ease
> of use,

I wrote to Steve.

> We set ourselves out to produce the best product there is
> for today's smartphone users and are focussed on doing one
> single thing really well. I strongly believe our focus on ease of
> use and our free account offering of a mobile on the go for
> twenty-first-century banking will be compelling.

As for investment, I explained:

> We've been backed by private investors and large supplier
> firms that have been involved in the process from an early
> stage and believe and support the innovative idea behind the
> disruptive proposition that is Starling.
> More than £4m has been invested in the business to date
> by these partners and we are now raising the £12m necessary
> for the banking licence.

Seeing it in black and white like that, it all looked so easy. The reality was, it was a hard slog. We were working with KBW, some investment bankers who were going to try to raise £15 million for us in the City, but we were a long way from signing anything.

At least I was now juggling multiple leads too, some of which seemed quite promising. This may have been why I initially ignored a message that came through from someone called Michael Boocher, who seemed overly keen to speak with me. I'd never communicated with him before and didn't know anything about him. When we finally spoke I learned that Michael was the son of Jim Boocher, the president of Kerzner International, the company behind such exclusive developments as The Palm in Dubai and the Royal Towers at Atlantis, Paradise Island in the Bahamas. Jim Boocher had died at just fifty-two, shortly after Michael had moved to Dubai to get to know him. Since then he had built up a string of restaurants in Dubai. Michael, it transpired, was an extremely bright and gifted mathematician. Which brings me to the most interesting part of his story. He was also a technology and venture capital advisor to the highly successful Bahamas-based investor Harald McPike.

Harald, or Harry as he is more commonly known, is invariably called 'a secretive billionaire' in the media, because he does not court publicity and has managed to keep a remarkably low profile. He is the founder of a private investment outfit called QuantRes and is always keeping a keen eye out for the next big thing. Quant traders, or quants, use trading strategies based on quantitative analyses, which themselves rely on mathematical computations and analytics to identify trading opportunities. McPike had been hugely successful at this, which is why Michael was getting in touch now. After reading an article in *Bloomberg* magazine about Tom's start-up, which was now our rival, Harry had become interested in the challenger banking market. He'd got his team to do some research and Starling had been pinpointed as the most interesting opportunity. (I later learned that one of Harry's colleagues had spoken to Tom over the phone. It was a brief call, the pair hadn't got along, and that was that. Mondo's loss was my gain.)

Interestingly, very few people knew much about Harald McPike. When I googled him (which I did straight away), I found almost no coverage of his trading activities whatsoever. I later discovered that McPike, who is Austrian, started trading independently in 1990 after attending the University of Vienna and seemed to have quite a talent for it, to say the least. He was now based in the Bahamas, trading more than $1 billion of his own money. Along the way he'd diversified into property, had homes in eight countries, including a 'modest' £4 million flat in London, and was known to be a substantial customer of Swiss investment bank UBS. Despite his success and immense wealth, he continued to take an active interest in investments and had an office in London's Gherkin.

I decided we'd lose nothing by meeting Michael and his colleagues and we set up a date. Michael said that at this stage Harald didn't want anyone hearing of his potential involvement and I suggested using the code name Salisbury. Salisbury was the luxury apartment block I'd lived in while in Ireland, and had been built during the banking boom. Henceforth, any oral or written correspondence was to give McPike the code name Harry Salisbury.

A few days later, Tony, Julian and I met Michael and his colleagues Craig Mawdsley and Marcus Traill. Craig and Marcus were both directors at QuantRes Asset Management, which was Harald's private investment vehicle. They'd been pals in New Zealand, before one answered an ad to go and work for Harald in the Bahamas as a trader and then the other followed shortly thereafter. It was a good move because both had done very well out of the association.

It was obvious from the start of our meeting that Michael, Marcus and Craig had done their research and they were very well briefed. They seemed keen to know about our progress with the regulator and where we were to date with our investment round. Before they'd arrived, I'd warned my team to be very careful to not say anything confidential. We'd only give them the basics for now, I said, until we knew they were all above board. Strangely, though, as the meeting progressed, I started to trust them. As a result, I found myself being much more open about the business than I'd intended to be. Not surprisingly, I quickly found the other members of the team glaring across the table at me, since I had contravened the very instruction I had pressed upon them!

For good measure, I also mentioned that I did not play golf. Ahead of the meeting, some people on my team had become convinced (erroneously as it turned out) that Harald might want to play golf while discussing anything further. This for me was a problem, since I don't play the game. I thought it best to clarify this up front.

Lack of golf skills notwithstanding, our presentation must have passed muster because, less than twenty-four hours later, an invitation arrived for me to visit the Bahamas and meet Harald.

My interest was sufficiently piqued by my conversations with Michael to get on a plane and fly to the Bahamas to make the pitch. It was all a bit surreal, arriving on the island and heading towards my accommodation at Sunrise Beach Villas. I discovered on arrival that my quarters were not one of the poolside, luxury villa variety. Let's just say they were reflective of our, as yet, unfunded start-up status. While the rooms were indeed villas, in that there was a kitchen diner downstairs and there was a little picket-fenced garden out back, each 'villa' was part of a terrace that faced the back of another building just off Casino Drive, rather than a sun-kissed beach. I wasn't particularly bothered. After all, I was not there for a holiday and frankly, after the flight I would probably have been able to sleep on a park bench.

Checking in was quite amusing, since I had a large amount of luggage. I hadn't been able to make up my mind what to wear during the trip (my thought process was: it was hot, but it was a business setting and I might have to go aboard Harald's yacht), so I'd taken everything. Well, pretty much everything. I had gone to Fluidity, my favourite clothes shop in Henley, and bought an entirely new wardrobe of 'cruise wear' with just about every combination possible. Most particularly, I'd also taken a large number of shoes, which, like handbags, are a passion of mine. There had been a running joke in the office for days about the fact I wouldn't be able to wear my usual high heels if I got aboard Harald's yacht, so I had reluctantly taken an assortment of flats, while also taking the precaution of having an immaculate pedicure.

I was hopeful. Certainly, hopeful enough to take time out of the office at a crucial moment when we were close to achieving our coveted banking licence. However, I was only expecting to raise £3 million at most. What I didn't have was the remotest inkling of the extraordinary events that were to follow.

Initially, I met Harald at his office, a chic, highly polished, luxurious block that looked quite European. I was told that the block next door housed the high-end apartments for all of his team. Michael Boocher and Marcus Traill, were already there and took me in to introduce me to Harald. I wasn't sure what I was expecting, but Harald didn't look anything like I'd anticipated. He was medium height, slim, with a neatly trimmed beard. If anything, he looked more like a smartly dressed explorer than a billionaire City trader, with his immaculately pressed Bermuda shorts and Oxford shirt. Even as we shook hands, though, I already knew he was not someone to be taken lightly. He had an intense presence about him that was hard to ignore. 'So, tell me about Starling,' he said, as we settled into our seats.

Harald was quietly spoken, with an Austrian accent, and utterly focussed on the matter in hand. He listened intently as I went through the deck, his face giving away nothing of what he was thinking. Michael and Marcus were also silent, deferring to Harald and waiting to see what he had to say.

When I finished, Harald nodded and thanked me. 'I just have a few questions, if that is all right?' he began. I nodded to indicate that I was very happy to answer anything he wanted to ask. What followed was one of the most intense few hours of my life. Harald, who in between all this had said I must call him Harry, asked the most intelligent questions I had ever been asked about Starling. I'd spoken to banking regulators, prominent investors and colleagues from the world's leading banks and yet not one person had ever homed in on the detail Harry tackled in that first meeting.

I answered each one as fully as I could. I'd been immersed in Starling so long, it was all in my brain. I just needed to pull the facts out and articulate them in the best way possible. But they kept coming. One after the other, like a barrage of machine-gun fire. The conversation was wide-ranging too, spanning everything from liquidity to yields, to risk modelling and Basel III.*

Harry was quite reserved when we first began to speak, even a little cold towards me, but as things went on he gradually lightened up. He genuinely seemed to like what Starling

---

* An international regulatory framework introduced in response to the 2008 financial crisis.

was about. Eventually, I appeared to have satisfied him. At least enough to get through to the next round. 'I think we should continue this on my boat,' Harry announced.

I spent most of the next three days in Harald's office and each evening aboard Harald's 92ft motor yacht, *New Life*, doing my best to answer the relentless barrage of questions. While aboard *New Life*, I had to pretend not to be distracted by all the enormous yachts that were moored around us, gleaming white against the magnificent and dramatic sunsets. It was like being in a scene from a James Bond movie. Mind you, it was not easy to be distracted for very long. I needed to be at the top of my game every second.

On day three, we headed towards the yacht's stern, which featured a large seating area. A member of staff in smart yet casual white uniform set about organizing drinks and, out of nowhere, carefully arranged seafood snacks appeared. By this stage I was feeling quite warm in the 40-degree heat. Despite having allowed for almost every eventuality in my wardrobe, it seemed I had somewhat misjudged it.

'Are you too hot?' Harry said, studying me. 'A little,' I said, doing my best to sound as natural and as at home as possible. 'Let's go inside for a moment then,' he said. 'There's aircon there.' He pulled open some large doors and the pair of us walked into a cool, large, luxuriously furnished saloon. 'So, tell me about Tom Blomfield,' Harry said, settling into a stylish pale tan leather sofa. It appeared that we'd reached the 'personal' stage in the discussion.

New Life's crew set about untying the yacht and readying the engines, as I explained the story of what had happened with Tom and the team. I left nothing out, outlining the disagreement I'd had with Tom, how he'd wanted me to leave, the sacking of the team and then how I'd come back into the fray to stake my claim, only to lose virtually everyone.

'Obviously, as you can see, I've rebuilt Starling and I now firmly believe that we are a stronger proposition than ever. We've got a brilliant team and are well on the way.'

Harry asked a few more questions about the period around Tom's departure and then seemed satisfied. In return, I asked Harry a lot more about his business, life, friends and ambitions, and he answered each question very openly.

He then seemed momentarily lost in thought. By now we were well out to sea and the sun was just starting to dip over a group of islands to the west of us. 'I don't want to invest £3 million,' Harry began. I tore my gaze away from the setting sun and looked at Harry questioningly. My instincts told me this was not his last word, but I wasn't at all sure what he might say next. 'I want to put in £48 million,' he went on. 'In three tranches. The first would be the £3 million, then £15 million and finally £30 million. This would be for two-thirds of the company.' I stared at him, not quite sure what to say. I'd known it had gone well, but had never anticipated this outcome. (I later learned that there had been much behind-the-scenes discussion to arrive at this exact figure.)

As we concluded our conversation, Harry smiled and walked over to an ice bucket containing a bottle of champagne. He poured two glasses and handed one to me. I realized then that this was probably the first time I had seen Harry smile. It was also the first time I'd seen him look relaxed. He'd obviously come to a decision and was pleased with his conclusion.

He leaned forward and clinked his champagne glass against mine. 'I know there will be part of you that will be thinking that what we have agreed here will close the door on so many other deals,' he said knowingly. This was true too. In all the jumble of thoughts that were crashing through my head right then, that one was right up there. 'Forget about that,' Harry went on. 'This deal is going to be the one.' We sailed around a bit more, while Harry moved on to discussing whether or not he should replace his boat with a better one, and then we returned to port. We arranged to meet at Harry's office the following day at midday and I returned to Sunrise Beach Villas feeling ever so slightly dazed. Had that all really just happened?

Harry had a highly unusual and unconventional way of doing business, but it worked. He was certainly very different from all the VCs I had previously seen, who never quite got either me or the business. He was an entrepreneur himself and understood and respected what I was trying to do.

We had supper together on my last evening in the Bahamas, as Harry's team scrambled to complete the term sheet, outlining our deal. I couldn't help noticing that the more Harry bought into the idea, the bigger his ideas became. As we sped over to the supper venue in his four-wheel-drive jeep, he floated the notion that we'd do a deal with a football club. Anyone who downloaded the app during a match would be rewarded with a £20 joining bonus. 'You could flash up how many people have done it on the scoreboard,' he said. 'When it reaches a magic number of X new customers, I'll donate a million pounds to charity.' I loved it. It was great to see someone as excited and enthusiastic about Starling as me and the rest of the team.

He was inspired by Starling because it had the potential to be something really big. A lot of the ideas that crossed his desk were small, or, to put it more accurately, didn't have the same capacity to grow as much as this proposition. For us though, the sky really was the limit. Not only could we increase our geographical reach as Starling became established, we'd also be able to add on facilities such as business banking and multi-currency. If Starling had the capital and could manage the risk, there was nothing at all to prevent us from becoming a very serious player in the banking market. Which was, of course, exactly what I was trying to do.

The other side to this was that Harry would inevitably be a dominant force in Starling. He'd want the biggest share possible because he simply wouldn't be able to see things any other way. This was something I needed to be aware of and prepared for.

The signed term sheet was in my hands one hour before I flew out of the Bahamas, feeling a little dazed after the whirl-wind of the previous few days. Even though I was utterly drained, I was consumed by an overwhelming sense of relief. All being well with the due diligence, we'd have funding in place by December.

When I finally arrived back at the office in London and tried to explain what had just happened, everyone was completely baffled. It didn't seem real. I had to admit, they did have a point. For a while I even started to wonder if it was all true, but it was and due diligence began straight away.

One week after my return to London it was announced that Atom had secured a £45 million investment from Spanish Bank BBVA. BBVA's 30 per cent stake in Anthony Thomson's bank, which valued our rival at £150 million, bought it two of the ten board seats at the online start-up. The deal was an interesting development. Despite receiving its licence in June, Atom had yet to take on any customers. This cash injection would surely see them accelerating towards their launch.

We eventually signed the deal with Harry on 22 December 2015, a little later than previously mooted, but impressively soon nonetheless. While I waited for the call I had been wandering around Fortnum and Mason, which was opposite our offices in Duke Street. When the call from Marcus came through, I was in the stationery department and sat down at one of the large desks there to take it. Afterwards I had to fend off questions from customers who seemed convinced I worked there! The £48 million investment, in three tranches, for two-thirds of the company represented the biggest ever seed round in London.

It was agreed the day before Starling submitted its application for a banking licence. As everyone headed off to spend time with their families over the festive break, I couldn't help musing on what a difference a year makes. Just twelve months earlier I had been on the Route 66 journey, heading for imminent disaster.

10. *Ship Your Product*

I glanced at my watch for what must have been the tenth time in as many minutes. The London traffic seemed worse than ever. It was at a complete standstill. The black-cab driver certainly didn't seem to think we were going anywhere and was delivering a monologue on who would pick his daughter up from school.

Maybe this wasn't such a good idea, I thought. On the spur of the moment, I had booked a dental check-up. It was the morning of Tuesday 12 July 2016. When I told people in the office where I was going, they all looked a little confused.

'You're going to the dentist? Today? Really?'

'Don't you think it is quite important that you are here? Today, of all days?' I understood their surprise. Today was a significant day in Starling's brief but intense history. It may even have been the most significant day so far. While getting the funding from Harald McPike had ensured our survival and future growth, this was the day that would decide whether we'd be able to trade at all. It was the day the regulator was due to make a decision.

I checked the time again and glanced at the traffic ahead. It was moving now, but only very slowly. I could have shouted with frustration. This visit to the dentist was supposed to be a brief distraction, to calm my nerves as we all waited. It was turning into a more stressful exercise than sitting at my desk checking and rechecking my emails in case something popped up from the PRA. To pass the time, I thought back to the events of the past few weeks. Activity around our licence application, which was already pretty all-consuming, had moved up another notch. There were now frequent communications asking for further details and emails confirming we'd passed through the various elements of the overall assessment of our application. On Friday 17 June, Starling went through the 'capital and liquidity' assessment, which we all knew was one of the final hurdles. Further requests were then made for an auditor's confirmation that capital was in place and available, as well as copies of bank statements showing our capital injection landing, minutes of board meetings and Companies House forms. There were now definite indications that an end was in sight. In fact, the letter re capital and liquidity signed off with the words:

> *Once we have received confirmation that a firm's capital is in place*
> *we will be in a position to fully authorize the firm.*

We were close to getting approval. Really close. The PRA's request gave Starling a deadline of 15 July for these last pieces of information.

'We're not running up to that deadline,' I'd said to the team. 'Let's get this across now.'

In the grand scheme of things, these last items were easy to organize for the authorities. Tony Ellingham and I pulled the documents together and sent them over to the PRA. 'And now we wait,' I said to Tony, knowing that saying it and managing to achieve this without disappearing under a mountain of nerves were worlds apart.

By then we were pretty certain that we'd be awarded the licence, but I had been around long enough never to take anything for granted. As I knew only too well, there can be last-minute surprises, just when you think you are finally getting somewhere. Even though we'd completely recovered from the Route 66 and Tom Blomfield debacles – indeed, had gone on to do far better things – they were still in my mind.

On 6 July I had received a rather welcome communication from HM Treasury:

I hope you don't mind me reaching out to you out of the blue, but the PRA mentioned that Starling is on the cusp of securing its authorization with restrictions. Congratulations, that's very good news!

I took a deep breath as I read these opening lines. I'd known we were close, but reading a note from the government official confirming it made it feel very real. I read on and discovered, to my surprise, that the government was making a request to be part of our licence announcement:

In the past ministers have sought to welcome instances when new banks have secured a licence by issuing a quote or tweet to coincide with the banks' announcements, so if they asked to do so again here I could suggest some lines they could take if that sounds reasonable?

I immediately replied, saying that Starling would welcome such a development and were very keen to coordinate any publicity. A comment from the British government would give Starling some real authority.

By now we were in almost constant touch with the PRA. We needed to know when they might be making their final decision. At last word came through that it would most likely be announced the following Tuesday, 12 July.

For the rest of the week we focussed on PR and marketing teams. In house, this was led by Terry McParlane, our enormously capable head of marketing, who could turn her hand to almost anything. Terry is from Australia and had previously

worked on the TSB spin-off from Lloyds. She was coordinating with our external PR consultants, Pagefield. To kick things
off, we met at our offices to plan our strategy for the announcement and beyond.

The challenge we faced was working out how best to
announce the news to the world and make the most possible
capital out of the story. It was an ideal opportunity to create a
great deal of noise about Starling and establish our place in the
market. Most important of all, we had to capture the imagina-
tions of our target customer group.

Through our earlier research we had already established that,
to begin with, our customers would be drawn predominantly
from the eighteen-to-thirty demographic. They'd be tech savvy,
aspirational and motivated and, of course, firmly attached to
their mobile phones. This was the generation that lived life
on their gadgets and knew nothing different. They weren't afraid
to try new things and downloading apps was second nature.

Our earlier research had also indicated that we needed
to take a positive approach with this audience. Any sort of
negativity about the competition grates with millennials.
They gravitate towards positive language, focussing on the
good things that are happening within the industry.

'So, we need to focus on engaging and exciting this audience by showing how Starling would deliver a positive vision
for the future,' Terry said, kicking off the brainstorming session. 'This means bright, positive language. The words we
need to emphasize are: simple, easy, digital, insightful, helpful
and intuitive design.'

'News-cycle wise, it is not a brilliant time,' Louise Fernley,
the consultant from Pagefield, pointed out. 'We need to take
that into account in our strategy too.'

She was right. It was just weeks after the 23 June Brexit refer-
endum result had determined we were leaving the EU. Banks

listed on the London Stock Exchange had been among the hardest hit in the aftermath, and the smaller challenger banks among them, such as Metro, Aldermore and Shawbrook, had taken the biggest blows. Investors panicking about 'what next' had wiped an average of 30 per cent off shares in new banks. The thinking went that they would be most exposed should the economy collapse.

On the plus side, PwC had come out with a report that seemed pretty optimistic for businesses like ours. In a statement it expressed the view that 'the UK is a market which embraces innovation [and] that has a progressive regulatory regime, a well-established and sophisticated financial system allied to a highly skilled and experienced workforce'. Or, as one journalist put it, 'Basically, despite Brexit, Britain is still the best country in the world to build a new bank.'*

'There is still a lot of unease in the markets and of course everyone is looking at the Tory leadership battle too,' Louise went on. 'We need to be mindful of this and cautious when we are pitching stories.'

'Agreed,' I said. 'I also think we need to set clear objectives around the announcement. What do we want to achieve?'

'Well, the first and most obvious is to introduce Starling to the market,' said Terry, counting off the points on her fingers as she went along. 'We want to attract customers to sign up for the testing phase thanks to the positive media coverage.'

The launch of Starling was going to be phased, as is usual in many technology applications. The plan was first to rope in friends, family and product testers and then roll it out with a so-called beta launch, which would expand it to a wider audience. Selected customers would be given the mobile app in

* Oliver Smith, 'Brexit: A Dead End for Britain's Digital Banks?', *The Memo*, 6 July 2016.

advance of the public launch in return for feedback. This was a great way to test the core functions so our team could continue to improve and develop the app once it was being used in a live environment.

'We also need to address scepticism about challenger banks,' Louise broke in. 'We can't forget, we're going to be one of the first to launch. We've already talked a lot about how reluctant consumers are to change banks and here we are talking about something completely new and untried. One of the objectives needs to be to explain what is different about Starling. We need to get across the advantage of switching to digital-only options. We need to emphasize that customer money will be protected by the Financial Services Compensation Scheme (FSCS). Funds up to £75,000 will be guaranteed by the British government.'*

'Plus there is the question of the name change,' I added. 'Let's not forget that on the day we finally receive this licence, Starling will no longer be simply Starling. We'll be Starling Bank.'

Everyone at the table smiled. The new name did sound good. We'd prepared for this and already had the new logo ready, as well as the website. All we needed to do was push the 'go' button once we'd got approval. 'That's quite a lot to get across,' Terry said, looking at her list.

'And let's not forget Faster Payments too,' I added.

Joining the Faster Payments Scheme had been one of my priorities when I had started again after Tom and the rest of the team had left. Tom had been dead against it, back in the Bank Possible days, preferring to piggyback on a bigger bank. I'd disagreed, but let it drop at the time. Now, thanks to the dogged persistence of our COO, Julian Sawyer, we'd been

---

* The figure has since been increased to £85,000.

named as the fourteenth participant in the 24/7 real-time payment service and were the only next-generation bank in that list. I knew this was the right thing to do: even though it had added another layer to the challenge of negotiating it, it would undoubtedly guarantee the best possible payment experience for our customers.

'OK, we'll add that to our list of primary messages,' Louise said, noting it down. 'We need to work on some secondary messages too. Some facts and figures you can give during media interviews to back up your arguments.'

Louise began to reel off a list of statistics, which all sounded pretty positive. 'The number of UK mobile banking users will double by 2020, from 17.8 million to 32.6 million. That's fifteen million more mobile banking users over the next five years.'

'Which means the opportunity is significant if we get the customer experience right,' Terry nodded.

Louise continued down her list.

'Today, a third of adults bank on their mobile. Our research has told us that more than half of customers will switch if the customer experience is good enough.'

As Louise carried on with her statistics, I considered the media interviews she'd mentioned. I'd done a few now, especially over the past few months, but the announcement of our licence would inevitably move things on for us. We'd be the second of the challenger banks behind Atom to be granted a licence and (satisfyingly) we were almost certain to get ours before Mondo. It was great to pip them to the post. Even though relations were now vastly improved with Tom and his team, there was still a great deal of friendly rivalry between our businesses.

We discussed some of the questions I was likely to be asked during interviews and Louise agreed to compile a list for me to go over ahead of the launch. She also said she'd send the first draft of the press release later that day.

The clock's really ticking now, I thought as the meeting came to an end. I headed off to speak with John and his team. I had to be sure that everything was ready on the technology side.

The first draft of the press release landed later that day, as promised. I opened up the email attachment and read:

STARLING BANK RECEIVES BANKING LICENCE AND ANNOUNCES FASTER PAYMENTS. LONDON – [DATELINE], 2016

- Starling Bank receives banking licence from the regulator.
- Confirms plan to become direct participant of 24/7, real-time Faster Payments Scheme through New Access Model.
- Unveils new brand identity.

Starling Bank today received its UK banking licence, with restrictions, from the Prudential Regulatory Authority (PRA) and the Financial Conduct Authority (FCA).

'We are delighted to have the confidence and support of the regulator, to move forward and introduce a new style of banking,' said Anne Boden, CEO, Starling Bank.

'Traditionally, customers have spread their finances over various accounts, loans and cards. Starling Bank will deliver a new level of control over spending and saving, using data and insights to deliver an unrivalled banking experience with the convenience of doing everything from one account.

'For the past year, our team has been focussed on building our product and technology from the ground up. Our absolute aim is to empower people to better manage their finances with an incredible app, purpose-built for those who happily manage their lives on their phone.

'Also today, Starling Bank unveiled its new brand identity and launched its new website, and announced it will join Faster Payments, the UK's 24/7 real-time payment service, later in the year . . .'

The two-page release covered all the points we discussed. I made a few changes and passed it around the senior team for their comments. After further discussion, we agreed we would tell the media we intended to launch in January 2017 following the next round of consumer testing. I then checked on all the other elements of the launch for the twentieth time, much to the chagrin of the rest of the team, and returned to my desk.

The waiting was unbearable. I wasn't at all sure how I was going to get through the weekend and then the following Monday. I did it as I always did, by immersing myself in work, even though I was a little distracted. I continually revised the press material, which must have driven Pagefield mad, but I just wanted to get everything 100 per cent correct.

By Monday, even the usual distractions were no longer working. I went through the motions, but was finding it more and more difficult to concentrate. Meanwhile, a steady stream of material was crossing my desk in preparation for the big announcement.

By Tuesday morning I could stand it no longer. This is why I decided to phone my dentist in Marylebone for an appointment. Fortunately, they had a cancellation for that morning, so I quickly hailed a cab and sped across town. At least, that was the plan. In reality, I was still only a few miles from my office and firmly stuck in traffic.

I checked my email. Again. There was nothing. Well, nothing from the PRA or FCA. By now my tension and stress were morphing into supreme boredom. Nothing was happening.

Anywhere. Out of curiosity, I fired up my browser and went to the FCA website. I wanted to know how they'd flag the licence when it came, so decided to check out the one that heralded the granting of Atom's licence. Would it be all bells and whistles, breathlessly announcing the official arrival of the latest challenger bank? Or, would it be mundane: 'The FCA and PRA confirm the granting of an AWR to Starling'?* I suspected the latter.

It took me a few moments to find the Financial Services Register. I typed in 'Atom Bank' and up came Atom's details with the words Status: Authorized, in bold type at the top of the page, along with a reference number. 'This is a firm that is given permission to provide regulated products and services,' it read, followed by a list of contact details and information about various parts of the operation.

After glancing up at the traffic ahead, which seemed to be moving more freely now, I idly typed 'Starling' into the search box. To my surprise, a list immediately popped up with my business's name at the top. Holding my breath, I clicked on the link and watched as the page opened up.

'Starling Bank Limited Status: Authorized.'

We were a bank.

'Turn around!' I shrieked at the startled driver. 'I need to get back to the office right now. St James's Square. It is an emergency.'

As the cab executed a rapid U-turn, much to the annoyance of the traffic around us and eliciting a cacophony of hoots and rude gestures, I began to type a hurried email to the team.

---

* An AWR is an Authorization with Restriction, which means it is an authorized firm, but there will be a requirement restricting the amount of business that can be done until the bank is fully operational.

I was about to click Send, when I reconsidered. No, I wanted the pleasure of giving them the news myself.

Fortunately, the traffic in this direction was not so bad and we reached the office in a matter of minutes. I leapt out of the taxi and positively sprinted into the office, which is not an easy thing to do in high heels. As one, the staff looked up in alarm, wondering what on earth could have happened to get me so excited.

'We've got it!' I said loudly, panting slightly from my sprint. 'The licence. It's on the website.'

There was a silence for a few moments as they took it in. Then there was a huge cheer. It had happened. It had finally happened.

I grinned. 'Champagne! We need champagne. And lots of it.'

As a couple of people were dispatched to procure as much chilled champagne as they could lay their hands on, other members of the team began to inundate me with questions. Where, when, how? Why hadn't they sent us an email? Did that mean we could go live?

'I don't know,' I replied again and again.

I really had no idea.

'I found it on the FCA website by accident,' I said, holding out my mobile, which was still open on the triumphal page. 'I've got nothing through directly yet.'

The official email notification didn't land until 3.48 that afternoon, by which time the celebrations were well in swing. It was from Michael Griffin, an associate at the PRA, who began:

Dear Anne,

I am pleased to inform you that we have approved Starling FS Ltd's banking application as of today, Tuesday 12 July 2016 . . .

Michael explained in the email that the authorization would go live as of the following day. I forwarded the authorization to the rest of the Starling board, with the note:

It is with great pleasure that I inform you that we are a bank!

Much of the rest of the day was given over to celebration, which everyone on the team deserved. We'd come so far in such a short space of time. In just over a year we'd managed to get Starling back on its feet, fully funded and now licensed. That was worth marking with a glass of fizz or two. We were also all very aware that this was only the beginning of yet more hard work. Tomorrow we would finalize the finer details of the big media announcement, which we agreed would be made on Thursday. Then, of course, we needed to work towards Starling going fully live.

The following day the office was a little more subdued than usual as many on the team no doubt nursed sore heads. Even so, everyone was very aware the show must go on and, amazingly, our tech guys were up at the crack of dawn to get our new website live. By the time the office rumbled into life early on the Wednesday, everyone was present and correct and the site was live. I sent a message out to all at Starling, urging them to go through the new site, page by page, checking for any errors, typos, or anything that didn't look right. Meanwhile, we went through the draft press announcement again and began to prepare an engagement email to send to anyone who had previously registered an interest in Starling. As well as the most recent developments at Starling Bank, the emails highlighted the fact we were now in proud possession of a licence and heading towards launch.

Everyone on the team was reminded that, while the announcement was live on the PRA website, it was not live as far as our own announcement was concerned. That would be happening the following day, when we would give the news maximum momentum. We told everyone to refer to me or Terry any media calls mentioning the news, but hoped the story would hold until the following day.

Louise Fernley got going on contacting the media, giving them the announcement under embargo and setting up interview slots for the following day. She came back to me quickly with the good news that BBC Radio 5 Live were keen to interview me for a slot on their morning show *Wake Up to Money*. The bad news? I'd need to be in the studio at 5 a.m. the following morning.

'I'll do it,' I said straight away.

After that, the confirmations for interviews came in quick succession. More than a dozen news outlets said they'd be keen to speak with me, including the *FT*, Bloomberg and Reuters.

'Any idea on the angle they are going to take?' I quizzed Louise. I really didn't want this to be a day when the media focussed on old ground. This needed to be a positive, upbeat news story that paved the way for what would come next.

'Well, it's impossible to say for certain, because you know as well as I do that journalists always like to lob one in from left field,' she answered. 'The impression I get, though, is they are going for the "challenger bank shakes up financial services" angle. The appetite seems to be for stories about breaking the dominance of major players.'

That figured. Until recently the four biggest high-street banks had taken 80 per cent of the market. Anything that offered consumers more choice could only be viewed as a step in the right direction.

By close of play on Wednesday we were fairly certain everything was in place. Starling Bank had reined in its social media and gone dark in preparation for the big announcement. We'd done all the background work we could possibly do to get us into a good position and the outcome was now in the hands of the news organizations. I was hopeful that they'd see the positive side to the story, but not entirely confident. Even without the hiccups Starling had faced on the road to where we were today, there was a relentlessly gloomy news cycle thanks to all things Brexit. There was little else I could do now, however, other than hope everyone saw the story in the same positive light that we did.

On Thursday morning I awoke in my St John's Wood flat before dawn. All trace of nervous anticipation had now evaporated. I just wanted to get out there and tell Starling Bank's story. I put on my favourite suit and scarf and headed out into the still-dark street to my waiting taxi.

As we drove through the relatively light traffic I checked our Twitter feed. I nodded with an approving smile: Malka Finkelstein, our creative and content manager, was already tweeting like a demon. Any tech-loving insomniacs looking to switch to a better bank would be in for a good day. I checked our website and noted it was working well too. Perfect.

If anything, that was the only 'relaxing' part of the day. The rest of it certainly passed in a whirl. First up was BBC Radio 5 Live, where I was interviewed alongside Danny Blanchflower, a former member of the Bank of England's Monetary Policy Committee. I'd already had a 'pre-interview' with the team the night before, so knew the discussion would centre around interest rates, how they would affect consumers and the banking industry. Most importantly, the direction of the conversation allowed me to talk about how Starling Bank was well placed to operate in this new environment and offer consumers much-needed simplicity to help them understand their whole financial situation. After my appointment with the BBC in Regent Street, I headed over to the office. The press release was sent out to the newswires at 7 a.m., whereupon I took a number of telephone interviews. I was then back out in the London traffic heading to a TV interview. This was followed in rapid succession by interviews with the *Daily Telegraph*, *The Times* and the *FT*. As a bonus, the *FT* was planning on doing two pieces, one for that day's online edition and another that would come out in the personal finance section of the (very widely read) *Weekend FT*. As I went from one to another, I was constantly receiving messages from Louise, who was squeezing in new interview slots wherever she could find a spare moment.

Whenever I had a gap, I checked in with the team to see how things were going elsewhere.

'Visitors to the website are already up,' confirmed Terry. 'Our average before today was somewhere between 250 and 500 and we're now off the chart according to Google Analytics. More than 300 have already registered.'

This sounded pretty good. Last year, over the whole year, we'd had 800 people registering, many of whom were probably tech journalists and freelancers. This was a definite sign we were being noticed.

Things looked good on the Twitter side of things too. By late afternoon we'd notched up 1.3 million impressions and 362 mentions, with a noticeable upswing as the working day drew to a close. Meanwhile, the email that had been sent to people who had already registered was also getting a better-than-expected response. Just over 40 per cent of the emails had been opened and read, while nearly 14 per cent had resulted in potential customers clicking through to the Starling Bank website. This was over double the industry-average figures for an exercise like this.

While all this was going on we couldn't forget to update our name at Companies House and change our email footer to reflect our new status as a bank. Our sign-off now needed to show that we were authorized by the Prudential Regulation Authority and regulated by them and the Financial Conduct Authority, with our registration number 730166. This was all crucial stuff, which we needed to relay to the entire team and make sure they switched over to the new footer immediately. Everyone was instructed to look out for rogue versions of our old logo popping up anywhere, so they could be changed to the new one. I couldn't have asked for a better day. It went exactly as we hoped and we secured a huge amount of coverage, with more features and stories planned for and expected in the coming weeks. Looking through the coverage as it came in, it was good to see it was overwhelmingly positive. There was virtually no mention of what had gone before, with only a couple of media outlets (the *Daily Telegraph* and *Finextra*) feeling compelled to rake over old ground and refer to 'some churn in its staff' and the fact Starling Bank had 'not had a smooth gestation', respectively. The rest of the coverage found the good news in the arrival of a new digital challenger. That, in my book, reflected just how far we'd come.

To celebrate, Terry and I arranged with the team to meet in the pub the following evening at 5 p.m. The drinks were most certainly on Starling Bank. What was very interesting in the aftermath was that now we had our licence we were, without a doubt, taken far more seriously by both the media and the wider world. Almost overnight I began to be asked to comment on banking issues. A few days after the launch, for example, I was invited to sit on the BBC *Breakfast* sofa in Salford to talk about an industry report into how many consumers were now using banking apps. Well, I say 'sit on the sofa'; they actually required me to sit on a stool to discuss the research. Initially, I was not very sure about this at all. I'm far too short to sit comfortably on a high stool, and I look ridiculous doing so because my legs are usually dangling in mid air! The team at Salford were lovely about it, though, and even brought a stool out for me to practise on. All that aside, it was a great piece and more good publicity for Starling Bank. We were definitely moving in the right direction.

11. Shout from the Rooftops

Securing regulatory approval was a giant step forward, but it was only the first on a long journey. Our licence came with a 'mobilization restriction' that meant we could hold no more than £50,000 in deposits. Obviously, we wouldn't be able to sign up many current accounts on that basis. Being granted a licence signals the start of a period working towards the time when the restrictions are lifted. This would be the final stage of becoming a fully fledged bank.

After securing the licence, the Starling team was more galvanized than ever towards the full launch of the app. The sense of urgency wasn't just eagerness to get the product out there at last. There was also the question of what our competitor challenger banks were up to: we were all moving forward at quite a rate and I'd be lying if I didn't say there was a healthy degree of rivalry between us. Plus, of course, I was always very aware of what one particular competitor was up to: Mondo. We'd pipped Tom's bank to the post in getting our licence, but only just. Mondo achieved its licence the month after we did.

Now we were both racing to be the first to be up and running properly.

If anyone asked about this ongoing rivalry (and people did all the time), both Tom and I would airily say it didn't matter one bit.

'There's more than enough room for two, three, four, or even five of the new-generation banks,' we'd say.

But it did matter. A lot.

This is not to say it was an unhealthy rivalry. In fact, at times it was quite funny. The most obvious manifestation of this (and the one I enjoyed most) came around the time we were awarded our licence in July 2016.

In June, Mondo had announced it would need to change its name following a trademark dispute. Although they had gone through all the normal checks, an unnamed third party had challenged the bank's name and, rather than opting to fight it through the courts, which could take a year or more, Tom and his team decided to change it.

This was not the first time Mondo had run into trouble over a trademark. A year earlier, the US-based Simple Finance Technology Corp. had issued the fledgling bank with a 'cease and desist' notice over Mondo's use of the phrase 'Safe to Spend'. Eileen Burbidge had tweeted screenshots of Mondo's app, which had subsequently been picked up by TechCrunch, and Simple had cried foul. The American organization had trademarked the phrase in the European Union months earlier, intending it for use in its online banking business.

At this stage, Mondo had already issued around 25,000 prepaid cards bearing the Mondo logo. In the run-up to receiving its licence, Mondo had opted to serve its following of would-be customers by issuing these cards, which had money loaded onto them through their app. It was a strategy that appeared to capture the imagination, since Mondo had a waiting list of 130,000 for its cards.

Characteristically, Tom played down the naming issue.

'It's annoying, but I think in two or three months we'll have forgotten that we were ever called Mondo,' he told one online magazine. 'It's an empty vessel that you bring meaning to . . . we've just got much, much better things to be doing like getting the banking licence, fully launching, making a product that people love.' The Mondo team came up with the neat marketing idea of involving its loyal fan base in the renaming process. Anyone who wanted to suggest a new name was invited to do so on Twitter using the hashtag #newmondo. The whole exercise was tightly policed to ensure that the bank didn't end up with something daft like Banky McBankface, after a similar exercise culminated in a ship narrowly avoiding being named Boaty McBoatface. Therefore it wasn't a pure vote, just a poll of names, which were assessed internally and then put through rigorous trademark checks. Plus, in order that the bank would not need to reinvent the wheel completely, with an entirely new logo and branding, all suggestions had to begin with the letter M. With everything going on in the run-up to Starling's licence announcement, I didn't have much time to think about Mondo's impending name change. However, towards the end of July I began to hear rumours that a new name had been agreed. The fintech industry is very close knit, so not much stays secret for long. It seemed the new moniker was to be Monzo, changing just one letter of the original. Tom and his team were now busily working on the rebrand, which was due to be unveiled some time in late August, so it seemed as though 'Monzo' had passed the various trademark tests.

I was in the office late one evening after another long day. As usual, there were loads of people still there and coming and going. Many of the tech team preferred to work late into the night since they were apparently useless in daylight hours, according to their own admission. A few of us were chatting about various things and the Monzo name change came up. I checked online to see whether they'd secured the domain name. That would be a sure sign that we were correct and that Monzo was definitely the new name. Sure enough, a number of permutations of Monzo had been signed up.

I'm not entirely sure why, but I then typed in 'getmonzo.

co.uk'. Mondo had been using 'getmondo.co.uk' to sign up new customers to its prepaid card. To my amazement, it flashed up as available.

'Hey, have you seen this?' I said, staring at the screen disbelievingly. 'They haven't secured getmonzo.co.uk.' A small group was soon crowding around my desk.

'How the hell did they miss that?' Terry said.

'Maybe they're dropping the whole get Mondo thing; or get Monzo,' Megan suggested.

'Possibly,' I said, putting the domain into my online shopping basket and typing a few details.

There were other variations too. It turned out that monzo-bank.co.uk, monzobank.info, monzobank.net, monzobank. org and monzobank.com were all also available. I really couldn't believe they hadn't scooped them up. I put them all into my basket.

'What are you doing?' Megan asked. 'You're buying them? Why?'

'I don't know, maybe we can have some fun,' I smiled.

Even as I said it, I wasn't sure exactly what I was going to do with the domain names, but it was too good an opportunity to miss.

Not everyone was enthusiastic about having fun with our direct competitor. Terry McParlane was worried that if we put something tongue-in-cheek about Starling on our newly acquired domains, it might confuse customers. She warned that raking up old conflicts could have a negative effect, even if it was done in jest.

'It would only make sense to the old Mondo team, or someone who knows the history,' she said. 'If I'm a person who's interested in Mondo, searching for them, but don't know about the Starling history, isn't it going to make them go and dig into what happened, at worst, or wonder what on earth Starling are about?

'We will need to be prepared for someone to pick it up and write a negative story about it, even if it is just meant as a bit of fun.'

Peter Rossiter, our risk officer, and Matt Newman, our general counsel, were also cautious. For them the worry was whether buying and using our rival's unclaimed domains was ethical, even if it was just for a one-off joke. The engineers' concerns centred around anything we put on the newly acquired domains. Even if it was just a landing page with a one-liner on, it had to be done properly, they said. If we executed it badly and something didn't work, we'd look incompetent as well as foolish.

I sat on the thought for a few days, mulling over what everyone had said. They each had a point. Sometimes it is best to leave well alone. The thing is, though, sometimes it isn't. Sometimes you need to take a few risks and it is better for people to notice and write about you than to ignore you altogether. We were so close to launching now, we needed would-be customers to know who we were.

There was something else too. I also wanted to break the taboo about talking about the Monzo and Starling connection. Whichever way we looked at it, there would always be a Starling and Monzo story and I didn't want it perpetually to come up as the slightly embarrassing question at the end of every press interview. I wanted to be open about our past and the fact that both companies had moved on.

At my request Malka Finkelstein organized a friend in Israel to do some very simple graphics for the 'new websites' and Dan Osborne worked on switching the domains. We produced a basic website. Resplendent in Starling's familiar purple branding, the landing page opened out, line by line, to say:

With a next generation **bank**
Anything is **possible**
Starling Bank

The screen then switched to the next page which said simply:

Congrats on the rebrand!
Lots of love, Anne.
Starling Bank

It was absolutely no coincidence that the form of words emphasized Bank Possible, the original iteration of the bank Tom and I had worked on together. We also included a sign-up link for Starling: there was no sense in missing out on a perfect opportunity to attract new customers, after all. We were, however, careful to make it clear that people were signing up to Starling, not Monzo, in case there was any confusion. We didn't want to be in a position of misleading customers. It was difficult to keep a lid on what we'd done, but although everyone in Starling Bank knew about it, I was determined to maintain the element of surprise in the wider world. For our prank to have maximum impact, we needed the tech community to find out about it on their own terms.

On the evening of 25 August, an event was held at Monzo's office to launch the new name and celebrate the 12,560 suggestions they'd received. It was live-streamed on YouTube. As soon as the announcement was made, we put the 'bank possible' congratulations messages on the half-dozen domains we owned. It didn't take long for Starling's prank to leak out. Pretty soon Twitter lit up with tweets and retweets highlighting the story. Half a dozen Monzo searches were opening up to a cheeky message from its arch rival Starling.

After we'd had our fun I agreed to let Monzo have the domain names for nothing but a small £1,000 donation to the financial literacy charity MyBnk. We matched the donation with £1,000 of our own. Tom was utterly silent about it and, as far as I know, has never mentioned it. I was a bit disappointed about that. I had hoped he'd embrace the joke, tweet something in return and we could publicly bury the hatchet. That wasn't to be.

The bit of fun with Monzo was a brief but welcome diversion in an otherwise extraordinarily hectic period. After winning the licence, we'd agreed to go all out to get the restrictions lifted by December. This was a challenge by any measure, but we firmly believed we could get everything in line by then.

There was a lot to do. The tasks we needed to complete now were divided into several categories. There was the ongoing work with the regulator, getting everything in line in the run-up to having the banking restrictions lifted. Then there was the challenge of aligning with the various payment schemes, from MasterCard to BACS to the Faster Payments Scheme to taking international payments. This meant working closely with the organizations responsible for each one and meeting their exacting standards, before being cleared to accept money via that route. Meanwhile, we needed to refine our day-to-day back-office operations by adding everything from a call centre to help customers with any problems that couldn't be solved in the app, to a comprehensive complaints procedure, to a code of conduct. None of this was to forget the all-important tech side, which covered everything from building the app our customers would use to the back end that would keep it all functioning smoothly. On top of all this there was a team dedicated to looking at the risk side of running a bank, which was naturally considerable since it involved large sums of money and multiple customers, plus finance so we could keep the service (and the company) flowing smoothly. Finally, we needed to keep tweaking the product itself and making sure it was exactly what the consumer wanted and expected. Each one of these elements had dozens of sub-elements, each of which was as important as the next. We produced complex, multilayered flow diagrams to show exactly where we were, or expected to be, from one month to the next. Even then, it all looked pretty challenging.

While I was fully immersed in each part of the process, the one that excited me most was the product itself: the app that our customers would download and use, hopefully not long from now. By this stage, we had done a lot of customer research and were pretty certain about our USP. There were now dozens of ways that people could spend their money digitally: PayPal, ApplePay, AndroidPay or contactless MasterCard or Visa. There were numerous new digital products to save and borrow money too, whether Peer to Peer, or new types of wealth management such as Nutmeg. Ironically, though, while the proposition behind the services was to make consumers' lives easier, the sheer number of options was starting to have the opposite effect. It was hard to know which app or service to choose and when. Which one was appropriate to which purchasing occasion?

It became very obvious to the Starling team that we had a real opportunity to simplify this new situation. We could put all these experiences into one account so that all consumers would need to make a purchase anywhere, at any time, would be their mobile phone, which, as we all know, is the one thing pretty much everyone has with them all the time these days. Spending and receiving money (and monitoring their accounts) would be as easy as sending a tweet or receiving a message from a mate. It was gratifying to see that my early vision of my bank becoming a marketplace for financial products was spot on.

One of the app's features was Marketplace, where we partnered with third parties, enabling them to offer Starling customers additional services from insurance to mortgages. I saw it as something resembling Borough Market, a favourite of mine that was not far from one of our earlier offices. Borough Market showcases a diverse assortment of top-quality products. The fact that there is such a good range on offer attracts high-quality customers, which in turn attracts more firms to come and sell their goods. However, the individual stalls are not branded 'Borough Market'. They all operate under the branding of the individual participants.

Obviously, we also had to pull off the delicate balancing trick of appearing extremely simple to use while offering a wide range of options. One of the simple yet compelling functions we were working on was based on a 'jam jar' idea, whereby consumers would be able to analyse their spend, manage their money and use predictive analysis to plan ahead in much the same way that people used to put money aside in jam jars for various planned expenditures such as an upcoming summer holiday or gas bill. (This eventually became the Spaces section of the Starling app.) We also needed to achieve all this while ensuring the most advanced security features and seamless interfaces with our partner services.

As I sat in on the weekly demos of new features of the app, I grew more and more excited. With each version I saw, I realized it was shaping up to be better than I had ever hoped.

Then, in August, we received bad news via the Faster Payments Scheme. Thanks to completely unrelated tech works at the Bank of England, there was no way we'd be able to join the scheme before Christmas. In fact, the date they were offering was 16 January. It was a huge blow, but there was nothing we could do about it. We just had to keep going. The next mile-stone, licensing-wise, was to make our submission to the PRA / FCA for lifting restrictions and this would need to be done by the middle of November. This would give them at least eight weeks' review time, allowing for the Christmas period.

In the meantime, we had a huge amount to do elsewhere. Plus, we had to squeeze in yet another office move. We'd been in offices in St James's Square since April 2016. It was an abso-lutely prime location in central London and we had the whole top floor with access to a balcony. We'd managed to get a great deal on the rent because the landlord had been given planning permission to tear it down (leaving the front facia intact) so we would only be there until all the paperwork went through. Short term or not, it was a great spot and as spring turned into summer, the team would regularly finish the day by head-ing out onto the balcony with drinks to talk about their vision for Starling while enjoying the breathtaking views of the city.

The team was still growing at quite a rate and, after we'd secured the licence, the pace of growth accelerated still more. It was soon apparent that we'd completely outgrown the sev-enth floor, so we needed to move even before the landlord announced that we had to. Luckily, there was room for us on the fourth floor of the same building, which was considerably larger, so we didn't need to go very far for the time being.

The day of the big move downstairs was set for 1 August. Everything went perfectly, except for one thing: the broadband connection to the Wi-Fi had been delayed. In the short term the only fallback available was to use 4G. However, there was practically zero 4G signal available in the new open-plan office. The only place we could raise a signal was in the small meeting rooms that were sited around the perimeter of the fourth floor. We ended up in the slightly ludicrous situation where the sixty Starling employees crammed themselves into the tiny rooms, practically sitting on top of one another, while the vast open-plan area was completely empty except for me, squashed into the one corner where I could just about get a signal. Visitors to the office during that brief 'pre-Wi-Fi' period were utterly perplexed! I tried to explain the reasons, but often I would tire of telling the story and just left them to think that we were all plain crazy.

What was interesting was, even though we were not a particularly conventional team (especially in banking terms), we were getting things done. And some pretty challenging things too. Somehow, we were building the technology for our new bank from scratch using the very best tools from some of the best companies in the world to produce something that would transform the consumer experience.

In terms of the business, the next big 'wow' moment was when our 'customer alpha' product became available. This was the prototype that would be used for testing by selected members of the team and their families. Most excitingly, it would be launched with a Starling debit card, in partnership with MasterCard. This card would not be a prepaid card, like the one Monzo had opened with, but a bona fide debit card that would be marked with its own Bank Identification Number and which would be accepted by over 28 million merchants around the globe as well as hundreds of thousands of cash machines. I was very impatient to make our first Starling transaction. It was such a significant milestone.

Finally, at the beginning of October, a box arrived at Starling's offices. It looked just like any of the multitude of brown cardboard boxes that get delivered to offices all over the world every second. But this one was different. It contained Starling's first ever batch of debit cards.

'Time to go shopping,' I said, my eyes glinting. 'Who's coming with me?'

I wasn't being entirely flippant. That's exactly what we needed to do. We needed to make sure the Starling card worked exactly as we expected it to in all circumstances, and the only way to do this was to take it out and spend some money.

It was agreed that Julian and another colleague would accompany me on the inaugural Starling shopping trip. The three of us grabbed our coats, buttoning them up tightly since it was a damp and windy autumn day, and headed for the door.

'Where to first?' I asked as we stood out on a corner of Regent Street.

'Well, I think we'd probably better start with something small,' Julian said. 'Just to make sure.'

'Agreed,' I said. 'Who's hungry?'

Without waiting for an answer, I darted into a small café and headed for the counter. I looked along the rows of pastries and sandwiches lined up there, taking in the prices, and then stole a glance at my colleagues, who had followed closely behind. I realized that I was feeling ridiculously excited. This was Julian's day – he had delivered this. Obviously it would be no big deal if the card was turned down, and we could simply walk away. It would just be so disappointing though.

Doing my best to ignore the butterflies in my stomach, I looked at the woman behind the counter.

'One brownie please,' I said.

She smiled and picked up some tongs and a paper bag before deftly scooping up the cake.

'One pound eighty, please.'

I held up the card and she nodded at the contactless payment terminal as she handed me the bag. Taking a deep breath, I tapped the card on the screen. I smiled as a familiar beep rang out.

It worked!

'Ta dah!' I said, much to the obvious confusion of the

assistant, who had clearly never seen anyone quite so excited about paying for a snack before.

'It's my new card,' I said, quickly realizing I was only making things worse.

'Shall we try it somewhere else?' Julian laughed, steering me out of the café.

Now we were off we embarked on an exhaustive stress test of the card. We followed the contactless payment with one via pin in another coffee shop. Then we went to an ATM and changed the pin, before going to another and taking out a small amount of money. Everything went swimmingly.

'But now we need to go bigger,' I said. 'Much bigger.'

I looked across the road and my eye fell on luxury leather goods and furniture maker Osprey. Osprey had long been one of my favourite brands and I'd often slowed to glance through the windows of its flagship store as I had hurried down Regent Street. From this extensive period of window-shopping research I had ascertained two things: the first was that I wanted pretty much everything in that store and the second that quality and style like that didn't come cheap.

'Come on,' I said, heading across the busy road.

The two others followed close behind. I had reached the pavement directly in front of Osprey when I stopped abruptly, almost knocking my colleagues back into the road.

'It's perfect,' I breathed. 'Totally perfect. In fact, it must be fate.'

They followed my gaze and began to laugh.

'They must have heard we were coming,' Julian said.

We walked slowly up to the window, never once taking our eyes off the object that had caught my eye. It was an exquisite polished croc leather handbag. But that was not what had my full attention. No, it was the fact that this gorgeous object was in the exact same royal purple as my Starling debit card. (The card colour later turned to teal, while the Starling corporate identity is still based on royal purple.)

The three of us looked at one another and simultaneously gave a well-what-can-you-do shrug.

'Although, that's got to be quite a bit more than one pound eighty,' Julian began to caution as I dived for the Osprey shop door.

Now was not a moment for caution. Handbags had always been my thing. A handbag in Starling purple and on a day like this? No contest. I had to have it. Besides, the £295 price tag would be a great test for the Starling card.

By the time Julian had followed us in I had already spoken with a very nice young man called Rafael, who had introduced himself as the store manager, and the handbag was being borne towards the counter. Rafael seemed quite keen that I spend some time examining the goods, but I admit I rather rushed that part. While I would normally be more than happy to give the luxury handbag buying process the due ceremony it fully deserved, now was not the time. I (a) wanted to test the card and (b) knew I wanted the bag anyhow!

I handed Rafael my Starling card and Rafael, being the professional he was, smiled broadly, scanned the bag's barcode and began to tap numbers into his screen.

'Can you enter your pin please,' he said, turning the card reader to face me.

I could feel the tension around me as I typed in my four numbers and stared at the screen. 'Pin OK,' it read and I held my breath.

For a few agonizing seconds nothing happened. Then the screen flickered onto the next page.

Transaction confirmed.

The three Starlings erupted into cheers and whoops. Poor Rafael didn't know where to look, he was so confused. I'm pretty sure he had never seen anything like it as the three of us punched the air and congratulated each other.

'We can't leave it like this though,' Julian said, when the excitement had subsided a little. 'While it is fantastic to see all our hard work paying off, we won't truly know it works until we make it fail.'

He was right, of course. While no consumer would actively seek out a bank card that is rejected at every turn, we needed to ensure it would be rejected in the right circumstances. In other words, if we didn't have the funds to cover a purchase, all the right checks and balances would be properly built in, so the card would be declined.

'Rafael, we need your help,' I said, turning back to the store manager. 'What is the most expensive thing you have in this shop?'

Rafael smiled uncomprehendingly. I wondered how often he received such odd customers.

I explained that we represented a new bank and that we were in the shop for the first ever test of our brand-new debit card, which, as he knew, had passed with flying colours.

'I now need to try it with something which is way, way above my limit,' I said. 'Something that no bank would ever authorize and, all being well, that you – well, we – would instantly reject.'

Rafael nodded.

'And I also need you to agree that if the payment does, by any chance, go through, you will give me an instant refund. Much though I would like to buy up pretty much everything here, it's probably not a good idea right now.'

Rafael agreed and immediately began to walk around the floor pointing out some of the pricier items.

'Why don't we do a bit of a trolley dash?' I suggested to my colleagues. 'You know, get a whole basketful of goodies to push up the bill.'

By now, we were all rather enjoying ourselves. Even Rafael was starting to see the funny side as he grabbed various pieces.

'Well, you definitely need one of these,' he grinned, passing it over to Julian, who was relaying stuff back to the counter. 'And have you seen this? It's one of our biggest sellers . . .'

The other customers in the store were beginning to stare. To be fair, we must have seemed quite an unusual group, cheerfully plundering Osprey of its stock.

'We're going to have to help you put some of this back afterwards,' I said apologetically.

'Oh, don't worry,' Rafael said, picking up a cashmere scarf. 'I'm enjoying myself.'

After about ten minutes, we'd gathered together an impressive haul and I decided enough was probably enough.

'Let's give it a try,' I said, waiting by the counter while Rafael scanned one barcode after another.

'Three thousand, five hundred and ninety pounds,' Rafael said, his eyes wide as he turned the card reader to face me.

I glanced at Julian, who shrugged. Leaning forward, I keyed in my pin and handed the terminal to Rafael. I could hardly bear to look as he stared into the screen. At last Rafael looked up.

'I'm very sorry, madam, but your card has been declined,' he deadpanned.

Pandemonium broke out. The Starlings were cheering and clapping and even Rafael raised his fist in the air triumphantly. By this time, the rest of the people in Osprey London must have been convinced our group was utterly deranged.

'It worked,' I said breathlessly. 'Or rather, it didn't work. Perfect.'

Daft though the experiment might seem now, it was a key moment in Starling's history. We had the licence, the technology, and now the card.

Just to make sure, we went to an ATM and changed the pin once again, before visiting another one and taking some more cash out. By the time we returned to the office, Greg, Steve and John were utterly perplexed. They'd been tracking our movements, or, more specifically, the card's movements, and couldn't believe what we'd been up to. We'd said we were going to test it in a coffee shop and now we were making transactions for many hundreds of pounds.

After that day, my next mission was for the team and me to undertake some intensive shopping with my Starling card. I needed to stress test it in conjunction with the alpha product and show a comprehensive history of transactions on the app. I should add that, while I greatly enjoyed doing so, it was nowhere near as pleasurable as that first trip to Osprey.

This intensive period was essential and showed up all sorts of unexpected glitches. During one thirty-minute period, for example, all shops whose name contained the '&' symbol stopped accepting our card. We couldn't make any transactions at M&S or H&M. Not surprisingly, everyone in the office quickly developed quite an obsession with cards and merchant terminals.

Meanwhile, we needed to update our growing fan-base on the progress we'd made. Ever since our licence announcement in July, there had continued to be an increasing amount of interest in Starling and its launch. It was part of the real buzz around challenger banks and it was important that we reflected as much of it as possible onto Starling, rather than on our main rivals Monzo, Atom and Tandem, as well as all the other soon-to-be challenger banks that were gaining ground.

Communicating well with customers was now more of a priority than ever. After all, that was what would make us a successful bank. We'd already signed up with a customer service software company to provide a 24/7, 365-day-a-year help desk across all platforms. We wanted customers to be able to contact us at any time of day or night.

All eyes were on the date when we would finally go live. We'd decided very early on that we were not going to have a big launch. We were simply going to *be*. If anyone wanted to pin down a 'launch date' then I suppose it would be when the app went live in app stores once the restrictions were lifted. But this was just one stage of many. There were so many fintechs launching products to massive fanfare and that was never how we thought of ourselves. There would never be a time when we had 'finished' our app. We'd be constantly evolving, keeping at the forefront of technology and innovating for our customers. Besides, it is possible to try too hard with a launch. Atom had a pop-up shop with an orchestra which serenaded people as they walked up to an ATM. I am sure most customers were as mystified as we were about it.

By early 2017, the team had grown to eighty Starlings and every one of us was focussed on building something extraordinary. Getting the app just right remained our primary focus. At times it really did feel like a case of one step forward and at least half a dozen back. We'd make one modification, put it in front of consumers in research, find out they didn't like it and change it again, but in doing so we'd disrupt a bunch of other things that had been working perfectly well beforehand. I often felt like I had to keep a real lid on things that were put up for change. Everyone meant well and we were all working hard towards getting it 100 per cent right, but sometimes it was just too much. We needed to slow down and examine closely the reasons for making a change, otherwise we'd tie ourselves in knots and might unwittingly chuck out some of the best stuff. I was constantly worried that we were overengineering the app too, which meant things didn't always go smoothly.

Ultimately, though, we were juggling two opposing issues. We needed to launch into app stores as soon as possible, but we also wanted our shop window, the Starling Bank app, to be clean and perfect. We couldn't accept untidy, unwieldy or truncated transactions. It had to look good at all times and keep things simple for our customers. Often it felt like a difficult trade-off and I found it hard to keep my impatience at bay.

It was frustrating when things didn't go to plan, because we wanted to 'go live' as soon as we could. We also managed to lose around six weeks through pre-issuance notification. This was to do with the way our backer Harry McPike was releasing capital into the business in tranches. As per the original agreement there was the initial £3 million, a further £15 million when we got authorization and £30 million would come when the restrictions were lifted. Naturally, there were many regulations about any sort of capital injections and the regulator had to approve all the legal documents around each additional tranche of capital. This took time.

As if to emphasize what a knife edge this business could be on, in early March 2017 we received news that Tandem Bank had had to relinquish the banking licence they had received back in November 2015. The venture had been waiting on an investment from Sanpower, the Chinese conglomerate that also owns House of Fraser, but it had been halted by the Chinese authorities, which were restricting outbound investments. Tandem had had to shelve tests of a savings product and return deposits. More frustratingly, it missed a deadline to fulfil some of the requirements of its banking licence, which meant it would have to reapply all over again in due course.

We didn't have much time to dwell on Tandem's issues. We launched our beta app at almost the exact same time that they took this backward step. Because of the nature of the way the lifting of regulations worked, our launch had multiple stages.

Alpha testing of the first version began in November 2016, and then, in March 2017, we were ready to launch Starling Bank's beta app. This was the version that would take us beyond the small group of friends-and-family private testers and that put the app in the hands of a wider, possibly less forgiving audience. We had to be very cautious with the launch, since we were still under restriction. This meant informing the PRA/FCA banking regulators of what we were doing and making sure we didn't go above £50,000 in our balances.

Coincidentally, on the morning of the beta launch I was booked at the Stock Exchange to ring the opening bell alongside a government minister. Following that, I had been asked to take part in a discussion there on Harnessing Data for the Customer. (Ironically, Tom was also on the panel and was not very friendly.) The two invitations were an indication of how far Starling Bank, and indeed I, had come. As soon as I was clear, I began to do a small round of media interviews. As ever, it was a delicate balancing act: we wanted attention for the development, but not too much attention. I was very conscious that there were some on the Starling Bank board who were already questioning whether it was too soon for the beta launch. Traditionally the approach to something like this would be to launch with a limited set of features and then get researchers to examine closely how every aspect had performed before taking it any further. I was adamant this wouldn't work in this case: we needed real customers with a real product in their hands.

Maintaining the balance of both creating and limiting excitement about the brand was not easy. We'd put a lot of thought into the presentation of our debit cards. There has always been a very big deal about the ceremony around unboxing Apple products in particular, and we were very keen to create a similar buzz and excitement among our new account holders because it is a great way to encourage viral adoption.

For our unboxing experience, we designed a very nifty pop-up wallet with a hologram, which was 100 per cent different from the usual form of debit-card delivery, namely glued to an A4 letter from the bank. Sadly, there were unintended consequences to creating such a covetable form of packaging. Our customers began to video themselves unwrapping the cards, with excitable oohs and aahs as they did so. Unfortunately, we then had to spend a lot of time contacting them after they posted their videos on Twitter and Instagram, sharing their bank details with the world at large!

Even though we needed to be cautious, it was crucial that we got our mobile bank tested by members of the general public, who might be more critical than people we knew and loved. And remember, criticism is what you need, if you wish to get the best possible product.

After brainstorming it for a while, wondering how we could get complete strangers to try out an unfamiliar banking app, we decided good old-fashioned bribery would be key. Well, bribery might be exaggerating somewhat, since we went for the lowest common denominator when it comes to stirring up interest: free ice cream. Our strategy was to buy a job lot of ice creams and to give one away to anyone who agreed to download our app and give it a go. After all, it was almost spring, and who doesn't like a free choc ice? Even as we firmed up the idea and ordered the stock, I was aware there were people on the team who were reluctant. You need to be a certain sort of person who can bowl up to a complete stranger and offer them something for almost nothing, even if it is a refreshing ice cream. It's a bit embarrassing. Most people have not been brought up to be pushy.

I decided that there was nothing else for it but to seize the moment, pick up the coolbox and lead from the front. I grabbed the handle, took a deep breath and strode confidently out of the office. It took me a while to get in my stride and overcome the somewhat startled looks I got when I walked up to people and offered them a frozen treat. After a while, though, I got used to it.

One 'successful' ice cream giveaway in particular made me relax and realize the situation was so funny that I may as well enjoy it. Starling was still in its St James's square offices, which is a great, upmarket location in central London. There were all sorts of characters working in the other offices there. One stood out in particular. He was a former digital entrepreneur and was very, very full of himself. He drove a flash Bentley, with a personalized plate, and was always immaculately turned out in bespoke, sharp suits, with his perfectly trimmed, slicked-back hair styled to a T. It was all a bit odd though, since the 'former' part of the digital entrepreneur moniker was key. He was not 'former' because he had triumphantly exited with a multimillion-pound payout. He was 'former' because the business had gone bust in a very big way. The small matter of insolvency didn't seem to have slowed him down much, though, because he still confidently strode the corridors of the St James's office like he owned the place. He never spoke to anyone at Starling, but had quickly become a figure of fascination for us all.

After pounding the pavements of Piccadilly with my box of ice creams for a while on an unusually hot spring day, I elected to cool off by seeking out the shade of our offices. I decided that I would offer what I had left over to the people who occupied the rooms around us. I had barely embarked on this mission when I ran straight into the former digital entrepreneur who was striding down the corridor in his usual bombastic style. Without skipping a beat, I diverted my course, stepped out in front of him with a bright smile and offered him an ice cream.

The man turned out to be quite charming and intrigued

about what we were up to. We chatted together for a while, then he chose an ice cream and, as he walked off unwrapping it, he promised to uphold his side of the bargain and check out our app. It was only when I rounded the next corner of the corridor that I stopped short and had to smile to myself. This character was currently embroiled in a very public court battle with his former partner, who had served him with a bankruptcy petition in a bid to recoup a substantial loan. If this case went the distance, this man couldn't legally open a bank account with us, or indeed any other bank for that matter. Undischarged bankrupts are barred from such activities!

The odd wasted ice cream aside, perseverance was key. This was not a one-time-only exercise. The object was to test the product, get feedback and adjust according to what we heard. This involved coming up with all sorts of creative ways to get it in front of people. Another of our promotional efforts to encourage trials of the app centred around gloves. We'd ordered 5,000 pairs of navy blue touchscreen gloves emblazoned with the Starling logo. These are the smartphone compatible gloves which you can wear and still swipe your phone screen: perfect for the colder months when you need to use your phone outside but don't want your fingers to go numb.

Once again, I sensed a certain reluctance among some in the team to get involved in the distribution effort. So much so, in fact, that by the time spring was showing signs of rapidly turning into what looked like a rather good summer, we still had boxes full of the things. Seizing the initiative once again, I shouldered a box of gloves as I headed home to Marlow for the weekend. I knew just the place where those gloves would go down a treat: my local rugby club. Each weekend, dozens of parents would hang around on the windswept touchlines, watching their kids play rugby: they were practically a captive audience.

That Sunday, I spent the whole day walking up and down the muddy pitches, giving out gloves. There were new matches beginning every hour or so, which meant an entirely new line-up of spectators, doing their best to shield themselves against the cold: perfect. Most people were pretty surprised to be approached by a cheerful and chatty woman offering a free pair of gloves. I am not the archetypal promotions person. However, they all recovered themselves quite quickly and were mostly willing to engage in conversation.

The strategy worked too. I'll gloss over the number of small businesses that approached me over the next week, with pitches along the lines of 'We met at Marlow rugby ground, and I think I might be able to help with your marketing strategy.' Aside from this, we had a marked uplift in downloads from Marlow.

You may be wondering if there was any point to this. It may even seem a little ludicrous. After all, no one is going to create the next Amazon by opening accounts one at a time in the wilds of Buckinghamshire. But, remember why I was doing this. The feedback from new accounts from this, and the ice-cream exercise, provided us with valuable intelligence. We saw the type of people who were most interested in opening a new account with us, the ways in which they used the app to open their accounts and then what they did with them subsequently. It was all essential stuff.

Ultimately, to find guinea pigs, you need to be creative and also to bare your soul.

Owners of iPhones who had already expressed an interest via referrals and who had been waiting patiently were now invited to download the app. An android version was due later in the month. On offer was the ability to sign up to the full current account and, once approved, customers would be issued with a Starling Bank MasterCard debit card that could be used in the UK and abroad. They'd also be able to set up regular payments such as direct debits and make one-off payments via the Faster Payments Scheme. Customers would be able to view their current account activity in real time via push notifications and the 'Starling Pulse' feed that displayed all their account activity.

To help publicize the next stage in the Starling Bank story, we got in touch with the ever-alert-for-a-scoop Steve O'Hear at TechCrunch and gave him exclusive access to the app. He seemed quite taken with one of the security features we'd included. In addition to the numerical password, the app now also boasted 'biometrical identification', which users could set up by recording a short video message of themselves reading out a specific phrase. This was all very innovative at the time.

Steve wrote a great article about the launch, which was good news. The tech market invariably took the lead from him, so I was hopeful we'd get good take-up of the beta. The staff, friends and family who were testing the beta very helpfully took overdrafts, so we didn't eat into the £50,000 limit. We then (very carefully) increased the numbers every day to stress test the system, but still watched the balances like hawks.

Our banking restrictions were finally lifted at the end of April, and on 9 May 2017 Starling Bank's app went live in app stores. In the run-up to releasing the app, we'd held a meeting with the Apple app store guys following a suggestion from someone on our team who had previously worked in San Francisco and picked up a few tactics that might get apps featured prominently in the store. We prepared a presentation that gave a high-level overview of Starling, the app and examples of early customer feedback/reviews. We also gave the Apple team a demo of the app and walked them through our marketing plans, including our go live date.

We began sending out invitations to 250 interested parties

the night before the app was released. These were the refer-
ees who had already signed up some weeks earlier. We also
supported the launch with a raft of tweets and social media
activity. From the moment it went live, we watched the
numbers like hawks. Within the first few hours 750 people
downloaded the app. I did my best not to eye the tech team
nervously. If there were any problems now, it would be all
down to them.

We were all glued to the app store screen, waiting for the
first ratings. We knew only too well that if the first few reviews
gave it just one or two stars, the other reviews would most
likely follow the trend. That scenario would be a disaster.
Companies like ours live or die by their ratings. It felt like ages
until the first ratings appeared, but people started to rate the
app remarkably quickly. Five stars! They liked it. It wasn't a
surprise, but it was certainly a very welcome endorsement. (I
now have an alert on my phone for every time someone leaves
a rating and, even today, my heart stops until I open it. If it is
five stars I am jubilant but if someone leaves a one-star rating
I am gutted.)

One month on from going live we hit £1 million in deposits. It seemed an incredible milestone, but was just one among
many. We certainly couldn't slow down now. I was on a mission to get as many people as possible to trial the app to keep
pushing the numbers up. First thing every morning we would
check just how many people had downloaded it. If the numbers seemed a bit low we would pull a few more safe names
from the waiting list and invite them. Some people on the team
thought it would be a good idea to send out invites to people
who worked at Atom, Tandem and Monzo, the logic being that
we were a bank and we couldn't pick and choose our customers for ever. Nevertheless, it was a bold statement: we were
ready, and if we were ready then we should be ready enough

to invite everyone, including our competitors. Of course, our competitors were very happy to oblige by downloading the app and stress testing Starling Bank in minute detail. They were completely shameless about it: one guy even used his business address and when we queried whether or not this was really his home, as you might expect for a current account opening, he insisted he actually lived on the company's premises.

Once our competitors had a copy of the app, we decided that we might as well ramp up our marketing campaign. Now was the time to really get Starling noticed. In my view we just needed to go large as quickly as possible. Over time, we would inevitably begin to grow through the personal recommendations of our customers. But in the short term we needed to build a solid foundation.

As we upped the ante, our ad campaign took off in a number of directions, from YouTube to Google. We also sought out trendsetters and influencers to make sure they were aware of Starling, and partnered with cultural events too. We didn't forget traditional media either, being sure to communicate regularly with the consumer press and financial journalists to get our message across.

As with everything at Starling, we began by thinking through what we knew, and then what was just wrong about what we knew. In seeking to boost the take-up of the app we were constantly experimenting to find what worked and what didn't. Key to this was keeping in close touch with our various stakeholders.

Very early on, we saw the need for a Starling Community Forum to give our customers more of a voice and to ask them for feedback. Customers were already very vocal about what worked and what didn't, so it made sense to listen to them and promote a dialogue. We were very conscious that Starling on its own couldn't solve real-world problems on a global scale, but together with the developer community and with our Marketplace offering services from like-minded companies we could enhance the financial lives of our customers. (We subsequently closed the Community Forum in September 2018. While it had been a brilliant idea, we realized some conversations opened up the potential to expose sensitive customer information. This was something we could not do, particularly in the highly regulated environment in which we operate. Like so many start-up activities, it was a useful experiment and well worth trying. We have since found numerous other, safer ways of continuing the conversation.)

Now we'd gone public with the launch we were also inundated by the software engineering community wanting to know how we'd built Starling. We recorded a series of podcasts where Jason Maude, our chief technology advocate, grilled the technology team, Jeremy Paxman style, about the big technology and engineering questions of the day. Greg Hawkins, John Mountain and Steve Newson were all put to the test. For day-to-day developer chat, there was the Slack channel, where Sam Everington, our lead engineer, hung out day and night ready to answer questions on the API (application programming interface).

We were constantly tweaking and improving the app too. Our focus had three main priorities. The first was to keep improving the quality and performance of the app by looking at the code and evaluating the mobile experience. Inevitably, we discovered all sorts of little bugs quite quickly, so we needed to log them and fix asap. Things like caching transaction data, so customers were able to see their balances even when offline, and automatic updates after transactions were fixed. Next, we were always looking at the features that delivered 'market fit', in other words, that solved pressing problems for our customers. Finally, the team prioritized optimizing the app to increase uptake. To do this we kept a daily review of just who our customers were and how they used the app. Once we spotted a trend, we quickly introduced new features or experiences to capitalize on the preference.

Try as we might to be treated as an individual entity, it was inevitable that people would always seek to compare us to the other challenger banks, and in particular Monzo. Since there was little we could do to prevent this, I decided to just go with it and embrace it for the advantages it brought. As an example, one of the early pieces of feedback on the app directly compared each of our features with Monzo. Under the 'positives' it included such things as our good product support and live chat, the easy set-up, and 'real bank' features such as direct debits and standing orders. Under the 'negatives', our user was critical of the speed of our card dispatch, and lack of a social forum. As a rule, I always focussed on the criticisms, since this was the stuff we needed to get right.

12. *Test, Retest and Pivot*

If you were to imagine the movie version of a digital entrepreneur's journey, the storyline might follow an uplifting narrative of one person bravely taking on the world to achieve their vision. The belief in the product/service is so powerful that the star of the show powers through, relentlessly seeing off all obstacles to achieve the goal. There would, of course, be a happy ending, where the entrepreneur's determination that their idea is better than anything, ever, is proved to be 100 per cent correct and all the naysayers have to eat their words.

It's a lovely story but, however successful any entrepreneur ever eventually proves to be, this narrative will always remain a fiction. There is never a triumphant denouement, where you know for sure you've succeeded. There is always, always something else to do. You can't stand still and benignly watch your products bask in all the glory. The moment any entrepreneur does that, their dream is over. There will always be others looking at a way to make a better version of what you've already done, and eventually someone, somewhere *will* succeed.

As a matter of necessity, all digital products are constantly under review. It is inevitable that they'll change from where they started, often markedly. In fact, in the digital world no company has ever made its name with the exact business model it started out with. Some have changed their strategy so much as to be virtually unrecognizable from the business they were initially. YouTube started life as a dating app, Groupon was a charitable platform and Slack, one of the biggest names in professional chat, was once a video game called Glitch.

Speak with any successful digital entrepreneur and they'll eulogize the importance of continually testing, retesting and refining their product. And rightly so. The feedback that is gained from each new iteration uncovers valuable pointers to correct your course, fix a flaw, or fulfil a previously unrecognized need.

When you've put your life, and most likely life savings, into an idea, it is not easy to change. It's perfectly understandable to feel protective of a vision, or to resist when being told that something about it isn't working. It's essential to learn to listen to feedback, though, and then implement it, even if it means discarding bits of the model you really, really like.

There are two options as to how you interpret and use feedback. The most drastic action is to pivot. This is what needs to happen when it becomes clear that little or no progress is being made. In other words if, following the test, test and retest process, the world is telling you that you had better go left, go left. Rather than making incremental improvements as you stoically travel straight ahead, you most likely need to go back to the drawing board and revisit the original idea. This is a radical course of action that may well involve the adoption of an entirely new strategy/idea/business model. The good news is, unless you are an extremely long way off track, pivoting is quite rare.

The alternative, indeed the most common form of action, and the one Starling has pursued, is to take the user views and make incremental improvements to an existing product. Unlike pivoting, this means persevering with the original idea, with each new iteration representing a progression of the last one. The product you put out for the next stage of feedback will still be recognizably based on the previous version, but with a number of small updates or changes. The idea is that each day you will have moved closer and closer to the best version of your product (a state you, of course, never reach). Unless the early feedback to your idea is overwhelmingly negative, this is always the preferred strategy.

The sort of changes that might be expected to result from the 'persevere' process would be tweaks to how customers use the product, based on their views on which features they liked or disliked. The issues could centre around anything from the number of steps taken to make a payment to the font used, to the most effective methods to convert visitors to the site into paying customers.

There is a skill to understanding feedback and responding to it. We are all individuals. Get a group of people in one room and there will be all manner of opinions and preferences. Which ones do you listen to and which ones do you ignore? If you are not selective and decide to revise your product in line with every piece of advice you get, you may end up with something that appeals to no one. You certainly don't want to be in a position where you are buffeted from one place to the next with no firm direction. My general rule of thumb is to hang on until I have heard the same comment at least a few times before examining whether or not it means a change has to be made. You are dealing with humans, after all. Someone could slam your product simply because they're having a terrible day and just want to vent forth about something.

Aside from clearing up any bugs we found, or that were reported to us, the changes Starling needed to make were all incremental. While our launch version already included a much wider range of features than the digital apps offered by traditional banks, we've continually added new ones. Thus, while the app's Marketplace section was there from the start, we have been bringing in new partners all the time. Each partner has to be fully evaluated before this can happen, to make sure they are suitable, so it is an intense process. We also took steps to pave the way for Starling to offer customers the facility to pay in either pounds or euros, a service that was launched in October 2019. No additional card is required, just switch between currencies in the app. We also launched a dedicated euro facility within the main app, which is handy for customers who are paid in euros, or who own property in Europe, or run a business and need to pay European suppliers.

One of the ongoing concerns highlighted by some customers is the need to deposit cash or cheques. To assist them in this Starling became the first mobile bank to partner with the Post Office, so customers can pay in or withdraw from any Post Office branch. It's a valuable service for many, at a time when some communities no longer have any bank branches close by.

While all these tweaks and innovations have been going on, I've focussed hard on retaining that start-up zeal that powered Starling to its launch, often against impossible odds. I've worked in big corporations and I know how easy it is for complacency to slip in. Before you know it, everything has slowed to a snail's pace, innovation has become a thing of the past and anything challenging is ignored. I never want that to happen to Starling. Right now, I think we're achieving our goal of continuing to think like a start-up and that's very well illustrated with the story behind Starling's business account, which is another innovation we introduced after the initial launch.

Developing a business account was always very much on the radar for Starling. It's the obvious progression when it comes to making money so much more transparent for all customers. An innovative digital business bank service, one that mimicked many of the most successful features of a Starling current account and more, would help companies stay on top of their finances, any time, anywhere – which is, of course, an essential element in running a successful business. We opened our first business accounts for sole traders in March 2018, less than a year after going public with our current accounts. The business accounts offered all the innovations our customers were coming to expect from a digital challenger, such as no monthly fees, in-app international money transfers, a set-up process that took just minutes and a new range of business-orientated Marketplace partners. Again, we were not intending to stand still. From the off, we had big ambitions to expand the business product, opening it up for larger businesses, limited companies and partnerships, as well as offering a wide range of additional features. However, we'd made a good start. Then something happened to really concentrate our minds. That something was the £775 million RBS fund which I mentioned in chapter one.

The fund was what had emerged after the Edinburgh-based bank failed to sell off Williams & Glyn to meet the measures brought in by the EU and European Central Bank to reverse all the mega mergers that had characterized the banking industry prior to the financial crisis. After spending millions on the unsuccessful sale, RBS suggested the alternative measure of a new fund to even the playing field and help other banks compete more effectively. The proposal was accepted and the Capability Innovation Fund (CIF) was born. An independent body called Banking Competition Remedies (BCR) was formed to implement the process.

News of the CIF emerged in May 2018, just weeks after Starling had launched its first business account. Details on the grant were thin on the ground to begin with. BCR were keeping their powder dry for the big announcement that was planned for September, where they would outline the entry criteria. At that stage, all we knew was that there was a significant amount of money on the table and that it was put there to encourage greater competition in business banking. I was, however, certain of one thing: I wanted one of those grants. Even as I began to formulate a plan in my head, I already suspected what my colleagues would say – that we were too far off being the sort of business bank that could apply for a grant of this scale. I was absolutely certain that the second-tier high-street banks, who were the most likely recipients of the grants, wouldn't give us a second thought as a possible contender either. The answer, I decided, was staring us in the face: we needed to be a big enough player in business banking to apply for the grant and be taken seriously.

I can still remember the ashen faces of some members of the team when I outlined the plan.

'Our business current account has to be as big as the rest by the closing date for the grants,' I told them.

This was a pretty tall order by any measure. With the fund due to be launched later in the year, the deadline for applications was months away. Beefing up our business offering was not as simple as saying, 'Well, we have sole trader accounts, let's just open up the Starling business account to large businesses.' Business accounts have an entirely different set of criteria to adhere to. First and foremost, a bank needs to check that the person opening the account is the registered legal owner of the business they are opening an account for. Then there is the need to safely give multiple sources access to the account, whether it is the in-house book-keeper or an external accountancy service. There were a lot more nuances besides. In fact, the best way to describe a business account is 'a current account with a lot of extras'. An awful lot of extras.

The obvious question to ask at this stage was how big Starling's business account needed to be if we were to be considered a credible contender. For some reason, I plucked the number of 30,000 business banking accounts out of thin air. My team looked even more ashen when I announced the target figure that I wanted to be in place by Christmas 2018, at the latest. To their credit, not a single one of them tried to dissuade me. Certainly no one mentioned that it took Starling almost twelve months to build up that number of current account customers. There had been a whole lot of development and marketing groundwork done in the months and years before that too. Now, we had less than seven months to reach that figure and we had not even expanded the initial version of our business account yet.

One of the things I love most about fintech as compared with big business is that no one is ever afraid to try the impossible. No one wasted time telling me why this was a preposterous idea, or that it couldn't be done, or that I was aiming too high. The team just got their heads down and started to work out how they were going to deliver a Starling business bank that met the very high standards of our current account and which would be able to attract 30,000 customers from businesses of all shapes and sizes before the end of 2018. There were lots of questions from the team, yes, but they all centred around the proposed features of the account.

In the weeks that followed, we steadily upgraded our business account, opening it up to a wider range of businesses and offering a larger bouquet of features. We also set about marketing it hard to bring in the tens of thousands of customers we needed. To our delight, businesses responded very positively and the number of account openings began to exceed our already quite lofty aspirations.

It wasn't until September that we knew exactly what it was that we would be applying for. BCR had decided to divide the grants into four different pools: Pool A focussed on banks that were offering to build 'more advanced business current account offerings and ancillary products for SMEs [small- and medium-sized enterprises]'; Pool B was dedicated to modernizing existing business current account offerings; Pool C looked towards expansion of business applications for SMEs such as lending, or payment services; Pool D was for businesses that could provide financial technology of relevance to SMEs. The size of each pool differed considerably. Pool A, for example, contained three grants of £120 million, £100 million and £60 million while Pool D was offering five grants of £5 million each. The clear expectation was that established, 'second-tier', high-street banks such as TSB, Santander et al. would go for the big Pool A grants, while smaller players would look towards Pools C and D. Pool B, with its one £50 million grant and two £15 million grants, would most likely attract the next layer down of established banks, or the second-tier ones who missed out on Pool A. Pool A was definitely the hot ticket and the one I firmly set our sights on.

Following the BCR 'information event' of 27 September, which was held in the Salisbury Wing Theatre at the National Gallery, the business pages of the papers were filled with news and speculation about the runners and riders for the generous CIF grants. I couldn't help noticing that Starling was hardly mentioned at all. In fact, despite the success of the Starling Business Bank campaign and the fact that our account-opening numbers continued to tick up nicely, no one seemed to be giving us a second glance. The *Telegraph* devoted a double-page spread to the banks competing for grants, featuring a giant roulette wheel showing all the possible winners. Again, we barely warranted a mention. I had to smile when I saw the newspaper's number-one tip for the big £120 million payout from Pool A. It was CYBG, led by David Duffy, my boss during my previous job at AIB. CYBG was formed out of a merger of the Clydesdale Bank, Yorkshire Bank and the digital banking service, and David had joined in June 2015. For me, this upped the ante even more. I have always been a hugely competitive person and I just had to win this face-off. The other hot tips were TSB, Metro Bank, Co-op and Santander.

The hotly tipped contenders were not shy in shouting about their prospects either. CYBG included details of their CIF bid in their annual report, declaring that they would be spending millions of pounds perfecting their application. The language coming out of TSB and Santander was unequivocal too. They each fully expected to come away with the £120 million grant, or at the very least the second-place grant of £100 million. I confess that whenever I saw the various pronouncements in the press, I wanted to shout. In my view, most of the established business banks had barely changed their offerings in decades. What was the point of giving them millions of pounds to innovate now? They'd had the benefit of hundreds of millions for years and yet hardly had a track record. How would an additional cash injection make a difference now, just because it was a grant? Starling's business account was new, yes, but we had already introduced a whole host of interesting and helpful innovations. Not least among them was the opportunity to open an account in seconds. In the business environment, where bureaucracy is a constant bugbear, the value of this feature could not be overestimated.

One thing I knew I had on my side was confidence. We were, by now, well into our next round of raising investment money and I often received quizzical looks from potential investors when I mentioned during our pitch that we were going to win this £120 million, or £100 million, grant (subtext: this woman is crazy!). It wasn't just bluff and bluster, though; I was convinced that my confidence was entirely justified. The stated purpose of the grant was to introduce new competition to an outdated and stale market. If the process was at all vigorous, as it should be, then Starling was the obvious winner.

Actions speak louder than words, so there was nothing for

it but to get my head down and make sure the Starling bid was the best one. I did not have millions spare to spend on perfecting our application, so I went back to square one and did what any ambitious entrepreneur should do: I got help for nothing. Or certainly nothing up front. I went back to the team I had worked with at PwC and persuaded them to assist me on a contingent basis once more. I would only pay them if we were successful. To their immense credit, they agreed and put a whole team on it. They obviously thought that since I had come through last time, I would most probably do so again.

As so often happens with these things, there were one or two bumps in the road. One of the worst was when I found out the names of the BCR board members who would be deciding on the grant allocation. One of them was Aidene Walsh. Aidene, the former CEO of The Fairbanking Foundation, had worked with me as a consultant in the early days of Starling. Although she was one of four board members, I did not want there to be accusations of unfairness, or vested interests. I immediately wrote to the BCR to declare the potential conflict. Fortunately, they responded by saying (a) they already knew and (b) that they had processes in place, so it was not an issue. (This did not prevent my competitors crying foul, both ahead of the grant awards and for a long while after.)

The date we were all working towards was 31 December 2018, when the fund closed for applications. By this stage we had met and exceeded our 30,000 business account openings, and were signing up a huge number each day, so full credit to the Starling team. I thought our application was pretty brilliant by the time it was finished too, if I do say so myself. The final few touches were all a bit tense as we toiled away in the office in the run-up to Christmas. Every detail had to be just so. We read and reread the criteria, just so we didn't make any silly mistakes and blow it at the last moment. We discovered at the eleventh hour that there was a complete ban on any font size in the submission being below 10pt. When we realized that some of our slides were at 9pt, we had to go back and change each one. Oddly, the final process of the submission was a tool featuring two buttons. One was to submit the application, the other was to say you didn't want to apply. If you accidentally clicked the 'do not want to apply' option, your entire application was null and void and you were out of the game. I'm not sure who decided that this button was a necessary addition to end the remarkably detailed online form, but it gave us pause for thought during the end stages. It was certainly a heart-stopping moment as our cursor hovered above the submission keys.

Once it was filed, there was little we could do but wait until 21 February 2019, when the Pool A awards were to be announced. After weeks and months of focus on this event, and of making sure our business bank account was up to scratch (or indeed up to better than scratch), the last few weeks in the run-up to receiving the results of all that hard work were agonizing. All we could do was wait. Partly to pass the time and partly to distract ourselves, our discussions turned to how we'd receive the news. BCR had decided to distribute the results to the successful parties via email the evening before the press was informed on 22 February. We resolved that we'd rather not be in the office when it landed. Everyone would inevitably be on tenterhooks and would watch us intently for our reaction. If it was bad news, we wanted time to process it, find a way to regroup and then present a positive front to the people at Starling who had worked so hard on it. Instead, we decided that a handful of people on the senior team would take up residence in a conference room in a hotel around the corner to hear our fate.

The new location didn't resolve all our problems. As we nervously settled down to wait, a lively discussion ensued about who would open the email and then how they would tell the others. Should we stand behind Alan Chandler, the elected email opener, and read over his shoulder? Or remain in our seats as he read it out? We all knew it would be agonizing if he read it really slowly.

Thank you for your application to the BCR grant. As you will understand, there have been a number of really strong submissions and . . .

All anyone wanted to know was, was it yes, or no? We were still going around and around the logistics when Alan shouted out that the email had landed. All our much-discussed but never-agreed-upon plans collapsed as we crowded around his laptop. We'd got it! We'd got £100 million in the Pool A fund. The largest grant of £120 million went to Metro Bank, which had made the powerful offer of a three-to-one multiplier. In other words, for every pound of grant they won, the bank pledged to invest two more of their own. Meanwhile, a partnership between ClearBank and Tide scooped the £60 million. The thirteen unsuccessful applicants included CYBG, TSB, Co-op Bank and Handelsbanken (Santander had pulled out at an earlier stage).

It was a huge boost to Starling Bank and its business bank offering, and not just in financial terms. It was also a big lesson in perseverance. What later emerged was that, while many second-tier banks had gone all out for the £120 million and £100 million funds, many did not bother to cover all the bases by putting in the separate applications required for the £60 million. Despite spending a great deal of money on the bids, others had decided that there was no point going for the smallest fund, even though £60 million is a significant sum by any measure. Starling certainly applied for all three and, while we were delighted with the £100 million, we would have been very pleased indeed to have come away with the smaller sum too. As it was, there were very few submissions for the £60 million, leaving the way open for ClearBank and its partner Tide, two banks that were comparatively little known at the time.

There is a clear lesson to be learned here. There are numerous grants available, in particular for tech businesses, and start-ups have nothing to lose by applying for as many of them as possible. In the same year as the Capability Innovation Fund was being run, Nesta, a UK-based innovation foundation, allocated a £2.5 million fund to companies who could help improve the banking experience for small businesses. The foundation, which was launched to advance innovation across a range of sectors, had the goal of encouraging companies to make full use of open banking APIs and this fund was a great way to draw attention to it. It also won backing from some of the UK's largest providers of SME banking, including Barclays, HSBC and Lloyds Banking Group. Grant opportunities like this are appearing all the time. Indeed, I am aware of a number of hugely successful fintechs that have made a strategy out of applying for and winning grants. A few million here, or £250,000 there, can make a significant impact on any business's growth plans. The £100 million has certainly been a valuable blast of fresh air when it comes to realizing the many plans we have for Starling's business account.

Conclusion

I've been to a fair few awards ceremonies over the years. While I never want to be rude, I often arrive late and leave early. I'll press the flesh, eat the dinner and then quietly slip away before the awards ceremony proper gets underway. I might even say I have an urgent phone call to make. Most of the time it goes completely unnoticed.

This was exactly my plan for the Card and Payments Awards 2018, which were being held at London's Grosvenor House on 1 February, just nine months after Starling Bank launched its current account. To be fair, there was (as always) a huge amount going on back at Starling, so I had a genuine reason for keeping my visit to the event brief. I was seated at a pleasant table filled with people in the banking industry I had met over the years, so it was good to catch up. Everyone seemed very keen to know how Starling was getting on now its app was well and truly in the public domain. I was pleased to tell them we were signing up a couple of thousand customers a week and that figure was climbing sharply. I pretended not to see the envious looks from some of my traditional banking colleagues.

Out of the corner of my eye I saw the stage being prepared for the awards. Finding a natural break in the conversation, I said that I must just nip out to deal with something important and got up to go.

It's never easy making your way across a room filled with crowded tables at an awards ceremony. This time it was even harder. As I weaved across the large room, squeezing myself between casually slung back chairs, people kept stopping me to say hello.

'Anne! How are you?'

'How is it going with Starling?'

'Love what you are doing with your app.'

I couldn't help noticing that the people approaching me were all the great and the good of banking and finance. Two or three years ago, when I was knocking on doors and asking for help in starting this exciting new venture, most of them didn't want to know. Now it seemed that digital banks were in favour.

Progress was slow as I paused, shook hands, exchanged pleasantries and moved on, often with a cheery agreement to 'get in touch' and 'catch up' shortly. By the time I reached the grand sweeping staircase the lights had been lowered and the compère had already started speaking. I was only half listening as I quietly climbed the stairs.

How odd, I thought, as I gradually tuned into a speech which was being made on stage behind me. The lady speaker seemed to be talking about a woman who had built a bank from scratch with the aim of making 'money management as streamlined as possible'. I vaguely heard her mention that this person had come up against 'a number of barriers along the way, not least lack of support from her peers'.

'Yet with huge amounts of fortitude and resolve, she drove the team at the bank to the success of today.'

For a moment I racked my brain to think who else in the business had had such a tough time. I felt sure I knew pretty much everything that was going on in my sector. How had I missed someone who had such persistence? And a woman too. That was sadly still unusual.

Then the penny dropped. It was me she was talking about.

I had reached the balcony by now and swung round in time to see many heads in the room swivelling left and right as though to see where I had got to. I started back down the steps, my head spinning with a heady mixture of shock, surprise and delight.

'This person is widely considered to be a role model for women in payments, positively encouraging more women to pursue senior positions,' the lady continued as I made my way towards the stage, to the sounds of claps and cheers from my peers. I saw now that it was Charlotte Duerden, the vice-president and general manager of American Express's UK Consumer Cards and International Currency Cards, who was speaking.

'Her entrepreneurial spirit and relentless strength of character have seen her succeed when she has struggled with gaining funding and credibility,' she continued. 'Anne has big expansion plans for the business with a strong team behind her. This award hopefully goes some way to recognizing her achievements of the last few years.'

I reached the foot of the stairs just as she announced that Anne Boden had been honoured with an Industry Achievement Award.

Obviously, I hadn't prepared an acceptance speech. It was a complete surprise. But, even so, I wanted to say something. Instinctively, I felt it was more than just a good moment for me and indeed Starling, it was also a step in the right direction for the industry as a whole.

'I am honoured to accept this award for Starling Bank,' I began, stepping behind the podium and getting closer to the microphone, my mind racing to find the right form of words. 'Starling Bank set out to change financial services for ever. We want to actually put right the wrongs of the past and put a lot of these people, who work so earnestly every day of their working lives for consumers, back in a place they deserve.

'We, as an industry, need to be centre stage, fighting for consumers and fighting for businesses. When I started in the banking industry, thirty-odd years ago, I was proud to be a banker. Today, I am back in that place.

'We are going to change the banking industry, the card industry and the payment industry and make it a place that we deserve. We have the courage to actually change banking for ever.'

It was a really special moment for me, and not just because I was getting a gong. I felt it was recognition for all that had been achieved in such a short space of time and often against crippling odds.

Starling isn't just about me. It is staffed by an incredible team of people, many of whom have not just contributed a great deal to our success but also won awards themselves. Since then, Starling has won numerous accolades. We've been named Best Current Account and Best Business Account (twice each) at the British Banking Awards. The Smart Money People Awards has voted us Best British Bank for three consecutive years and we have become a *Which?* recommended supplier. Starling is a member of the Tech Nation's Future Fifty cohort for 2019 and *Forbes* named us on their World's Best Bank List. FStech declared us 'consumer finance product of the year' while to AltFi we were the 'digital bank of the year'. I have also been named Tech CEO of the year in 2019, which is something I am really proud of. While I have also won a clutch of 'women in business' awards, it is good to be judged against the entire industry, and not on the grounds of my gender.

We've also had plenty of support from investors. To date, Starling has raised £263 million in funding. This includes the £60 million raised in a Series C round led by Merian Global Investors, including Merian Chrysalis, in February 2019. At the same time, our original investor, Harald McPike, put in a further £15 million.

It's hard to believe that just six years ago, when Starling

appeared on the scene with the radical idea of reinventing banking, barely anyone knew anything about fintech. The growth in public recognition of our brand is testament to how far we have come on this front. In November 2019, 38 per cent of adults in Great Britain were aware of Starling Bank, up from 12 per cent in December 2018 and 8 per cent in September 2018. In London, the figure stood at 47 per cent. Nearly a quarter (24 per cent) of British small businesses were aware of the Starling brand. By the time you read this, I fully expect those numbers to have been boosted considerably after our multimillion-pound television advertising campaign airs. We hit our target of one million accounts opened in November 2019.

I won't say that our success has been without its challenges. There is certainly another side to Starling and the other challenger banks coming out of the shadows, which is not as enjoyable as seeing our ideas finally realized. The founders of all the main players are now firmly in the public eye. We are regularly quoted in the media and everything we do is picked over very publicly. This is great when we launch fantastic new products, or announce a wave of new people signing up to accounts, but not so comfortable when we make mistakes. There is no longer any room for manoeuvre. We have lost a lot of that early start-up freedom to move fast and break stuff in a bid to keep making things better. I should add that we have always had fewer opportunities to break stuff than the average start-up, because the banking sector is, quite rightly, highly regulated. We had to meet extremely high standards of operation from the off, or we'd never have been awarded a licence. However, we've never been afraid to push things as far as we could in our mission to offer our customers the best possible experience. Now, though, the days when we could make any sort of mistake and then adopt the fallback position of saying that we were 'still figuring out strategy' are long behind us. Not only are customers, the media and big investors watching, they are quite rightly very unforgiving if we fail to live up to our promises. I am occasionally asked to sit on Treasury Select Committees as a representative of a bank that is both resilient and reliable. Even as I do so, I am fully aware that there may well be one day when I am on the defensive. I need to be prepared for that.

Someone from the start-up world once told me: when the world thinks you are doing well then you are probably not. This works the other way round too. The point is, there is never room for complacency. Success and growth are never linear either. There will be very good days and there will be very bad days. All start-ups will go through periods of bad press, even if they have not done anything particularly wrong. In December 2018 we had a situation where what at first seemed like a molehill grew into a mountain in a matter of hours. A customer complained on Twitter that Starling 'does not take security seriously' after we sent an image of his passport photo page to him via an internet link contained in an email. Despite our assurances that the URL was tokenized, which meant it would be unguessable to outsiders and others would have been unable to access the information unless the link had been shared with them, the story rapidly grew legs. After the press gleefully picked over it, we announced a review of how Starling stores sensitive information, but even then it took time to die down. Our competitors have also had their moments in the spotlight. Monzo has been criticized for loaning customers money to buy its own shares and for unwittingly exposing customer information to unauthorized staff. It also drew flak for axing its Monzo Plus premium bank account just five months after it launched, admitting it was not 'the best it could be'. Revolut, another mobile-based current account, which launched after Starling, came under fire for 'single-shaming' in its promotions and for expecting staff to work weekends and well into the night. The point in each case is that the media's response to any perceived shortcoming can be swift and brutal. We all need to be prepared for it and to react quickly. The good thing (if there is a good side to this challenge) is that now Starling is no longer a start-up, we have plenty of positive things to talk about too. We've got lots of pithy soundbites about our business which we push home at every opportunity, even during the tough conversations. We're also sure to follow all the relevant journalists and opinion formers on Twitter, so when a storm is on its way, we know about it as early as possible.

Often, the negative exposure is not based on anything we've done wrong. It's a sign of how far Starling has come that every time a senior figure leaves the bank, it is always reported in the press. I won't comment on the usual terrible puns on our company name, where 'flying the roost', or 'taking flight' appear with predictable regularity. I will also dwell only briefly on what feels like a certain amount of sexism in the coverage. I detect an undercurrent of prejudice against female bosses, as each time someone goes it is written up as though there has been some sort of personal argument based on strategic differences. Female bosses suffer from boiled-egg syndrome. We're either too hard or too soft, but never quite right. I don't think male bosses ever endure anything close to this level of scrutiny.

The truth is, in any start-up, whoever founds it, the reality is more nuanced. It is the nature of the beast that any start-up team is transient. All being well, things will move quickly. It is inevitable that some people who were 100 per cent perfect for one part of the journey will not be as suited to the next stage. It can be heartbreaking to part company with loyal members of the team who have not put a foot wrong in getting things off the ground, but who simply don't have the right skills or experience for the high-growth developmental phase. Just as you recruited each person for their very specific set of skills, when those skill requirements change, often the person will need to change too. As a founder, this means you will have to have difficult conversations and you will need to part company with people to whom you have grown very close as you navigate this extraordinary journey. As all founders will come to learn, titles and promotions that you prioritize today will not seem so relevant or prudent tomorrow. But you have to make such appointments nonetheless, partly because with a start-up you can never be completely sure that there will be a tomorrow.

It is a sad fact of start-up life that people will lose out as the business restructures to facilitate growth. One example was when I realized that we had grown to such an extent that I now had direct reports well into the double digits. It was completely unmanageable. The solution, which made perfect business sense, was to put in new divisions with new line managers. However, some of my reports inevitably felt sidelined by the changes. Those who were on the original team particularly, and understandably, resented being layered in this manner. Some even felt that, since they were no longer reporting at the top level, they needed to leave. Losing good people is something I will never get used to, but the important thing is to make sure they are well looked after financially and don't lose out.

It'll happen the other way too. Some of those wonderful, awesomely talented people who are attracted to a forward-thinking start-up will want to move on to the next thing entirely of their own volition. Often this is because other businesses have seen the incredible things our team members have achieved and want some of that magic for themselves. Now that Starling is successful, we've seen many people tempted away with offers of double or even quadruple their salaries. It's hard to turn that sort of incentive down or question their motivations. Alternatively, people also move on because they feel they have run out of road with your business. While I may have committed my life to achieving my goal of turning my idea into a successful business, their number-one goal is, understandably, themselves. They want to improve their career and their position in life. Starling may simply not have what they are looking for in the next stage of their career.

It can be tough saying goodbye to people you've worked with. All you can do is accept it, be grateful for the huge value that they have brought you and the rest of the team and wish them well. Not every departure is unavoidable. To keep people around as long as they are needed, you have to make sure they love their jobs. It's also useful to consider some sort of employee share scheme that will encourage people to stay for a certain number of years. My intention is to give 10 per cent of Starling to employees. Of course, this adds a layer of pressure for me to make the next generation of Starlings rich, rather than just *hopeful* of riches. But, it does ensure we are all in it together.

I am acutely aware that the way I communicate with my team has changed completely since the Starling adventure began. In the early days I used to sit in the middle of the room, working on my laptop. New recruits were handed a MacBook Pro and told to get on with it. 'Build a banking app. We need to launch asap. If you have any questions, ask Anne. She's that lady in the middle of the room.' Today, Starling is a very different organization from what it was when our tradition of Wednesday lunches first began and we used to nip round the corner for a plate of bacon sarnies. At the time of writing, we are preparing for our numbers to surpass a thousand. In fact, we have just opened two large offices outside London. The new

Starling Southampton office, which has a plum position on the marina, is a million miles away from the various, less-than-glamorous places we occupied or squatted in during the early days. Housing 150 new Starlings, mainly working in engineering, customer service and operations, it looks every inch the modern fintech with its open-plan setting, along with work booths and fantastic facilities (as well as an incredible maritime view). Our Cardiff office opened in March 2020, welcoming 400 new Starlings in our data science, fraud and customer services teams. I felt very proud to be returning to the country of my birth and ensuring that the exciting growth in fintech is not confined to London. This is just the start of our growth though. We already have a skeleton team in an office in Dublin, and in the not too distant future we'll be expanding into continental Europe, with bases in the Netherlands, France and Germany. Aside from all the other logistical and procedural challenges this represents, the growth also tests how the culture of Starling persists.

I am still deeply reluctant to produce culture decks* to spread the word about 'how we do things around here'. I'm keener to give people the physical and mental space to work out how they are comfortable working, whether they are introvert and prefer to be alone and contemplative, or extrovert and like working in noisy groups. As long as everyone understands the core message that the customer experience comes first, everything else builds from there. We have a few rules, such as a ban on people doing PowerPoint presentations for each other internally. I think everyone sees it for what it is – symbolic avoidance of doing things that waste time or replace the real work of running the bank for the optimum benefit of our customers.

* A short document that outlines how a company operates and what it stands for.

Our recruitment needs have changed entirely too. Rather than seeking out people who can be flexible across a number of functions, we now look for individuals who are the best in their field at specific roles. This in itself presents another learning curve in terms of hiring, managing and delegating. There is also an issue that the battlefield for talent is ever more intense in a successful sector like fintech. It's hard to attract the right people and hard to hang on to them too. At the same time, any growth in staff needs to be in line with cash flow. There is a delicate balance between the pace at which a company expands and the number of people employed to manage that expansion. Get it wrong and you will run out of money very quickly.

With rapid growth comes the demand for more funding to support that growth. Despite our track record, each funding round has been tough. I should say, though, they are tough for other reasons than before. By this latest stage, Starling was up and running with tens of thousands of customers, and more signing up each day. Our figures were no longer numbers on a spreadsheet, predicting the growth of the UK's first ever mobile bank. We had credible data about how customers signed up with us, how much money they entrusted with the bank and how that money performed day to day. Lots of data.

The Starling team that went out to seek our most recent round of investment was much larger. As well as me there was Declan Ferguson, the chief strategy officer, and John Mountain, the chief information officer. Accompanying us on our so-called 'road show' around Britain and the US were two executives from JP Morgan. We discovered this time around that many more doors were open to us and we did over forty pitches, which was pretty arduous by any measure, although the offices we were seen in were a little larger than before, possibly to mark our 'established' status. After each meeting the pair from JP Morgan would carefully coach us on what to say at the next, even down to what jokes to tell.

Not every potential investor 'got' Starling, which in their eyes seemed to be such an unusual business, but many more did. Some of the reasons that we were turned down were just risible. One billionaire investor who sallied forth into Starling's offices with an entire entourage, complete with his wife sporting a very lavish fur coat, turned us down for the most extraordinary reason. Apparently, I did not grovel enough.

In the end our road show was hugely successful and, ironically, we received investment from Merian Global Investors, one of the first organizations we'd seen in London before leaving for the US. Merian are not VCs at all but an asset management company and, in particular, a crossover investor. They normally invest in public markets, but have a strategy for crossing over into the private markets so they can get greater exposure to companies prior to an IPO. I'd got on very well with Richard Watts, the manager of Merian's UK Mid Cap fund, who was also from Wales. We had a lot in common, thanks to our background, confirming my long-held view that investors generally invest in people with whom they can empathize. Ironically, after our first meeting with Merian, to kick off the road show, John had said, 'Why don't we just go with them?' We were encouraged to continue the road show as it was not considered a good idea to go with the first offer, but as it turned out, that is exactly what we did.

But what of our goal to disrupt banking? I did, after all, start out with the intention of transforming the way everyone saw the once stale, unfriendly world of banking. I wanted to pioneer a new era of customer focus. How did we do? Aside from our growing customer numbers, there is surely one acid test of our success in this direction: the reaction from traditional banks. In the early days, they completely ignored what any of the challenger banks were doing. They barely seemed to give us a second glance as one after the other of us launched. Interestingly, as I noted in the previous chapter, we were still entirely under the radar when we applied for the BCR grant in December 2018, more than a year and a half after we first launched.

Today, this has most definitely changed. Starling and our rival challenger banks are without a doubt on the radar of the established banks, who are clearly watching our every move and innovation like hawks. As any readers who are still with a mainstream bank will recognize, over the past year banking apps across the board have seen all sorts of improvements. It's now possible to log onto some banking apps using face ID. Other apps offer the facility for customers to see all their bank accounts on a single app, including those of rival banks. Visual representations of spending patterns, where bank customers can instantly see how much is going out and on what, are becoming more mainstream. Granted, these are all things that Starling has been offering since launch, but welcome to the party, as they say. The more the merrier. The main beneficiaries are customers, so that's fine with me.

Of course, while big banks are playing catch-up, we're innovating all the time, staying one, two, or several steps ahead. We can't be complacent though, since major banks still have far deeper pockets than we do. Our one big advantage here is the same as the one we've had from the very beginning: we are fleet of foot. Traditional banks are still reliant on outdated technology, bolting new tech onto old systems. They will never be able to move as fast as we can.

It would be easy to imagine that now the established banks have woken up, the obvious response would be to start again and do what we did. They could build their tech from scratch and use the latest APIs to create something that would be a worthy rival to the speeding challengers. Then, once they had a credible digital banking product, they could migrate their millions of customers over to the new service. Voilà! Bye bye challengers. I can tell you now, this is never going to happen. Let me explain why.

You might perhaps remember the TSB IT fiasco of April 2018? You might even have been one of the 1.9 million customers who were locked out of their accounts. The debacle had its roots in the sale of TSB from Lloyds Banking Group to Spanish bank Sabadell. There needed to be an accompanying IT upgrade, so the records and accounts of 5.2 million customers could be migrated to Sabadell. TSB warned all its customers in advance that there would be some disruption to services such as online banking and money transfers, but it would be minimal. At 4 p.m. on Friday 20 April, someone pressed the button to begin the changeover process.

It wasn't long before customers began to see the disruption was anything but minimal. Some reported accounts showing the wrong balances, while others who logged in could see accounts belonging to other customers entirely. In the chaos that followed, TSB made one PR gaffe after the other, claiming that it had 'successfully completed' the technology migration when it was plain this was not the case. Panicked customers were unable to get through to the jammed helplines as stopped payments caused chaos in their lives. It emerged that TSB turned down the offer of help from its previous owner Lloyds, which got in touch at the beginning of the crisis. One month on, some customers were still locked out of their accounts. The problem cost the bank £350 million to fix, but the actual cost to its reputation cannot be quantified. Certainly, it lost 80,000 accounts in the immediate six months following the botched switch.

So, put yourself in the shoes of the CEO of Big Battleship Bank. Your amazing IT department has been working hard for months, perfecting your amazing new digital banking service. It's brilliant, they assure you. It does everything the challenger banks do, and more. Now, ask yourself this: are you prepared to push the button and migrate all your customers to this new service? Even if you are feeling particularly courageous, and have the utmost faith in the skills of your team, there is one more aspect to consider. Since the financial crisis of 2008, it is now a criminal offence to make such a colossal mistake with your customers' money. Steering a battleship while incompetent is a huge, potentially career-ending, issue. Who would be prepared to take that sort of risk?

With their hands tied, established banks have turned to plan B. In November 2019, RBS launched the mobile-focussed Bó brand after apparently trying and failing to buy Monzo two years earlier. Bó, which boasts a bright yellow payment card, is billed as a 'new breed' of financial institution, targeting customers with tight budgets who want to take control of their spending. It's the first in what is expected to be a wave of new mobile products introduced by established banks. The new digital apps will be owned by their larger parent, but operated separately.*

Do we fear the competition? Not really. We're far more interested in looking forward, to see where we can innovate next, rather than backwards to check on how mainstream banks are getting on. I still have tremendous respect for the people who work in high-street banks, who are generally highly intelligent and committed to doing a good job. If pressed, though, I'd probably say that however much established banks *pretend* to be start-ups, which is what they are clearly doing, they will

---

* Bó was unexpectedly wound down in May 2020.

never have that all-important start-up mentality. It's impossible to have that urgency and creativity if you have to answer to a larger parent company. It doesn't matter how separate these new divisions are, they will still be subject to the inevitable committees and discussions that continue to slow down the organizations that have invested in them. More importantly, if you are starting a new digital bank today, you are six years behind the curve. It's too late to jump into the market with something new and innovative. That happened six years ago. Six months is a lifetime in fintech. Six years feels like a different century.

It's not easy to build a truly innovative app either; it takes time and a very talented team. I'm pretty confident that the new generation of big-bank small-bank apps will not have the same number of features as the challengers', not least because they are starting from a point so far behind us. Certainly, I have seen no evidence so far of anything very innovative, or indeed new at all. All of this may sound like I fear change. Or that I worry about major banks catching up. I don't. In fact, as per my initial aim of offering customers a truly rewarding banking experience, I am delighted with each new improvement, however incremental. However, my sincere view is, it is the challengers that will always be the most innovative and will, therefore, offer the best choice. Big banks may well be able to copy everything the start-ups do, but they will never get close to imitating our cost base.

What I do need to think about is the next generation of challenger banks. When Starling first launched, there were just four companies vying to capture the mobile banking market. Today, new banking apps are appearing all the time. Those innovators and early adopters who flocked to Starling because it was new and exciting are already eyeing the next best thing. Retaining their interest as customers has to be a big consideration. While it is gratifying to realize we achieved what we set out to do and did truly disrupt banking, we don't have the luxury of declaring victory just yet. Indeed, we never will. Now we have opened up the sector and raised customer expectations, the new innovations will keep on coming. Starling won't be the only 'bank that does'. We won't be the only bank to offer our customers everything they always wanted from a bank, but never got. We need to be ready for that.

Afterword

Unicorn status is a big deal in fintech. The symbolism celebrates the statistical rarity of a private company achieving a valuation of more than £1 billion. At the start of 2021 there were just seventy fintech unicorns in the whole world,* from N26 to Revolut to Wise, representing a fraction of the 20,000 plus fintechs that launch each year.† Starling Bank, in its seventh year of business, achieved the goal in March 2021, after a £272 million funding round where we once again approached outside investors, inviting them to invest cash in exchange for equity in the business. The round had been oversubscribed too, which meant the following month we also announced an extension, with an additional £50 million investment from Goldman Sachs. It was the biggest signal yet to the outside world that the digital bank is a force to be reckoned with. The calibre of our new investment partners spoke volumes. The lead investor was Fidelity Management and Research, one of the largest mutual fund companies in the world, and then there was the Qatar Investment Authority, global investment firm Millennium Management, and RPMI Railpen, the investment manager for the £31 billion Railways Pension Scheme. And the exclusive financial advisor on the funding round? Rothschild. This was the same Rothschild that I once noted wouldn't look twice at a tiny start-up like New Bank. How things have changed.

* https://sifted.eu/articles/10-quickest-fintech-unicorns/ – 11 January 2021.
† https://www.statista.com/statistics/893954/number-fintech-startups-by-region/.

While the announcement generated many headlines and warm messages of congratulation, the signs of our coming-of-age had been there for a good while. In October 2020 we announced that Starling Bank had gone into profit. At that time, we had nearly 1.8 million accounts, £4 billion in deposits and £1.5 billion of lending. For an indication of how fast things were moving in the right direction, by the time we became a unicorn four months later, we'd exceeded 2 million accounts, including more than 300,000 small business accounts, and deposits were over £5.4 billion, with £2 billion of lending.

Step away from the raw stats, though, and I think Starling has changed immeasurably in the year since this book was first published. Like all other businesses around the world, we were impacted by Covid-19 and had to find new ways of working. Initially, this involved rapidly setting up the whole team to work remotely, all while ensuring there was no gap in our services. In uncertain times, our customers needed to know they could rely on us. It was inevitable that the lengthy series of enforced lockdowns would speed up the switch to digital banking, and it has. We had a role to play in reassuring people that we'd be there to keep the financial side of their lives moving smoothly, when everything else was so tough and up in the air.

As time went on, we had to find new ways to support our teams. Many Starlings were working on the front line in customer services, dealing directly with the needs of tens of thousands of individuals and businesses who were extremely anxious about money. Measures were put in place to ensure that, while they were working alone, they always felt the full weight of the company support behind them. This could be the three-times-a-week online 'Ask Anne' sessions, or our 'Never Home Alone' broadcasts on a range of subjects from psychology to mental health to nutrition, all presented by expert guests.

When it came to our customers, we were able to use our

tech abilities to quickly design and introduce new products to meet the needs that emerged out of the unprecedented situation. Within weeks of the first lockdown we launched the Starling Connected card to make things easier for people who were helping self-isolating friends and neighbours. These additional cards could be connected to the accounts of personal account holders via the Spaces section of their app, and then handed over to a trusted shopper to pay for goods on their behalf. Elsewhere, we introduced a facility whereby account holders could pay in a cheque by simply taking a picture of it using their phone.

Perhaps the most pivotal point for Starling, though, was the launch of the government-backed lending for businesses, the Coronavirus Business Interruption Loan Scheme (CBILS), and the Bounce Back Loan Scheme (BBLS). Starling was overlooked not once but twice in the government's rapidly assembled emergency plans to help businesses through the Covid-19 crisis. We had to justify our place on the roster of banks offering loans, firstly for CBILS and then BBLS. There were solid business reasons to make sure we were included. We'd been steadily building up our business-account side for months before this and it would have been a huge gap in our range if we couldn't offer customers the benefit of these loan schemes at such a crucial time. If we left it all to the big banks, we could easily haemorrhage customers, just at a time when we'd made some real gains.

There were risks involved too. While government backing for the schemes was in place to protect the lenders, rather than the borrowers, Starling would still be lending its own money. We recognized very early on that the rapid way the loan schemes were designed meant they were by no means perfect. Indeed, there was real potential for spurious applications. If there turned out to be a large number of them, default rates were going to be off-scale. To me, though, it was never an option to simply walk away, not least because there were also thousands of genuine businesses in need. Therefore we took a two-pronged approach. I was sure to articulate my concerns to government, however unpopular that may have been, writing to them, outlining my concerns in detail. At the same time, Starling used the best of its know-how to make sure our fraud controls were second to none. We also set ourselves the challenge of making sure our application process was entirely automated. If too much human interaction was required, it would slow things to a crawl or stop them altogether. This was a time when speed was of the essence.

Despite all our well-laid plans, the roll-out of the scheme was not easy. My worst fears were realized when, through no fault of our own, Starling faced a slew of negative headlines for the first time in its existence. Things had started smoothly, except we very quickly recognized that the firm limit of £20 million in loans that we'd been given by the British Business Bank, which administered the scheme, hopelessly underestimated the scale of demand. We'd had to immediately petition to raise the limit – by a factor of ten. Even then, the applications still kept coming. After nearly two weeks we introduced a waiting list, where customers could register interest for Bounce Back Loans. We also announced that we would be considering applications only from established customers who used Starling as their primary account. For a few weeks, social media was alive with criticism: why was Starling (and indeed the other banks) being so slow, just at the moment when they were truly needed? Then, just as things were beginning to settle down a little, we received a further influx of applications from an unexpected source.

Money Saving Expert Martin Lewis has long been a staple of our small screens, advising households on how to make the most of their cash. His Money Tips email boasts 12 million subscribers and the Money Saving Expert website offers a comprehensive source of information on everything from mortgages to loans, and there's a lively forum to go with it. Martin had always been very supportive of Starling, and whenever he gave us a positive mention, we'd always get a welcome surge in account applications. I liked Martin too, since his sensible words of advice very much chimed with what we were trying to do at Starling, which was to help people get on top of their finances by managing their money better. Towards the end of May, Martin appeared on TV to talk about BBLS. In a special edition of *The Martin Lewis Money Show*, live from his London home, he had some words of guidance for those people he felt had fallen through the cracks when it came to the various government schemes to help people through the financial burden of the pandemic. He said that Bounce Backs could be taken out by almost anyone, and were a cracking way to get a year-long interest-free loan.*

'When this came out, I started to look at the terms, and realized that some of the people that missed out on the self-employed help scheme, this might actually be a way to get some support.'

In what felt like a thorough, A–Z explanation on how to claim a significant sum, Martin explained that it was possible to be a 'very new business to get this', with the scheme offering loans of up to £50,000.

Taking out a loan was, he conceded to his Twitter followers in a discussion following the show, a far from ideal solution, but an interest- and payment-free loan to help people over the worst was a viable option. He did, of course, reinforce that

---

* https://www.dailyrecord.co.uk/lifestyle/money/martin-lewis-explains-how-almost-21993965.

Bounce Back was a loan, not a grant, so would need to be repaid.

While Martin's stance was intended to help the many small businesses and sole traders who had found themselves in real trouble, the announcement did have some unintended consequences. In the days that followed, Starling received a surge in CBILS and BBLS applications from newly formed businesses applying for substantial loans. Since these brand-new businesses didn't have a trading record, but could estimate their own turnover, we began to see some quite toppy forecasts. Even to the untrained eye it seemed quite optimistic that Joe, a one-man-band window cleaner, was expecting to make £250,000 in the coming year, or that a sole trader massage therapist would bring in £150,000. We were not the only bank to experience this sudden increase in loan activity, but needed to act fast to make sure we weren't overwhelmed.

By now, it was clear that the major banks were reaching breaking point with the scale of demand for government-backed loan schemes, both legitimate and otherwise. Big banks were always set up to be branch-based businesses and the technology at the back end was simply never equipped to be able to cope with tens of thousands of small businesses applying for loans online almost simultaneously. They also didn't have the staff numbers to cope with their more manual, hands-on process of dealing with BBLS, and it certainly didn't help that nearly everyone was working from home. A backlog quickly grew, with applications being processed at a snail's pace. Twitter was perpetually awash with tweets from frustrated businesses claiming they were waiting for weeks even to get an acknowledgement. To slow down the pace of applications, the big banks began to close their books to new business accounts one by one. By 2021, Starling Bank was alone in still accepting new business customers for Bounce Back Loans, as rival banks sought to distance themselves from the difficult-to-administer schemes. It had been a roller-coaster ride in every way, but I believe that we established ourselves as the leading bank supporting SMEs.

This experience, and the impact of Covid on our business overall, showed me how far we had come. We'd long since left behind our persona as a plucky start-up, since we were now an established (not establishment) business boasting millions of customers with both business and personal accounts. It occurred to me that, up until now, I'd always marked our progress against Monzo, since they were our rival challenger bank and had launched at almost the same time. The fact that I had history with Tom Blomfield always upped the ante, competition-wise, too. The extraordinary experiences of the year 2020 made it clearer than ever that our competitors are now Lloyds, Barclays et al. Our lending performance during the pandemic has already proved that we are their equals and we have ambitious plans to keep growing our lending. The high-street banks are the organizations I need to keep gaining ground on and looking to overtake. I'm already convinced that Barclays is now in our sights, since it has around 15 per cent of the business banking market and Starling has a 6 per cent share of the market for SME banking. At the rate of growth Starling is now experiencing, overtaking them is not just doable, it is a strong possibility.

When *Banking On It* was first published in November 2020, I noted that many of the traditional banks were starting to wake up to the threat of digital banks. RBS had launched (and then closed) a mobile-focussed brand, Bo, and there were other establishment-bank challengers in the pipeline. The consensus now is that the whole banking industry is completely wide-awake to the rise and rise of the so-called 'neobanks'. This is hardly surprising, since between 2018 and 2020 digital banks grew their base from under 10 per cent of the adult population to over 25 per cent.* Those numbers are still rising every day, as demonstrated by account-switching data which shows major banks are losing tens of thousands of customers each year.

It was inevitable that established banks would eventually throw a great deal of weight behind their response, and they have. This reaction has manifested itself in a number of ways.

Followers of Starling's fortunes will have noted that there was speculation in the media at the end of 2020 that we had caught the attention of two suitors who were interested in acquiring us: JPMorgan Chase and Lloyds Bank. Other interest has gone unrecorded, but the strategy was neatly summarized to me during a conversation with an executive at another leading bank.

'We've had a look at what digital banks do and it seems really complex,' he told me. 'It seems to make more sense to buy one of the challenger banks than build ourselves from scratch.'

Well, quite. Except, Starling is not for sale and I very much want to lead it to floatation and beyond. Thanks to the latest round of fundraising outlined at the beginning of this chapter, it is full steam ahead towards an IPO.

We don't have room to be complacent, though. Fintech sub-brands from the traditional banks are proliferating. Goldman Sachs has put its considerable resources behind Marcus, a separate brand offering online loans and savings accounts. Other digital offerings include Openbank from Santander, BNP Paribas' Hello bank! and the fledgling scheme from JP Morgan codenamed 'Project Dynamo'. The models that have been launched so far bear many similarities to what we've done, focussing on customer-friendly features, improved financial

---

* 'Neobanks – Butterflies or Fast Caterpillars?', confidential research report, Keefe, Bruyette & Woods Europe, 16 October 2020.

management and innovations such as card controls and gambling blocks. (I have been told that consultants run workshops where they study how Starling operates.) There have also been numerous reports of banking executives leaving blue-chip banks to explore the potential of setting up their own digital banks.

What does this mean for Starling? We do, of course, need to keep moving and innovating. As time goes on, expect to see the Starling name further afield. At the time of writing, we are still pursuing our banking licence from the Central Bank of Ireland, which will be our passport into opening in several European markets such as France, Germany and Spain. We also continue to grow our Banking as a Service (BaaS) offering, opening up our API to enable a broader range of fintechs, retailers and brands to use our banking licence to develop their own customized financial products, such as savings or current accounts and debit cards. We expect to see a lot of growth in this area.

On a personal level, while I have achieved so much, I feel that there is still much for me to do. Just as Starling has changed immeasurably over the past year, I believe I have too. Early on, when I was pounding the streets looking for investment and getting knock-back after knock-back, I never allowed myself to think beyond a six-week timeframe. My mantra was: *If I can just survive for the next six weeks, I will be OK*. If anyone started to talk to me about things on an eight-week time horizon, or even further ahead than that, it would be interesting, but not really on my radar. I now feel certain about Starling's future. That short-term thinking and vague rumble of desperation that niggled away at the start have completely disappeared. I have acquired the luxury of long-term thought.

While, of course, this gives me the freedom to devise ambitious plans for the future of Starling, I can also use this new-found breathing space to my advantage elsewhere. There's an opportunity to use the knowledge and experience I have gained from both the new and old worlds of banking to greater advantage. I can influence change.

In recent months I have watched new developments in online fraud with increasing alarm. It appears that many criminal gangs made use of their pandemic lockdowns to work out ways to exploit weaknesses in the financial world. While the latest figures available show that the £738.8 million fraud losses in 2020, across payment cards, remote banking and cheques, were down 5 per cent compared to 2019,* the statistics don't tell the full story. While many individuals are becoming savvier when it comes to protecting themselves against fraud, and banks are using better technology to stop many fraudsters in their tracks, the criminals are becoming more creative. Sophisticated social engineering tactics are being increasingly deployed to trick people into circumventing bank security and giving away sensitive information. Impersonation scams *doubled* in 2020, with criminals claiming to be from trusted organizations such as the NHS, Royal Mail, the police or the government. The consequences of this criminal behaviour can be far-reaching too, well beyond the absolute horror of losing your life savings to fraudsters. In a new twist, people are being tricked into letting their legitimate accounts be used as so-called 'mule accounts' for money laundering. When the ruse is exposed, the account holder faces the prospect of a black mark against their credit history that can prevent them from ever opening another bank account or accessing loans for their entire lives.

Starling, like all banks, is powerless when it comes to stopping scammers persuading people to take all their money out of

* https://www.ukfinance.org.uk/system/files/Fraud%20The%20Facts%202021-%20FINAL.pdf.

their accounts and put it somewhere for 'safe keeping', after which, sadly, they'll never see it again. Despite prominent warnings on every Starling account, we've seen and heard far too many heartbreaking stories of bank customers being tricked in this way.

To date, measures to crack down on fraud have been ad hoc and, frankly, pretty uninspiring. There is a voluntary code of practice, which was introduced in May 2019, signatories to which commit to reimburse victims of organized payment scams in any scenario where the customer has met the standards laid out in the code.* A great deal of the onus seems to have fallen to banks to sort it out, when in reality, this is a far wider problem. It's online, over the phone, face-to-face, anywhere and everywhere. No one seems ready and able to organize a meaningful, coordinated response, when this is what is really required. With my new thinking space, I have decided to take control and start getting people together. I have been consulting with search engines, telephone companies and government ministers in a bid to get us all on the same page to help rein in the fraudsters. It's early days, but I am determined to make a difference.

There are other things that I can do elsewhere too and, for me, this is only the beginning. Digital banking is here to stay. We've gone beyond the stage of just being able to offer customers a truly rewarding banking experience. Think about what else can be done to give everyone the secure financial future they have worked for and deserve.

I am.

* http://researchbriefings.files.parliament.uk/documents/CBP-8545/CBP-8545.pdf.

Acknowledgements

My success owes everything to the unique spirit and extraordinary talent of so many people who have been closely involved in Starling Bank's journey from being a brilliant idea to becoming one of the UK's most successful digital banks. I am very grateful to Teena Lyons, the friend, journalist, author and special person I trusted to turn my recollections, along with a thousand emails, into this story of how it all happened.

My thanks must go to Harald McPike who understood my vision for Starling Bank straight away and backed the idea. He made so much of what we did possible.

Many of Starling's exceptionally skilled people are mentioned in this book, but I am conscious that I have not said much about the board. These people all put their reputations on the line because they too believed in the notion that banking could be better. I am therefore eternally grateful to our chairman, Oliver Stocken CBE, and our independent directors, Mark Winlow, Steven Colsell, Marian Martin and Victoria Raffé. Also, our investor directors, Lázaro Campos, Marcus Traill and Craig Mawdsley, and, of course, our advisor, Michael Boocher, who spotted the potential of Starling from the very beginning. Special thanks to Richard Watts and Nick Williamson of Merian for their insight and ambition.

It goes without saying that if Ken Blackman hadn't been there to give his advice on a very difficult day and if Alan Chandler had not dropped in for coffee and stayed at my side then Starling wouldn't be here today.

Thanks to Tony Ellingham and Julian Sawyer, who brought

everything together and became the solid pillars of Team A, and to John Mountain and Steve Newson, who built the foundations for the finest software engineering team in Europe.

Special mention should also go to Matt Newman, Starling Bank's company secretary and general counsel. He played a much bigger part in the Starling story than this book suggests, but for legal reasons his role must remain largely unsung.

I would also like to acknowledge Gareth Christensen and Andrew Doughty, who each played an important role in making Starling Bank a reality.

I would love to list every single person who works at Starling Bank by name, but space doesn't allow. So let me just say a big thank you to them all and reiterate that they should all be exceptionally proud of what we have built.

Elsewhere, there are also hundreds of people who did their bit to help me create Starling and then moved on. Some helped in a small yet hugely significant way, perhaps with an introduction or recommendation, or by reviewing some documents. Others gave me hours of invaluable free consultancy time in some of the earlier incarnations of the bank. As is the case with all start-ups, people come and people go. Not everyone can put their heart and soul and financial future into a venture without much certainty of success. To all of you who in some way played a part: thank you. I couldn't have done this without you.

I am also hugely grateful to the team at Penguin Business, who encouraged me to write my story and helped me to get it into print. Martina O'Sullivan and Celia Buzuk did a brilliant job with the editing. Thank you also to Jeff Scott at Platypus PR for his advice, Starling's head of corporate affairs, Alexandra Frean, for her calm, measured approach that kept everything on track and Kam Hudson, my executive assistant for her help in coordinating it all.

And finally, to the person who first said to me: it can't be done. Thank you. I do respond well to a challenge.

Index

AB indicates Anne Boden.

Index

He just wanted a decent book to read ...

Not too much to ask, is it? It was in 1935 when Allen Lane, Managing Director of Bodley Head Publishers, stood on a platform at Exeter railway station looking for something good to read on his journey back to London. His choice was limited to popular magazines and poor-quality paperbacks – the same choice faced every day by the vast majority of readers, few of whom could afford hardbacks. Lane's disappointment and subsequent anger at the range of books generally available led him to found a company – and change the world.

'We believed in the existence in this country of a vast reading public for intelligent books at a low price, and staked everything on it'
Sir Allen Lane, 1902–1970, founder of Penguin Books

The quality paperback had arrived – and not just in bookshops. Lane was adamant that his Penguins should appear in chain stores and tobacconists, and should cost no more than a packet of cigarettes.

Reading habits (and cigarette prices) have changed since 1935, but Penguin still believes in publishing the best books for everybody to enjoy. We still believe that good design costs no more than bad design, and we still believe that quality books published passionately and responsibly make the world a better place.

So wherever you see the little bird – whether it's on a piece of prize-winning literary fiction or a celebrity autobiography, political tour de force or historical masterpiece, a serial-killer thriller, reference book, world classic or a piece of pure escapism – you can bet that it represents the very best that the genre has to offer.

Whatever you like to read – trust Penguin.